The General's Slow Retreat

The publisher gratefully acknowledges the generous support of the General Endowment Fund of the University of California Press Foundation.

The General's Slow Retreat

CHILE AFTER PINOCHET

MARY HELEN SPOONER

UNIVERSITY OF CALIFORNIA PRESS
Berkeley Los Angeles London

University of California Press, one of the most distinguished university presses in the United States, enriches lives around the world by advancing scholarship in the humanities, social sciences, and natural sciences. Its activities are supported by the UC Press Foundation and by philanthropic contributions from individuals and institutions. For more information, visit www.ucpress.edu.

University of California Press
Berkeley and Los Angeles, California

University of California Press, Ltd.
London, England

Library of Congress Cataloging-in-Publication Data

Spooner, Mary Helen.
The general's slow retreat : Chile after Pinochet / Mary Helen Spooner.
p. cm.
Includes bibliographical references and index.
ISBN 978-0-520-25613-2 (cloth : alk. paper)
ISBN 978-0-520-26680-3 (pbk. : alk. paper)
1. Chile—Politics and government—1988– 2. Pinochet Ugarte, Augusto. 3. Democratization—Chile. I. Title.

JL2631.S67 2011
983.06'6—dc22 2010036098

Manufactured in the United States of America

20 19 18 17 16 15 14 13 12 11
10 9 8 7 6 5 4 3 2 1

This book is printed on 50# Enterprise, a 30% post consumer waste, recycled, de-inked fiber and processed chlorine free. It is acid-free, and meets all ANSI/NISO (Z 39.48) requirements.

Once again, for Alan, Daniel, and Alexandra

Dictators ride to and fro upon tigers which they dare not dismount. And the tigers are getting hungry.

Winston Churchill,
from a letter dated November 11, 1937

The spirit of democracy cannot be imposed from without. It has to come from within.

Mohandas K. Gandhi,
statement to the press, September 17, 1934

I said to Felipe Gonzalez once, "Imagine what it would be like to be president of Spain with Franco still alive. I am with my Franco. It's General Pinochet."

Patricio Aylwin,
president of Chile, 1990–94,
New York Times, April 30, 1992

Contents

Illustrations

Following page 94.

Acknowledgments

Returning to Chile after so many years seemed a daunting task, and I am deeply grateful to Odette Magnet, whose encouragement, friendship, and extraordinary networking skills helped reconnect me with the country, and to my editor, Naomi Schneider, who gave me this opportunity. In addition to those interviewed for this book, I would like to thank Barbara Thompson for giving me a better understanding of banking practices and money laundering, as well as Juan Carlos Roman and Genaro Roman, Daesha Friedman, Judy Ress, and Francisca Donoso. Jimmée Greco showed great patience with me while meticulously editing this book. My husband, Alan Stephens, supported me through this project, and our children, Daniel and Alexandra, are the most precious gift Chile gave us.

Introduction

The Chilean presidential palace, La Moneda, began life as a Spanish colonial mint in 1805, five years before the country was even a republic. During Chile's brutal 1973 coup, the palace survived a military bombardment, which destroyed the beams supporting the upper floors and reduced much of the Italian-designed edifice to a shell. For several years afterward La Moneda was boarded up, until General Augusto Pinochet, having won a dubious referendum extending his rule for another nine years, moved his headquarters into the palace in 1981.

La Moneda continued to project a grim image: the previous occupant, socialist president Salvador Allende, had committed suicide there during the coup, shooting himself after instructing his most loyal staffers to leave the building. His corpse was removed by soldiers and firefighters through a side door, which had been the private entrance for Chilean presidents. The military regime repaired much of the internal damage to the palace and added an underground bunker, where Pinochet conducted business. But the presidential side entrance remained blocked up with concrete, an architectural eyesore and sad reminder of the country's once-proud democratic tradition.

Chile returned to democracy in 1990, and today entire sections of La Moneda are open to the public. The palace's exterior has been brightened, with the once-grayish outer walls now painted white. A replica of the original carved pine door has been installed in the restored presidential side entrance. Casual visitors may walk up to the main entrance of the palace and, after submitting to a brief security check, wander through two exquisite courtyards filled with fruit trees and outdoor sculptures.

La Moneda also hosts concerts and guided tours, and the former dictator's bunker has been transformed into a new museum and cultural center, which opened in January 2006. But shortly after the cultural center was inaugurated, a controversy erupted over souvenirs sold in the gift shop. A series of postcards, "Presidentes 1970–2010," included the ill-fated Salvador Allende, three civilian presidents who served after military rule ended, and the newly elected Michelle Bachelet, Chile's first female president. Conspicuous by his absence was Pinochet, and when some visitors to La Moneda complained, sale of the postcards was quickly suspended.

Chilean officials offered mixed explanations: some said that the postcards were the work of a private company offering what it thought visitors would buy, while others explained that the postcard series was limited to democratically elected presidents. The culture minister suggested that it might be more appropriate to have a set of postcards featuring all heads of state dating from the nineteenth century. It was a mistake to exclude Pinochet, he said, for Pinochet had been president of Chile for seventeen years, "whether we like it or not."[1]

Had it been up to Pinochet and his most determined supporters, his regime would have lasted a quarter of a century. The one-man presidential plebiscite on October 5, 1988, to extend his rule for another eight years was one he fully expected to win. His defeat at the polls paved the way to free elections and Chile's readmission into an international community that had held the country at arm's length during the military regime. But Pinochet continued to cast a long and intimidating shadow as army commander until 1998, and he had begun an indefinite term as "senator for life" when his arrest in London shattered his indestructible image.

He returned to Chile a weakened figure, or as one congressman put it, "politically dead."[2] And yet he still managed to dodge a series of judicial investigations into some of the worst crimes of his regime as well as an inquiry into an illicit fortune he had built up during his rule and hidden in bank accounts abroad. Pinochet may have left office, but the remnants of his power and his authoritarian legacy would take decades to dismantle.

"Now that he is gone, I feel I can finally write my memoir," a former cabinet minister who had worked with Pinochet as army commander told me.[3] He shook his head, as if to convince himself that the coast was finally clear. But the Pinochet legacy was still not dismantled, and the former official had reason to be cautious: had he published his book a few years earlier, he might have faced prosecution under state security laws leftover from the regime. Not only had there been no immediate repeal of such laws when Pinochet left the presidency, but some politicians in Chile's emerging democracy would find them useful for their own ends. Dictatorship would not disappear overnight.

Chile's democratic changeover was, as several people emphasized to me, *una transición pactada,* a negotiated transition in which democratic leaders had to engage in an elaborate and prolonged bargaining process with the former dictator and his supporters. In neighboring Argentina, military rule was discredited by the country's devastating loss in the 1982 Falklands War. Chile's military, on the other hand, had never known defeat, and it would take years of skillful domestic diplomacy to separate the country's armed forces from Pinochet's enduring influence. Coaxing the bull back into the pen would not be easy or without dangers.

"It is not for vanity that I want to remain commander in chief, or for comfort, nor because I want to get myself something," Pinochet told an interviewer in 1989. " I could peacefully retire. I can be a senator for life. But I have people in the army, people who could be annoyed."[4] Though it was never clear whether the army's officer corps and soldiers would support another coup, Pinochet often implied he might take such a course if the situation warranted. That he was prevented from doing so is a testament to the political skills of Chile's new leaders and support from an international community that no longer saw regimes arising from military coups as lawful governments.

In many ways, Chile is a profoundly changed country. An example of those changes is provided by the *Guia Silber,* a directory of virtually every public and private institution or organization in the country and an essential tool for anyone wanting to conduct business or establish contacts. The guide was first published in 1986, the year the regime launched a repressive crackdown in the wake of an assassination attempt against Pinochet. This first edition was barely bigger than an address book, and the only advertisers were two Santiago restaurants, whose owners paid the young publishers with meal vouchers. During this time of extreme political tension, many of those listed in the guide were nervous about having their names appear in print, as if old enemies might be tempted to locate them.

Today's *Guia Silber* is published twice a year, is nearly eight hundred pages long, and is also available in a CD version. And everyone wants to be in the *Guia Silber,* the Who's Who of Chile. The country has also become Latin America's biggest per capita consumer of digital technology, including Internet broadband, cell phones, and cable television. Small cafes attached to gasoline stations along the Pan-American Highway in rural areas south of Santiago offer WiFi service, and nearly one in ten Chileans use Facebook, more than any other Latin American country and many European countries as well.[5]

Transparency International ranks Chile, along with Uruguay, as the least corrupt country in Latin America, while the United Nations Human Development Index, which measures life expectancy, educational opportunities, and living standards, ranks Chile as the best country in Latin America in which to live and 44th out of 182 countries in the world. And in 2010 the Organization for Economic Cooperation and Development (OECD) admitted Chile as its first South American member, citing "nearly two decades of democratic reform and sound economic policies." At a signing ceremony in Santiago, Secretary General Angel Gurría said the "Chilean way" would enrich the OECD on key policy issues and praised the country for "combining robust economic growth with improved social welfare."[6]

Along with economic development, Chile has begun to face social dilemmas of the sort industrialized nations know only too well. The country's relative prosperity has attracted thousands of migrants from Peru, Ecuador, and Bolivia hoping for a better economic future. They are often smuggled across the northern border in refrigerator trucks and later housed in crowded, substandard dwellings. Some of these migrants find domestic work and other low-wage jobs no longer filled by Chileans, while others struggle in the underground economy. They are often blamed for an increase in crime.

Santiago's newly extended highway runs farther east toward the Andean foothills, past endless modern apartment blocks and shopping centers and into the wealthiest residential areas. A taxi driver pointed out a multistoried mansion visible from the highway, built by Pinochet as a presidential residence but never used due to security concerns. "Crime was much lower when Pinochet was in power," he said. It is a view frequently expressed by the dictator's former supporters but also acknowledged across Chile's political spectrum. The country's crime rate is still far lower than most, with gun crime and kidnappings being relatively rare occurrences. Santiago remains Latin America's safest capital. According to Fundación Paz Ciudadana, an independent think tank that monitors crime, the country's crime rate has remained fairly flat since 2003, but fear of crime has steadily increased. The foundation published a survey in 2008 in which 52.1 percent of respondents said they felt unsafe in their own neighborhoods, and 47.8 percent believed they would be victims of crime within the next twelve months.[7]

"Nothing is as it seems. What you see on the surface is not going to give you much information about what is really going on," Marta Lagos, director of Latinobarómetro, a polling organization, warned me. She said that fear of crime in present-day Chile was higher than fear of the military had been under Pinochet. "If you kept your head down you could avoid trouble with the military. Crime, on the other hand, affects anybody and everybody," she observed. "Chileans are as fearful of crime as any residents of more violent cities."[8]

A poll by another organization, the Centro de Estudios de la Realidad Contemporánea (CERC), revealed that Chileans' chief concerns were crime and unemployment. Asked which of the country's institutions they trusted, Chileans put the country's paramilitary police force, the *carabin-*

eros, on top of the list, followed by radio stations, the Catholic Church, and the navy and air force. The Chilean judiciary, congress, and political parties were the institutions least trusted. The carabineros are something of an anomaly in Latin America, a highly professionalized force trained at a police academy at which admission is competitive. One comparative study of police forces noted that although starting salaries for carabineros and their Russian counterparts were roughly the same, along with similar costs of living, the latter were notorious for corruption and links to organized crime while the Chileans had a reputation for honesty and discipline. Growing numbers of overseas visitors to Chile at one point prompted the carabinero's official Web site to post an advisory in six languages, and this is the English version: "If you commit a fault or a crime during your stay in our country—according to the in force Chilean legislation—NEVER try to bribe a Carabinero, since only trying to perform this action you will incur into a crime. If it is the case you will be detained and the background of the case will be delivered to the court concerned."[9]

The carabineros' relative efficiency combined with the increase in crime has resulted in Chile having more prisoners per capita than any other country in South America. New, privately contracted prisons have been built, but the inmate population has grown faster, with some facilities holding more than double their planned capacity.

Santiago's La Legua neighborhood takes its name from its location one league south of the capital's central square, the Plaza de Armas. It was settled by displaced migrants from northern Chile looking for work after the nitrate industry collapsed in the 1920s and 1930s. In the years leading up to the 1973 coup, La Legua was a leftist stronghold where the Chilean Communist Party not only kept a branch office but a social club as well, with dances held on weekends. But today it is considered one of the Chilean capital's poorest and most dangerous areas, with political activism overtaken by the urban drug trade.

"There's no doubt that poverty has decreased in Chile," Isabel del Campo, manager of the Catholic charity Trabajo para un Hermano, said. "But for many young people these improved prospects have been undermined by drugs."[10] I visited the charity's center in La Legua, which offers job skills, training, and counseling along with a crafts course in mosaics.

The center's director apologized for not being able to give me a tour of the neighborhood—it was too dangerous to do so, he said. One of the women enrolled in the mosaics class wanted me to know that her community had many good, hardworking people. She belonged to La Legua's residents' association and said that job applicants from the area often face discrimination when potential employers notice their address.

Then there are the communities known for other kinds of crime. Paine lies on the southern outskirts of Santiago, a small country market town with the unenviable record of the most disappearances and killings in a single community after the 1973 coup. The local association for families of the disappeared reported at least seventy *detenidos desaparecidos,* but more than three and a half decades later, investigators have yet to establish the fate of the victims. In 2008 a memorial to Paine's missing was inaugurated, an austere concrete walkway with rows of wooden poles representing the victims. Nevertheless, the group's president, Juan Maureira, said that not all victims' families have been willing to take part in the group's activities. Some did not like reliving the trauma, and many of the missing victims' children have moved away and in some cases even married into families of Pinochet supporters, he said.[11]

The disappearances and killings occurred in wake of the bitter agrarian reform disputes of the late 1960s and early 1970s, with politicized farm workers attempting to take over large agricultural estates. Some landowners became vigilantes after the coup, joining the military in making the arrests. Such scenes would seem out of place in Paine today, as the town has become more like a Santiago suburb, with farmlands converted into tract housing and a metro bringing commuters to the capital. Paine's annual watermelon festival is one of the few reminders of its rural heritage. A teacher at the local high school told me most of his students had no idea about what had happened in their town in wake of the 1973 military coup, though occasionally some ask him about life during the regime.[12]

At the monthly meeting of the Paine association for relatives of the disappeared, two government functionaries presented a report on progress to date of the investigation into the disappearances. One of the officials, a representative of the coroner's office, described the forensic work at a nearby site where bodies had been buried in makeshift graves and later clandestinely removed. Investigators had found spent bullets, shell casings, bone fragments, pieces of clothing and shoes and were conducting further laboratory tests. They were considering sending the material to a lab in either Germany or the United States for additional tests, he said. Several of the women at the meeting immediately demanded to know whether they could view the scraps of clothing and shoes. "We know exactly what they were wearing on the day of their disappearance," one woman said.[13] The official said they could not but promised to have more information for them at next month's meeting.

Afterward I asked some of the women about local attitudes toward the disappearances. After so many years, after the publication of a government report on killings and disappearances after the coup, had anyone who had shunned them in the past offered any kind of conciliatory gesture? Had a neighbor or acquaintance ever approached to say, "I'm sorry—I had no idea"? Their response was a categoric "no."

The widow of a shopkeeper who had been detained and never seen again told me she still encounters one of the civilians who took part in her husband's arrest. They occasionally cross paths in stores or other public places, and the man invariably makes eye contact with her and smirks, she said. A hairdresser whose father had disappeared when she was two years old said her earliest memory was of her mother leaving her and her siblings home alone to search for him. At the salon where she works, many of the customers are still very vocal about their admiration for Pinochet.[14]

At the opposite end of Chile's political spectrum, there is a support network for the families of military officers charged in human rights cases. An organization of "politically imprisoned soldiers and relatives of terrorism victims" maintains a Web site that praises the Chilean military as the true founder of the country's democracy.[15] In 2005 retired army colonel German Barriga, a former agent in the regime's secret police, leapt to his death from the eighteenth floor of a building near the military academy. He had been the subject of a judicial investigation into the disappearance of twelve Chilean Communist Party members in 1976 and had been implicated in at least three more cases but not yet formally sentenced. Barriga left behind an eloquent letter describing how he had lost three different jobs after human rights campaigners had exposed him in public demonstrations at the places where he had worked. A devout Catholic, he said he had recently gone to confession and taken communion but could no longer endure his situation.

The practice of publicly naming and shaming accused human rights violators began in 1999, the year after Pinochet was detained in London. Inspired by a similar organization in Argentina, the group called Funa sought to unmask "those participating in human rights violations during the dictatorship." Its tactics were controversial: one of its videos shows demonstrators gathering outside the Chilean labor ministry, with some entering the building and confronting the accused functionary, a grey-haired man who professes bewilderment and terror.[16] The group's slogan is "If there is no justice, there is Funa!"

The Chilean interior ministry has an entire department devoted to human rights, offering legal assistance and social support to families seeking redress. The pace of judicial investigations can be agonizingly slow and the results far from satisfactory. In one incident, bodies found in unmarked graves in Santiago's general cemetery were exhumed, identified, and returned to their families for reburial, but later officials admitted that in some cases families had received the wrong bodies. Meanwhile, more bodies continue to appear. In late 2007 work on a new supermarket in Santiago was halted when workers found skeletal remains at the building site, land that had once belonged to the Chilean air force. The following year the mummified body of a Uruguayan woman was discovered in a military training zone in northern Chile. She had worked for the local municipal government during Salvador Allende's presidency. Establishing the truth and laying the dead to rest seems a never-ending task in Chile, even as the country prepares to join the community of developed nations.

On the second anniversary of his death, Pinochet's admirers opened a museum in his honor. For someone who held the Chilean presidency for seventeen years, the museum seems tiny, just four rooms in a suburban house in eastern Santiago. The centerpiece is a re-creation of Pinochet's office—not the one he used at La Moneda or at army headquarters, but the office he occasionally used at the Pinochet Foundation: a desk with framed photographs of his wife and mother, the pens and other items positioned just the way the general arranged them. There were sabers and knives on display as well as a collection of toy soldiers. "We want to allow Chileans to get to know Pinochet, the man, the general, the president, and what better way to do that than by opening a small, boutique display of his personal effects," explained General Luis Cortes, executive director of the President Pinochet Foundation.[17] He showed visitors a packet of breath mints of the brand Pinochet preferred, the uniform he was wearing the day of the coup, and even the bathroom he used, with his combs, soap, and favorite cologne.

There were several glass cases displaying his medals and decorations and a white bust of Pinochet sitting on an antique table. But the most jarring exhibit is the metal sculptures of Pinochet's head and those of the former commanders of the Chilean navy, air force, and carabineros. The four original members of the junta who seized power in the 1973 coup are mounted in a row on a red background, and the sculptor captured their features in close detail. But the sculpted heads are not to scale, and the row of small faces gives the impression that the junta members might have come to an untimely end at the hands of aboriginal headhunters.

There is Admiral José Toribio Merino, his mouth slightly open beneath his mustache. Then comes Pinochet, set somewhat higher, who appears to scowl into the distance. Air force commander Gustavo Leigh, whom Pinochet forced out of the junta in 1978, gives a slight smile, as does carabinero general Cesar Mendoza, the least formidable of the military commanders, who resigned in disgrace in 1985 when a court found that carabineros had kidnapped and assassinated three leftists. The military junta that ousted a democratically elected president has ended up as a strange display in a small museum.

PART ONE An Uneasy Transition

ONE Transferring Power

I

Around midnight on October 5, 1988, the commanders of Chile's air force, navy, and national police entered La Moneda. They had received a summons from General Pinochet, who had just lost a one-man presidential plebiscite, in which Chileans had been asked to approve an eight-year extension of his regime. But there had been no official announcement, and the partial returns broadcast on Chile's controlled television channels suggested that Pinochet was winning. The three military commanders did not believe these reports.

Outside La Moneda, the streets of the Chilean capital were subdued and tense. Two buses belonging to the paramilitary police, the carabineros, were parked outside the palace and near the defense ministry one block away. Another carabinero bus was stationed near the headquarters of the Comando del No, a multipartisan coalition that had campaigned for a vote against Pinochet. Tear gas trucks had been positioned at major intersections, but there were few pedestrians, let alone demonstrators, anywhere to be seen.[1] Leaders of the Comando del No had urged their supporters to vote, then to go home and stay indoors the rest of the day.

The junta had serious misgivings about Pinochet as a presidential candidate, believing that a conservative civilian might have a better chance of winning. In the months leading up to the vote, Pinochet had traveled extensively up and down Chile's narrow territory, ostensibly on government business but actually to campaign for his own reelection, even before the junta had officially nominated him. His secret police, the Central Nacional de Informaciones (CNI), had even organized a political party, the Avanzada Nacional. The group attracted few adherents other than those with ties to the military, but they appeared wherever Pinochet did, cheering, waving Chilean flags, and holding up banners. And the country's state-controlled television stations were careful to avoid images filmed from a distance that might expose the limited extent of Avanzada Nacional's membership.

During one such tour Pinochet claimed to have narrowly avoided an assassination plot when explosives were discovered at an airport where he was scheduled to land. He had canceled the visit the previous day, claiming he had a premonition that something was amiss, and the episode appeared to have been staged to boost his popularity.[2] At times during his campaign Pinochet appeared in civilian dress, but he had no intention of ever giving up his role as head of the Chilean army.

According to air force commander General Fernando Matthei, the junta members had insisted that if Pinochet was going to prolong his presidency for another eight years, he should do so as a civilian and retire from his post as army commander. It was their role to nominate the regime's candidate on August 30, 1988, and they informed Pinochet they would only do so if he agreed to this condition. The dictator seemed to agree, saying he would announce his departure from the army in a speech on September 11, the anniversary of the coup that brought the regime to power. But Pinochet's speech that day contained no such announcement.

"That old gangster, he didn't say a word about this," Matthei said.[3] And relations between Pinochet and the other service commanders cooled considerably in the weeks leading up to the vote, which Pinochet believed he would win. The Chilean economy had recovered from the severe slump it had suffered during the early 1980s, when low copper prices and high foreign debt gave way to mass protests against the regime. The country's gross internal product was growing by 7.3 percent that year, up from 6.6 percent the previous year, and most economic indicators seemed to augur well for Chile.[4]

Pollsters, however, were detecting a different mood. One conservative research group, the Centro de Estudios Públicos, had taken a poll in June of that year and found that only 14 percent of those surveyed described their economic situation as good, with 56 percent reporting it was average and 30 percent describing it as bad or very bad. A quarter of respondents said they were worse off than they had been a year earlier. And most important, only 33 percent said they would vote for Pinochet if he were the regime's candidate in the forthcoming plebiscite, while 37 percent said they would not.[5]

After seizing power in 1973, the regime had declared an indefinite "political recess," closing the Chilean congress and unleashing a campaign of arrest, torture, and imprisonment against the left-wing political groups supporting the Allende government. Thousands of Chileans sought political asylum abroad, fleeing to Europe, the United States, Canada, the Soviet Union, Australia, Cuba, Mexico, and Venezuela.[6] The Christian Democrats, Chile's largest political party, also became a target of persecution, with some of its leaders forced into exile and at least one the victim of an assassination attempt in Rome.[7]

But Chile's political parties survived, with the help of their foreign counterparts, such as Europe's Socialist and Christian Democratic Parties. Within Chile, political party leaders often met under the cover of large social events, such as baptisms and weddings. Rafael Moreno, a Christian Democrat charged with clandestinely reorganizing his party in the mid-seventies, said that he and his colleagues quickly learned how to elude the security forces' surveillance and listening devices. "We had some of our best meetings in the bathroom, with the shower running," he recalled.[8]

The shared experience of persecution probably helped to ease long-standing rivalries and tensions among Chile's left and political center and to pave the way for the sixteen-party coalition that formed in early 1988 to campaign for a "no" vote in the regime's one-man presidential plebiscite. The coalition's ideological range extended from Salvador Allende's Socialist Party (which had split up into three differing factions) to the moderate wing of the National Party, which traditionally represented landowners and other conservatives. The bitter political disputes leading up to the 1973 military coup were now replaced by a well-organized, purposeful drive to bring democracy back to Chile. Led by Christian Democratic Party president Patricio Aylwin, the coalition began with a voter registration drive, followed by a grassroots campaign to urge voters to cast "no" ballots.

Chile's electoral registry had been destroyed during the coup. The regime's two previous plebiscites—one in 1978 to support Pinochet in the wake of a United Nations condemnation of the regime's human rights record and another in 1980 to ratify the new, authoritarian constitution and to extend Pinochet's presidency for eight more years—had been held without lists of registered voters or electoral safeguards and, as was inevitable, showed a majority of votes cast in favor of the regime. But this third plebiscite would be different, with voter registration beginning several months earlier. Approximately 7.4 million Chileans, over 90 percent of eligible voters, had registered. Political parties could finally be officially recognized, if they gathered at least 33,500 signatures. And every political party was entitled to have observers at polling stations watching the voting and the counting of ballots. These provisions, along with the hundreds of foreign observers arriving in the country, convinced most political leaders that the voting process itself would be clean. But how would Pinochet react to an electoral defeat?

There were fears that Pinochet might use any available pretext to overturn the plebiscite, including sabotage by his own security forces. Two weeks earlier the director of the CNI had met with the intelligence chiefs of the Chilean navy, air force, and carabineros. He described Pinochet's plan for the day of the plebiscite "in case something goes wrong." Between five and six in the afternoon the voting would be interrupted, all the country's television and radio stations would be connected to a government broadcasting system, and a state of siege would be declared. Upon hearing this news, air force commander General Fernando Matthei called his naval counterpart, who told him he had received the same report. The service commanders then requested a meeting with Pinochet.

The meeting was held over lunch on September 27. The head of the carabinero police, General Rodolfo Stange, told Pinochet that the reports he had received showed that in several major Chilean cities, a majority of voters would be casting "no" ballots. Pinochet seemed surprised at this news and began taking notes and muttering that he was not going to leave. The other service commanders reminded him that the country's constitution must be respected, but then Pinochet repeated what the CNI director had previously stated: "If 'something goes wrong' he would give orders to send troops out into the streets, to set up a national broadcasting system, and request a state of siege. . . . Our reaction was silence."[9]

Five days before, the plebiscite leaders of Civitas, a nonpartisan voter education program, had met with the army general commanding Santiago's military zone to discuss security protection for their offices on voting day. General Jorge Zincke was initially cordial but then began warning the civic leaders about "a communist plot" to disrupt the voting process: there would be various types of explosions and other terrorist incidents, goon squads would attack polling sites, massive power outages would take place, and the army would use tear gas and rubber bullets to break up any crowds that failed to disperse. The army, Zinke said, did not have the manpower to protect electrical towers but did have candles and matches to allow the election boards to do their work. The general's relaxed demeanor convinced the Civitas leaders that he was actually talking about a Chilean army plan to sabotage the plebiscite, not a plan by communists. They reported their conversation with Zincke to U.S. ambassador Harry Barnes, who sent an urgent cable to the State Department saying the embassy "took this information extremely seriously and urge[d] Washington to do so as well." This incident, along with two suspicious blackouts, prompted the U.S. State Department to call a meeting with Chile's ambassador in Washington, D.C., and to issue a statement requesting that the vote be respected.[10]

Young campaigners for a "no" vote had reported numerous instances of police confiscating their identity cards, thus preventing them from voting, and a pile of around five hundred Chilean identity cards, torn into pieces, had been discovered in a hillside park in downtown Santiago. Opposition leaders had received reports that two carabinero buses had mysteriously disappeared from police installations, which looked like part of a plan to provoke disturbances in poor neighborhoods of Santiago. "We met with General Stange, who told us he had the same reports," recalled Ricardo Lagos, a socialist who would later become Chile's president in 2000. "He told us he had ordered that the roofs of all carabinero buses be painted with reflective paint, so as to be visible from the air. We never did find out exactly what was going on."[11]

II

On the eve of the vote, Pinochet invited the junta members back to La Moneda and showed them the vote tally computers installed in the palace basement. This system, an army colonel explained, would allow a rapid computation of voting returns as soon as they were reported, and he predicted that a likely outcome would be available as early as one hour after the first voting tables closed. The returns from every voting site would be monitored by officials, regime supporters, opposition activists, and hundreds of foreign observers throughout the country. The Comando del No and Chilean political parties would keep their own vote tally, but the only official returns would be announced from La Moneda.[12]

On the day of the plebiscite the offices of Generals Matthei and Stange and Admiral Jose Merino were connected with the computers in La Moneda's basement. The service commanders watched the returns come in and heard reports that the Comando del No was expecting a victory based on their own estimates, but then at 7:00 p.m. their connections were cut off without warning. Repeated phone calls to La Moneda yielded only vague or evasive answers even as the first official announcement on national television reported that with a miniscule fraction—0.36 percent—of the votes counted, Pinochet was ahead with 57 percent. Another bulletin was promised by 9:30 p.m., but this was delayed by an hour, causing speculation that officials were tinkering with the results. What had happened to the efficient computing system?

At 10:30 p.m. the regime released a second set of very partial returns, showing Pinochet ahead by 51.3 percent. A government spokesman promised a third announcement within an hour, but as midnight approached, there were no more official bulletins. The regime, according to a cable sent by the U.S. embassy that evening, "is obviously sitting on the results and releasing them very slowly."[13]

Meanwhile, leaders at the Casa del Si, Pinochet's campaign headquarters, were asking that they be allowed to celebrate this "victory" with a public demonstration in the center of the capital, though a ban on mass gatherings was in effect. Such actions would invariably spark counter demonstrations from "no" vote supporters, lending the regime a convenient pretext for launching a crackdown and suspending the plebiscite. General Stange refused this request and threw a police cordon around a twenty-block area of downtown Santiago, blocking the entry of any vehicles. Carabineros also arrested a group of men wearing balaclava helmets, who turned out to be agents of the CNI, and refused to release them. The army general commanding the Santiago garrison also refused the Pinochet campaigners' request that the ban be lifted.

Admiral José Merino was preparing to go home when the summons finally came from Pinochet. As the three service commanders arrived at the presidential palace, air force commander Matthei detoured away from his colleagues and did something that would forever earn him the opprobrium of Pinochet and his hard-line supporters. It was time to "pull out the detonators," as he later described situation. He approached a group of reporters standing in the palace's inner patio, waiting for news.

"It looks to me like the 'no' won," Matthei told the press. "And we are going to analyze this now." As the journalists scrambled to report this official acknowledgment of the regime's loss, the junta members descended to Pinochet's bunker underneath the presidential palace. The dictator, dressed in a suit and tie, appeared calm, but his volcanic temper would soon manifest itself. He was accompanied by his interior minister and another army general who acted as chief of his cabinet. The interior minister opened the meeting by saying that the plebiscite showed that Pinochet was still the most important political figure in the country, with 43 percent of Chileans voting for him. The opposition, on the other hand, consisted of multiple parties and political leaders.

Matthei sarcastically suggested opening a bottle of champagne to celebrate, and the interior minister fell silent. General Stange indicated that the regime should begin to make contacts with political opposition leaders and announce the free elections as stipulated in the constitution in the event of a plebiscite loss. Pinochet rejected this proposal, saying he was not going to leave and that if necessary he would fill the streets with troops and "sweep away the communists." He also threatened to fire "any general or admiral who speaks to the communists."[14]

An argument then ensued, with Generals Matthei and Stange and Admiral Merino insisting Pinochet had no power to undertake such actions. The discussion turned to the plebiscite's results, which had come as a deep shock to Pinochet, as he had been convinced by his sycophantic advisors that he would win. The service commanders suggested that it might be time for a cabinet change. Pinochet seemed to agree, and then asked the junta members to sign a document that contained the minutes of the meeting they had just completed. Surprised that such a written report had been produced so quickly, the junta members examined it carefully and saw that it was not a record of their meeting but a document granting Pinochet extended powers, including greater control over the navy, air force, and carabinero police. Matthei picked up the document and tore it up; the other commanders also refused to sign.[15] And with that, the slow process of ending one of Latin America's longest dictatorships began, with Pinochet fighting a fierce rearguard action every step of the way.

III

Many Chileans had gone to bed that night thinking that Pinochet would be declared the winner of the plebiscite, regardless of the vote count.

The news that the dictator had lost and would be leaving the presidency after sixteen years seemed extraordinary. Small groups of onlookers began congregating near La Moneda, staring at the presidential palace almost in disbelief. By midday the crowds had grown to the thousands, filling the plaza and the surrounding streets in the center of Santiago. Rumors began to circulate: a helicopter was about to land on the roof of La Moneda to take Pinochet to safety; or Pinochet had already fled the country, possibly to Paraguay. The mood was calm, but the sheer number of people seemed to overwhelm the carabinero police. At one point an opposition politician, Alejandro Hales, approached one of the police vans and addressed the crowds on the loudspeaker, urging them to disperse.[16]

That evening Pinochet appeared on national television, dressed once again in his army uniform. He said that the plebiscite had not altered the existing order and that his regime's constitution would be upheld. He dropped from public view for a few days, spending time at the seaside before returning to Santiago. He held a luncheon with leaders from the Avanzada Nacional and spoke to a conference of military wives, comparing those who voted against him in the plebiscite with the biblical mob that preferred Barabbas to Jesus Christ.[17] During this speech and others he would make in the coming months, Pinochet blamed his electoral defeat on the Soviet Union, the United States, Europe, and Cuba and other Latin American countries along with unnamed politicians "who sold their souls abroad."

"The regime had no plan B," recalled Genaro Arriagada, a Christian Democrat and leader of the opposition Comando del No.[18] Having convinced himself that he would win, either by electoral victory or military fiat, Pinochet was now casting about for a new strategy. According to the terms of the 1980 constitution, if the regime's single candidate were defeated in the plebiscite, free elections would be held the following year.

"He was a very worried man about human rights," General Matthei said. "He tried to persuade us that we could never turn over the country to civilians because we would end up accused."[19] On the other side of the Andes, his Argentine counterparts had been tried and sentenced for their part in the massive human rights abuses during that country's dirty war. Chile's victims were fewer in number, with those who disappeared or were killed perhaps a tenth of Argentina's thirty thousand *desaparecidos.*[20] But Argentina's dirty war featured a rotating cast of generals; in Chile, Pinochet was very much the lead actor. And the United States was exerting renewed pressure to resolve the 1976 car bomb assassination in Washington, D.C., of Chilean exile leader Orlando Letelier and an American coworker. U.S. investigators had charged the regime's former security chief, retired general Manuel Contreras, and two other army officers with planning and organizing the killing; the regime's refusal to extradite them to stand trial had further worsened relations between the two countries.

If Pinochet was "a very worried man," Contreras was even more so. He had been Pinochet's closest advisor and the man responsible for helping him consolidate power following the 1973 coup, moving him from junta member to supreme leader. In the wake of the Letelier case, Pinochet had removed Contreras and reorganized the security forces under a new name in 1978, but the former intelligence chief, who now ran a private security agency in Santiago, was still widely feared.

In February 1989 Contreras, through intermediaries, approached the U.S. embassy in Santiago bearing a strange message. He claimed to have had four separate meetings with "gringos" prior to the October 5 plebiscite. As a result of these meetings, it was agreed that neither side would reveal any information damaging to Contreras himself, Pinochet, the U.S. government, former CIA director and then–presidential candidate George Bush, or then-ambassador Harry Barnes.

The United States had broken this agreement with its recent initiatives on the Letelier case, and if a new understanding was not reached by the end of the month, Contreras would take unspecified actions against the United States. He indicated that he was prepared to give a sworn statement in Chile on the Letelier assassination, provided that he and U.S. representatives could agree on "an appropriate story" to explain the case, such as stating that the Chilean exile had been a pro-Castro Cuban agent, killed by Cuban exiles. As if to show he could still provide information of interest to U.S. officials, Contreras also indicated that one of his agents indicted by a U.S. grand jury in the case had been involved in drug trafficking with one of Pinochet's sons. Contreras's threat was reported in a cable written by embassy deputy chief of mission George Jones, who noted that the former security chief was "the most dangerous man in Chile" and that the possibility of a "a Contreras-initiated terrorist act" could not be excluded.[21]

While his former security chief was attempting to blackmail his way out of trouble, Pinochet returned to his support base, the Chilean army, visiting regiments around the country for five weeks. He then spent a week touring a part of southern Chile that had been one of only two regions in the country where a majority had cast "yes" votes in the plebiscite. Pinochet told supporters that his regime would provide the area with improved healthcare facilities as "a prize for patriotism" and that he would soon advise them who to vote for in the forthcoming presidential elections.[22] He did not discount the possibility of running himself, which would have involved bending the rules of his own constitution.

The regime's 1980 constitution envisioned a protected democracy for Chile, in which the armed forces would be given an explicit role as guarantors of the institutional order. One-third of the seats in Chile's new senate would be appointed by the government, making any future reforms difficult. Other authoritarian provisions included a ban on political party membership for labor leaders and a presidential prerogative to dissolve the lower house, the chamber of deputies.

It is unclear whether Pinochet actually believed a rerun for the Chilean presidency was feasible; in any case, he wanted to avoid being viewed as a lame duck. Aside from a shrinking pool of die-hard supporters in the Avanzada Nacional, there was little backing for a Pinochet candidacy. Chile's other conservative and right-wing parties had supported a "yes" vote in the plebiscite on the grounds that this would ensure stability and continued economic growth. Like the junta members, most conservative leaders would have preferred the candidate in the regime's one-man election to have been a civilian, and discussions were already underway to select a candidate for president as well as candidates for seats in Chile's soon-to-be-reopened senate and chamber of deputies.

IV

On March 11, the date that began his final year as president, Pinochet gave a speech reversing his earlier, adamant pronouncements that there would be no tampering with his constitution. He said he had instructed his interior minister to hold discussions with Chile's political parties on possible modifications to the charter. He even went so far as to mention some reforms being considered, such as shortening the eight-year presidential term and eliminating the president's power to expel Chileans from the country. He also promised to boost spending on health care, housing, and education, without raising taxes, and urged the few thousand regime supporters "to prepare the way to defeat the rainbow," a reference to the opposition coalition's campaign symbol.[23]

The speech suggested that Pinochet would not seek reelection in the forthcoming election and was preparing the governmental apparatus to help a conservative candidate win the presidency. His hard-line backers were still making their presence felt within the regime—there had been some discussion of Pinochet's wife, Lucia Hiriart, running for president—but more pragmatic officials had managed to persuade him that a second defeat would be disastrous. Constitutional reform and increased social spending were likely to be major themes in the campaign, and what better way to steal some of the opposition's thunder than to take control of these issues first?

If Pinochet appeared to be loosening his grip in some areas, he was tightening it in others. On March 21 he named a new head of the regime's constitutional tribunal, a seven-member body charged with interpreting the charter and approving new laws. Two more Pinochet loyalists were also appointed, one replacing a relatively independent jurist who had helped create the procedures for clean voting in the 1988 plebiscite. These appointments, according to one diplomat, effectively converted one of the more independent entities in the Chilean judicial system into "a mouthpiece for Pinochet."[24] Two weeks later Pinochet gave another speech in which he said the military would remain the best defense against those seeking to return the country to the "pseudodemocracy" of the Allende years. This last remark prompted assertive criticisms from opposition leaders, with the Christian Democrats issuing a statement calling Pinochet's words "treasonous" and stating that they contradicted his own constitution.

Renovación Nacional was a Center-Right party founded in 1987 that had reluctantly backed Pinochet's reelection in the plebiscite. The party had already begun talks with the opposition coalition to discuss constitutional reforms and the country's political future. Several leaders on both sides had known one another since their days in Chile's congress before the 1973 coup and had maintained informal contacts during the military regime. In what seemed a promising display of political cooperation, Renovación Nacional, opposition leaders, and the regime's civilian interior minister, Carlos Cáceres, had worked out a proposal for constitutional reforms to be presented later that year to voters in a referendum.

Pinochet's response to his minister's hard work was predictable. He rejected almost all of the suggested reforms, prompting Cáceres to offer his resignation the following day. Two other cabinet officials offered—or threatened—to resign as well. On April 26 Pinochet requested the resignation of his entire cabinet, and that evening he held a previously scheduled meeting with members of the junta. The junta objected strenuously to Cáceres's departure from the government and insisted that the process of constitutional reform continue. The meeting, according to General Matthei, soon deteriorated into a shouting match with Pinochet. "At one point he got up, causing his chair to fall over and, striking the table with his fist, shouted 'I am the only one to speak here. You have no right to say anything!'" Matthei said. Admiral José Merino shouted back at Pinochet, and the atmosphere became so tense that Matthei and two other service commanders walked out of the room, leaving the admiral and Pinochet still shouting at each other.[25] The next day Pinochet announced that Cáceres and all but one other minister would remain in their posts. Cáceres later said that there had never been unanimous agreement within the government on the issue of constitutional reform and tried to downplay the cabinet crisis as a short-lived disagreement.[26] But it was clear to most observers that once again the junta had forced Pinochet to back down.

Trying to save face, Pinochet lashed out at Renovación Nacional, publicly criticizing the party for working "with political parties that join with Marxists."[27] He also issued an unusual written statement accusing the opposition coalition of trying to drive a wedge between himself and the armed forces.

Constitutional reform was going ahead, with or without Pinochet's backing, but the dictator found another way to help preserve his authoritarian legacy. On June 17 the regime published a new law offering a retirement bonus equivalent to US$43,000 to any Supreme Court judges over seventy-five if they would leave. Six judges promptly accepted the offer, while three others who were eligible—the only ones not appointed by Pinochet—did not. The jurists appointed to replace the retiring judges were all viewed as sympathetic to the regime and not noted for originality or independence.

On July 30 Chilean voters went to the polls and approved, by 85.7 percent, a package of fifty-four constitutional reforms presented by the regime. The reforms were less than the original proposal worked out among Renovación Nacional, the opposition coalition, and Caceres but still represented a first, tentative step toward political liberalization: the reforms eliminated the president's right to dissolve the chamber of deputies and to send Chilean citizens into exile and limited the executive's powers under a state of emergency and a state of siege. It is likely that Pinochet and other regime hard-liners did not relish the prospect of an opposition civilian president having such powers. The presidential term was reduced from eight years to four, and an article used to ban Chile's Communist Party was replaced with one providing "norms which guarantee political pluralism." Pinochet appeared on television that evening, looking fit and healthy despite a recent hernia operation, and gave an address to the nation in which he interpreted the vote as ratification of his 1980 constitution.

V

Of much greater interest to the Chilean public was the election campaign, the first democratic presidential race since 1970. The opposition coalition, now enlarged to seventeen parties, had become the Concertación de Partidos para la Democrácia and had nominated Christian Democratic president Patricio Aylwin as its candidate. The nomination had been expected, for Aylwin was not only president of the Christian Democrats, the largest of the Concertación parties, but had been one of the most visible leaders of the Comando del No in the plebiscite. A moderate, old-fashioned politician, he had been a member of Chile's senate since 1965 and had served as its president from 1971 to 1972.

The regime's candidate was its former finance minister Hernán Büchi, a man who had been a mining engineer but who also held an MBA from Columbia University in New York. At first glance, he seemed an odd choice for a conservative, right-wing campaign: at forty he was barely old enough to run for the office, and his long blond hair made him look more like a pop singer than a potential president. His favored mode of transport was a bicycle, and he was said to be separated from his wife and cohabiting with a girlfriend.

Büchi had held various economic posts within the regime but was a reluctant candidate. In May he said he was suffering "a vital contradiction" and would not run, only to formally register as an independent candidate two months later.[28] He was backed by the Union Democrática Independiente (UDI), Chile's second-largest right-wing party. Büchi also enjoyed the support of much of the country's business community, and his campaign manager, Sebastián Piñera, was a moderate conservative who had voted against Pinochet in the plebiscite. (Piñera would make an unsuccessful run for president in 2005 and then win the presidential election four years later.)

The Concertación had published a detailed, forty-eight-page policy document, which began with a list of further constitutional reforms, such as an elected (rather than appointed) congress and reigns on presidential control over the military. It pledged to fully investigate human rights violations since the 1973 coup and would support the Chilean courts in prosecuting the most egregious cases. The document also promised sound macroeconomic policies but indicated that the minimum wage would be increased and that a reform of the regime's labor code would give unions more bargaining rights. There were also detailed sections promoting stricter environmental policies, along with sections extending the rights of woman and Chile's indigenous minorities.

The Chilean Right was suffering from serious internal divisions, as seen in its much shorter, sixteen-page program document. The economic section was more expansive than the Concertación's and was difficult to reconcile with Büchi's reputation for careful fiscal management: there were promises of a million new jobs, better salaries and working conditions, a hundred thousand new housing units built each year, and access to private health care for all, with some subsidies to help the poor pay for treatment. There was a section on human rights containing a vague condemnation of violence. The UDI and Renovación Nacional had signed an electoral pact, Democrácia y Progreso, but there were rivalries among their various senate and congressional candidates as well as a lack of consensus over how much distance to place between themselves and the Pinochet regime.[29] The Aylwin campaign was already attacking Büchi as a continuation of the regime. Complicating matters further, another Chilean businessman, Francisco Errazurriz, had registered to run for president as an independent candidate. His candidacy was likely to siphon votes away from Büchi but not from Aylwin.

Both candidates, to their credit, had filed full financial statements disclosing their holdings. Aylwin, who came from a family of prominent lawyers, turned out to own only one car; Büchi had investments worth around US$100,000 plus holdings in two small companies. Neither could reasonably accuse the other of ill-gotten gains.

Aylwin had been acting like a presidential candidate months before he received the nomination. He had delivered an address on his coalition's economic and social programs to the U.S.-Chile Chamber of Commerce, a group largely supportive of the regime's economic policies. He said that the Americans there understood that economic freedom also required political freedom and that in economic terms Chile was divided into two countries: one whose people had incomes of between one and two thousand dollars per month and another whose people had incomes of between fifty to one hundred dollars per month. Although in the 1960s even the Chilean Right favored strong state participation in the economy, the world had changed and so had the opposition's thinking—the coalition believed that 90 percent of the economy should be in private hands. There would be more social spending and wealthy Chileans would have to pay higher taxes, but an Aylwin government would resist the kind of populist pressures that had undermined other Latin American countries. A question-and-answer session followed, with Aylwin referring some of the more technical queries on matters relating to foreign investment and taxes to an aide. Much of the reaction was critical, with some in attendance dismissing the economic proposals as old-fashioned, "soak the rich" rhetoric.[30]

Büchi's support from business groups did not seem to boost his confidence in other settings. His first official campaign appearance occurred in a small town in southern Chile where a majority of voters had backed Pinochet's reelection. A few days later he was photographed taking part in an equestrian show, winning an amateur jumping competition astride a horse named Oligarch.[31] Büchi also gave a speech in a low-income area of Santiago but left almost immediately afterward, as if he wanted to avoid mingling with locals. Other events, such as a series of visits to factories, received little publicity, and his campaign did not always inform the press of his plans.

The polls showed Aylwin enjoying a healthy lead, with one conservative research group reporting Aylwin ahead 51.6 percent to Büchi's 35.8 percent in October. An even higher percentage of respondents—60 percent—believed that Aylwin would win the forthcoming election.[32] Even Pinochet seemed to think the opposition victory was inevitable, and it appears he was spending most of this period devising ways to protect himself and the military under a future opposition government.

On the anniversary of his promotion to army commander sixteen years earlier, Pinochet delivered a hard-line speech stating that the armed forces were standing by to "rescue Chile" if the situation warranted. He warned against any tampering with a 1978 amnesty for human rights abuses his regime had imposed and indicated that service commanders could not be removed from their posts by a future president. The military would determine its own budget and system for promoting officers; these provisions were nonnegotiable, he said.[33]

Several weeks later Pinochet presented a new law to the junta that would create a military council to preside over the armed forces and take charge of all dealings with the executive branch. The proposed law effectively sought to construct an additional barrier between civilian and military authority, with the commanders of the different armed services reporting to this new council rather than directly to the Defense Ministry. "He wanted to establish a kind of parallel military government," General Matthei recalled. The Chilean navy and army were willing to go along with the measure, which required unanimous approval by the junta. Another thorny issue for Pinochet was what to do with his security forces.

Matthei said the air force's chief accountant had come to him with the news that the service's budget had been unexpectedly increased. At a subsequent junta meeting Pinochet informed the service commanders that he needed to redistribute CNI officials and employees among the different branches of the armed forces—hence the budget increases. The Chilean air force was to incorporate about three hundred individuals, some military officers and some civilians, into its ranks. "Obviously, I got angry and told the president there was no way we were going to take charge of these people or these funds and that I was returning the extra budget monies assigned to me," he said. Matthei was irritated that the proposal had been presented as a done deal, as had so many of Pinochet's past schemes. The dictator later requested a meeting with the air force commander, which took place at a military club near an army base in Santiago's southeastern outskirts. Pinochet "said that we had to face the eventual human rights problems together, and that each one of us had to do his part," Matthei stated. Matthei had assumed command of the air force in 1978, when Pinochet had forced the removal of his predecessor, who had argued for an earlier transition to democracy. Eighteen other air force generals had resigned in support of their commander, leaving only Matthei and one other general. As commander, Matthei had successfully weeded out air force officials or employees working for the security forces and informed Pinochet that he was unwilling to reverse this policy.[34]

Pinochet moved much of the CNI into an army intelligence unit, and his defense minister said the former security forces' files would all be destroyed before the new president took office. However, the CNI had one last operation to perform. On the evening of September 4, 1989, Jecar Neghme, a twenty-nine-year-old spokesman for the moderate wing of the Movement of the Revolutionary Left (MIR), was shot dead as he left the organization's offices in Santiago. The MIR was founded in the 1960s out of university student groups and was a principal target of the regime's security forces. A few days earlier Neghme had spoken at a MIR rally in support of Aylwin's candidacy (though the MIR, like the Chilean Communist Party, was not part of the opposition coalition). "Pinochet cannot ignore us, we have survived, we are not dead," he told the crowd. Perhaps the CNI interpreted Neghme's remarks as a provocation, but whatever the motive, his was the regime's last killing. More than sixteen years later a judge would charge six former CNI agents in the killing; all but one confessed to involvement. According to an attorney representing the victim's family, the decision to kill Neghme was made to spend unused "special projects" funds before the agency was disbanded.[35]

VI

On September 11, the sixteenth anniversary of the coup that brought his regime to power, Pinochet gave an emotive ninety-minute farewell speech. He listed his regime's accomplishments in such areas as road and bridge building, mining production, and the reduction of infant mortality rates and lashed out at "those looking for money and foreign philosophies abroad." He also announced a 12 percent pay increase for government employees. Choking back tears, he said he "loved Chile more than his own life."[36]

It was not, however, Pinochet's farewell to the Chilean army. Over the years he had increased the number of generals, bringing their total the previous year to fifty-six. This gave Chile a ratio of almost one general to every thousand soldiers, or double the U.S. equivalent. On October 9 he announced new promotions and appointments, retiring twelve generals but appointing another seven. He also replaced his vice commander, General Jorge Zincke, with another general. Zincke was well respected among his fellow officers but had shown perhaps too much independence when he refused the Pinochet campaign's request to allow a premature celebration in the streets of Santiago the night of the plebiscite. He was also said to have a plan to purge the more notorious human rights abusers before a new civilian president took office in March. Zincke expected there would be human rights trials in the future and wanted to lessen the army's involvement.[37]

Pinochet was having none of this. A few days after the new appointments, he made another visit to southern Chile, where he gave a speech warning that the armed forces would never "allow any of their members to be vilified and humiliated for their actions aimed at saving Chile" and said he would remain as army commander to protect his officers. "The day they touch any of my men will be the end of the state of law," he said. Aylwin's reply to Pinochet's threat seemed like that of a patient adult dealing with an ill-behaved child. "What is one to understand by touching a man? Is it to apply the law and justice?" he asked.[38] "I believe that phrase was an unfortunate one pronounced by this gentleman in an outburst, without really thinking." Were he to take Pinochet's statement seriously, it would constitute sedition, a punishable offense.

On November 13 Pinochet held a luncheon for right-wing political leaders where he suggested that army headquarters might be moved to Iquique, a port city in northern Chile. Any dealings with the future civilian president could be handled in Santiago by Pinochet's vice commander. He also indicated that he expected Aylwin to win the election, even as some right-wing leaders were hoping that businessman Francisco Errazurriz's candidacy would result in a second round between the opposition leader and Büchi.

The polls continued to give Aylwin a commanding lead, and his team was making plans for his future government as well as conducting informal discussions with Renovación Nacional politicians on how constitutional reform might be continued. Aylwin presented himself as a bridge builder, at one point appearing onstage with the daughter of the late socialist president Salvador Allende and a politician from the most conservative wing of the opposition coalition. Privately, some coalition leaders were worried that Aylwin could be the target of an assassination attempt by right-wing hard-liners. Should this occur in the eight days leading up to the election, the coalition would be prevented by law from running another presidential candidate, leaving voters with a choice between Büchi and Errazurriz.[39]

On December 14, 1989, over seven million Chileans took part in the first presidential election to be held in nearly two decades. It was also an election for the country's new congress, composed of thirty-eight elected senators (plus nine appointed senators) and one hundred twenty members of the chamber of deputies. There were fifteen officially registered political parties, with another twelve with applications pending, a remarkable situation when one considers that the regime's constitution demanded that each party gather at least 33,500 signatures from voters unaffiliated with any other political group.

The voting process went smoothly, and there were no suspicious delays in announcing the results. The first returns were reported at 7:30 p.m., showing Aylwin clearly ahead, and there was a definitive announcement by Interior Minister Carlos Cáceres shortly before midnight that recognized the Christian Democrat as Chile's president-elect. Nearly two hours earlier Büchi made a gracious concession speech in which he promised to "maintain constructive criticism" of the new civilian government, and then he proceeded to Aylwin's campaign headquarters to present his congratulations. Independent candidate Francisco Errazurriz followed suit. The final returns showed Aylwin with 55 percent of the vote, Büchi with 29 percent, and Errazurriz with 15 percent. In a brief address to his supporters, Aylwin promised to be president "of all Chileans."

The election itself had been peaceful, and most Chileans turned their attention to Christmas and the southern hemisphere summer ahead. But Chile's angry, disaffected youths made their presence felt in the election aftermath. By late afternoon there were scattered clashes between the carabinero police and groups of rock-throwing youths, some wearing emblems of the Far-Left. At one point the demonstrators blocked Santiago's main avenue for an hour and were eventually dispersed with tear gas and water cannons. And in the coastal resort city of Viña del Mar, similar groups of youths attacked what they charged was a building belonging to the CNI. The violence was easily contained but was still a worrying taste of what Aylwin would have to confront in the near future.[40] He spent much of that day at his campaign headquarters in Santiago's San Francisco Hotel, receiving international delegations, journalists, and diplomats. U.S. ambassador Charles Gillespie was among the visitors. "He's a good, decent man who clearly senses the heavy responsibilities he now faces," Gillespie wrote in a cable to Washington, D.C., following their meeting. "He shows every sign of having the qualities necessary to guide this country through the difficult times ahead. Certainly the majority of Chileans think so."[41]

TWO The Conciliator

I

March 11, 1990, was the day Pinochet actually handed over the presidential badge to his successor, if not all the power that office was meant to signify. According to protocol, the departing president is supposed to be the first to greet the new president, but Pinochet arrived a few minutes late.[1] A photograph taken in La Moneda shortly after the inauguration is suggestive of the conflicts ahead, though outwardly the two men appear to be engaging in polite conversation. In the photograph Pinochet wears the army's white dress uniform and stands less than two feet from Aylwin. Though slightly shorter than the new civilian president, he looks the more confident: his posture erect, his hands folded neatly behind his back as he gazes directly at his successor. Two younger army officers standing behind Aylwin and Pinochet are also staring at the new civilian president; one is unsmiling, while the other seems to be smirking. Pinochet may have surrendered the Chilean presidency, but he would continue as army commander and do everything possible to keep his authoritarian system in place.

"I think he believed that my government was going to fail and that he would return in all his glory and majesty," Aylwin said. The two men first crossed paths during the presidency of Christian Democrat Eduardo Frei (1964–70), when Aylwin was a member of the Chilean senate. There was a reception at the senate library that Pinochet attended as representative of the army; Aylwin still possesses a group photograph of the event. The second meeting occurred a few years later, when then-president Salvador Allende summoned the senate president and other Chilean leaders to La Moneda.[2]

The meeting had been called to discuss the assassination of a former cabinet minister who had served under President Eduardo Frei Montalva, Allende's predecessor. Edmundo Pérez Zujovic had been driving along a Santiago street, accompanied by his daughter, when his car was intercepted by a leftist extremist group that shot the Christian Democrat with an automatic weapon.[3] At the meeting Aylwin recalled that he urged Allende to turn the case over to the carabinero police rather than the civilian detective police, Investigaciónes, whose left-wing director seemed too politicized to undertake an impartial inquiry. But Pinochet rebuked Aylwin, saying that the Chilean army had full confidence in the leftist-led detective unit. "It was the first time I had an exchange of opinions with Pinochet," he said. That year Aylwin became president of the Chilean senate and led the political opposition to the Allende government, even as Pinochet appeared to be a neutral officer unlikely to participate in coup plotting.[4] This opposition culminated in a congressional resolution, the Declaration of the Breakdown of Chile's Democracy, on August 22, 1973. The resolution called for "an immediate end" to Allende's constitutional abuses, accusing the Socialist leader of ruling by decree, of supporting illegal land seizures, and of ignoring rulings by the Chilean judiciary.[5] The next day Pinochet became army commander, taking over from General Carlos Prats, a strict constitutionalist who resigned when a group of right-wing Chilean women staged a demonstration outside his home.

Their next encounter would not occur until a few months after the coup. Aylwin and other leaders of the Christian Democratic Party had requested an audience with the junta to discuss the human rights situation and the decree banning Chile's political parties. The meeting was long, civilized, but uncomfortable, he recalled. Pinochet barely spoke, but other junta members had harsh words about the Christian Democrats and the Frei government, accusing them of enabling a near-Marxist takeover of the country under Allende.

The two met again on December 21, 1989, as Aylwin reestablished the protocol of president-elect visiting the departing president. Aylwin broached the subject of Pinochet's future, telling the general that while he recognized that the constitution allowed him to remain army commander for eight more years, it would be for better for the government and the Chilean army if he would retire. Aylwin would never forget Pinochet's response, which contained an implied threat: "But no one will ever protect you better than I will!"[6]

Aylwin was happy to have air force commander General Fernando Matthei and carabinero police director General Rodolfo Stange remain in their posts as counterweights to Pinochet. The fourth member of the junta, navy commander Admiral José Merino, resigned shortly before the inauguration in a maneuver designed to ensure that his successor would be sympathetic to the outgoing military regime. He had drawn up a list of five like-minded admirals from which Pinochet could make the appointment while he was still president. Pinochet selected Admiral Jorge Martinez Busch, who by law would remain naval commander for eight years before becoming an appointed senator for eight more years.[7]

II

The Pinochet regime allowed Aylwin's staff less than twelve hours to prepare La Moneda for its new occupant. Late in the evening of March 10, 1990, an advance team was finally allowed to enter the presidential palace, where they found no government documents or archives and only a few computers whose files had been wiped clean. The regime had constructed an extensive underground wing, nicknamed "El Bunker," containing at least forty offices and a broadcast studio where Pinochet gave his television speeches, but little of this equipment was left for the new government to use.[8] "I recall they had even taken the phones, cut the wires," Aylwin said. "It was incredible."[9] U.S. embassy officials visited La Moneda that night to inspect security arrangements for Vice President Dan Quayle's planned meeting with the new president. They found "a scene from Fellini" as Aylwin's team explored areas of the presidential palace previously unknown to them, moving furniture and trying to establish the new government's physical presence.[10]

The actual inauguration ceremony was a simple affair held in the port city of Valparaíso, where the Pinochet regime had decreed Chile's new congress should be located. Work on the building had not even been completed when Aylwin entered the chamber, where the new senate president administered the oath of office and draped him in the presidential sash. An assembly of newly elected parliamentarians, foreign dignitaries, and officials from both the previous regime and the Aylwin government watched as Pinochet handed Aylwin the star-shaped brooch he had been wearing, which had belonged to Chilean independence hero Bernardo O'Higgins and had been passed from president to president for one hundred fifty years. Many of those present were weeping openly. After shaking hands with Aylwin and his wife, Pinochet and his entourage left the building as the new cabinet was sworn in.

Thousands of cheering supporters lined the route as the new president's motorcade made its way back to Santiago, where Aylwin was greeted by celebratory crowds gathered in the plaza and the streets surrounding La Moneda. He and his wife, Leonor, briefly appeared on the balcony, where he promised to work "with all [his] energy and ability" toward building a true democracy in Chile. He then began receiving visitors, including Allende's widow, Hortensia Bussi. She was accompanied by Veronica Ahumada, who had been a young member of Allende's staff and whom Aylwin had offered a job at La Moneda. "It was very moving to reenter La Moneda through the very doors I had exited sixteen and a half years earlier," she said. Ahumada had been among the last to leave as the Chilean air force's Hawker Hunter planes began strafing the palace. Allende told her to save herself, that she was part of Chilean history and that she needed to remember those moments. Ahumada was arrested, and brought to the defense ministry, "but fortunately not tortured," and given twenty-four hours to leave the country. Now she and the president's widow were returning to La Moneda. "We could hardly believe where we were," she said. "It was magical."[11]

III

Other scenes from that day were less than dignified. U.S. vice president Dan Quayle paid a visit that morning to Pinochet at his army commander's residence and was booed and jeered by several hundred pro-regime demonstrators who blamed the United States for the regime's defeat in the plebiscite and who viewed even a Republican administration as part of an international conspiracy against Chile. "Go back to Cuba!" some of them shouted. As Quayle's motorcade departed, some of the demonstrators even rushed up to the vice president's limousine, screaming obscenities and kicking and punching the vehicle.[12]

In downtown Santiago the festive atmosphere gave way to disruptive clashes between the carabinero police and the drunken hooligans throwing rocks and bottles at them. The new government charged that some members of "the overexcited political left" were partly to blame for the incidents, in which over one hundred civilians and seventy-nine police were injured.[13] Traces of tear gas lingered in the air around the presidential palace.

Aylwin wrote his inaugural address himself and saved the speech until the next day for an extraordinary ceremony at the National Stadium, the site of mass detentions, torture, and execution following the 1973 coup. The names of the missing and the dead were scrolled across the stadium scoreboard. In the field below, Chilean folk dancers representing various regional and cultural groups converged and symbolically pulled the country together. A group of women dressed in black and white carried pictures of some of the missing. And in a precisely choreographed presentation, hundreds of youths unfurled an enormous Chilean flag covering the entire field, an act that sought to heal some of the scars of the past and unify the country.

In his speech, Aylwin said Chile's poor would be his government's first priority and that he had instructed his cabinet to begin talks with the country's largest labor organization, the Central Unitaria de Trabajadores (CUT), about a new labor code. But he cautioned that it would take time to meet the country's "many long-postponed needs" and urged patience, asking, "How many years did it take us to recover democracy?" Aylwin also called on Chileans to reestablish "a climate of respect and confidence among all Chileans, whether civilian or military." At the mention of the word *military,* some of the assembled crowd began jeering, but Aylwin turned the crowd around in an electrifying show of leadership. "Yes, *señores.* Yes, my compatriots," he said, gesticulating forcefully and looking defiantly into the crowd. "Civilians *and* military. Chile is one nation." The jeers turned to cheers and applause, and he paused for a few second before continuing. "The sins of a few cannot affect all. We have to reunite the Chilean family!"[14] There followed another crescendo of applause and cheering, causing Aylwin to pause once again.

Until that moment, Chile's new president had not been viewed as an especially charismatic figure or dynamic public speaker, yet here he clearly showed he could inspire an audience. His critics on both the Right and the Left may have dismissed him as a leftover from the political past, but Aylwin was about to demonstrate considerable skill and diplomacy. His placid demeanor would help project a public image of calm as Pinochet plotted ways to undermine the new administration and as extremist groups unleashed a disturbing cycle of violence. No government ever accomplishes all its goals, and the Aylwin administration would disappoint many Chileans, but it would succeed in moving Chile away from dictatorship and toward a democratic future.

After the speech Aylwin, his wife, his interior minister, and carabinero commander General Rodolfo Stange visited the hospitalized carabineros injured in the previous day's disturbances. The next day Aylwin attended a reception given by CUT and made a point of shaking hands with almost every trade unionist present. He cautioned those present that they would not always be in agreement, but that he and CUT president Manuel Bustos respected each other and would continue to seek common ground.

IV

Chilean labor had suffered its share of repression under the Pinochet regime. In 1982 the president of the public employees' union—a man who had initially supported the military coup—was found a few days after he had held a press conference calling for a campaign to oppose the regime's economic policies with his throat cut and five bullet holes in the back of his head.[15] More recently Bustos and the CUT vice president had been sentenced to internal exile several weeks before the 1988 plebiscite. Now, with a popularly elected president in office, would Chilean labor unleash an avalanche of pent-up grievances and demands that the economy could not sustain?

This was the fear of many Chilean business leaders, who, as mentioned in the previous chapter, would have preferred the Pinochet regime's candidate, former finance minister Hernán Büchi, as president. Aylwin's new finance minister, Alejandro Foxley, was a Christian Democrat with a PhD in economics from the University of Wisconsin. His economy minister, however, had the kind of background that might give conservative investors nightmares. Socialist Carlos Ominami, who held a PhD in economics from the University of Paris, had once been active in the Movement of the Revolutionary Left (MIR), a Marxist group whose members had participated in land and business seizures during the Allende government. But neither Ominami nor Foxley had any populist economic illusions. In neighboring Argentina a new elected government taking power after years of military rule had just struggled through a round of hyperinflation, riots, and looting, causing President Raul Alfonsin to declare a state of emergency and later resign before his term ended. In Peru another popularly elected president, Alan García, was presiding over an inflation rate that would reach a whopping 7,649 percent that year and an economic collapse that had left Peruvians even poorer than they were when he took office. Would this be Chile's fate?

It would not. One early, hopeful sign was the fact that Aylwin's economic team did not encounter as much obstructiveness from their outgoing counterparts as other cabinet ministers faced. Foxley said that during the period between the elections and the inauguration he had good relations with the official in charge of the transition.[16] Information on the Chilean economy was shared, and the two sides easily reached agreement on a new president for the country's central bank, which under the military regime had become an autonomous institution akin to the U.S. Federal Reserve.

The Aylwin administration's initial approach to the economy would be one of fiscal caution rather than populist spending. Chile's gross domestic product had grown by 7.3 percent in 1988 and 10.6 the following year, causing concern that the economy was overheating. Inflation was also growing, from 12.7 percent in 1988 to 21.4 percent in 1989—low by regional standards but worrisome to Chileans.[17] Foxley and others have attributed this in part to the regime's more lavish expenditures during its last two years in power. "We did something that nobody expected from a Concertacion government," he recalled. "We said, 'we are going to have fiscal austerity, we are going to have not only a balanced budget but a fiscal surplus, we are going to be hard, we are going to reduce spending everywhere possible."[18]

Foxley was committed to fiscal austerity, but Aylwin and his cabinet had also made a sincere pledge to reduce poverty, which, according to United Nations figures, affected 40 percent of Chile's thirteen million people. In April the government presented a tax reform proposal to Chile's new congress. Corporate income tax would be increased temporarily from 10 to 15 percent, and total profits—not just distributed profits—were to be taxed. The highest maximum tax rate was extended to a larger group of taxpayers, and the value-added tax was increased from 16 to 18 percent. This last provision was less controversial than it might seem, for Chile's value-added tax had been 20 percent during most of the military regime and only reduced to 16 percent as a vote-getting ploy in the run-up to the 1988 presidential plebiscite.

Getting legislative approval to increase taxes is hardly easy in the best of circumstances, but the Aylwin government faced a congress that was just beginning to function after sixteen and a half years of inactivity and had to legislate in the unfamiliar surroundings of the still-unfinished building in Valparaíso. The Chilean senate had nine members designated by the regime, and of the thirty-eight elected senators, twenty-two were members of Aylwin's political coalition, which also held seventy-two of the one hundred twenty seats in the lower house, the chamber of deputies. And according to the terms of the regime's constitution, any reforms required a two-thirds majority.

But the Center-Left coalition already had a working relationship with Renovación Nacional (RN), the Center-Right party with whom it had successfully negotiated a package of constitutional reforms the previous year. RN's leadership described the economic proposals as moderate and balanced, and after a few months of negotiations, the tax increases were passed on July 20, 1990. "Most of us were aware of the immense responsibility we had to build a democracy based on accords," said Alberto Espina, an RN deputy in the new congress. "The initial feeling was one of urgency."[19] The increased tax revenues gave the government an additional US$600 million for spending on housing, healthcare, education, and support for small businesses.

Labor relations were another critical component. The Pinochet regime had initially banned all strikes and severely restricted trade union activity, later issuing a labor code allowing some limited rights. Aylwin's labor minister proposed a series of talks between the CUT leadership and the head of Chile's politically powerful manufacturers' association, the Confederación de Producción y Comercio (CPC). CUT leaders Bustos and Arturo Martinez were receptive to this initiative, in part because CPC president Manuel Feliu had called for their release when the two men were serving internal exile sentences. Many Chilean business leaders were decidedly unenthusiastic, noting that the CUT only represented some 10 percent of the country's labor force. But Feliu managed to convince them that it was in their own best interests to work out an accord, which might help future labor-management negotiations. The meetings resulted in the signing of an agreement to raise the minimum wage on April 27, 1990.[20]

V

Chile was also beginning to enjoy the fruits of renewed or improved relations with the rest of the world after enduring years as a diplomatic pariah. Pinochet had received few invitations to travel abroad, and his last attempt to do so, in 1980, had ended in disaster: Ferdinand Marcos rescinded an invitation to visit the Philippines after the dictator's plane had already left Chile and was heading toward Manila. But those days had come to an end. At least eighty foreign delegations arrived to attend Aylwin's inauguration, and Spain signed a $2 billion economic cooperation agreement with Chile that very day. The delegations included several from countries that had broken off relations after the coup. Relations were quickly restored with the Soviet Union, four eastern European countries, four Caribbean nations—Trinidad, Suriname, Jamaica, and Guyana—and Mexico, whose embassy had sheltered hundreds of asylum seekers in wake of the 1973 coup and whose diplomats had been repeatedly harassed by the military.[21] Mexico and Chile also signed a free trade agreement at year's end.

Aylwin soon received an invitation to make a state visit to Washington, D.C., and President George Bush promised a reciprocal visit to Santiago before the end of the year. The high level of good will would be needed to resolve some of the thorny issues between the two countries. The most tangled of these was the Letelier case. In September 1976 an American expat residing in Santiago helped assassinate a Chilean exile living in Washington, D.C. The American, Michael Townley, had arrived Santiago as a teenager with his parents, later marrying a Chilean woman and moving to Miami, where they became friendly with Cuban exiles, many of whom were involved in violent anti-Castro activities. Viewing Allende as another Castro and wanting to be a player in the fight against world communism, Townley approached the CIA, offering to work for the agency in Chile. The CIA later said it rejected Townley as an agent, although declassified U.S. documents suggest he was in at least indirect contact with the agency and a frequent visitor to the U.S. embassy.[22] Townley and his wife were active members of Patria y Libertad, a right-wing extremist group responsible for bombings and other acts of sabotage against the Allende government. After the coup, he began working for the regime's feared security agency, the Dirección Nacional de Inteligencia (DINA), as did many other former Patria y Libertad members.

Acting on orders from DINA, Townley detonated a bomb that killed Pinochet's army commander predecessor, General Carlos Prats, and his wife in Buenos Aires in 1974. The following year he took part in two more assassination attempts. First, he tried to blow up a building in Mexico City where several prominent Chilean exiles were attending a convention. Second, he attempted to assassinate the Christian Democrat and former Frei government cabinet minister Bernardo Leighton and his wife in Rome. The couple was critically wounded but survived.

On September 21, 1976, a bomb attached to a car driven by Orlando Letelier exploded, killing him and an American coworker and injuring her husband. Letelier had been Chilean ambassador to Washington during the Allende government, later becoming a cabinet minister before enduring detention and exile after the coup. Townley had organized the assassination with help of anti-Castro Cubans, and he later made a deal with the FBI to testify in the investigation in exchange for witness protection.

Letelier had lobbied hard against foreign assistance to the Pinochet regime, and two months before Letelier died, the U.S. congress had approved the Kennedy-Harkin amendment banning all military assistance, credits, and cash sales of weapons to the regime. U.S. officials later sought the extradition of DINA chief Manuel Contreras and two other Chilean agents and compensation for the victims' families, which the regime adamantly rejected.

In 1987 the Reagan administration had withdrawn the duty-free status of some Chilean imports, citing violations of international standards of workers' rights. Chile had been one of one hundred forty-one countries granted this status under the Generalized System of Preferences (GSP), a program to aid developing economies by stimulating trade. The move did not amount to a major economic blow, for only about $60 million of the $818 million in goods Chile exported to the United States that year was covered by the program. Chile was also suspended from programs under the Overseas Private Investment Corporation (OPIC), which helps U.S. businesses investing abroad. But the mere fact of a democratically elected president taking office in Chile did not automatically result in a lifting of these sanctions.

At his meeting with Bush and other officials in Washington on October 2, 1990, Aylwin raised the issues of trade and the arms embargo and was told that a press release announcing the restoration of OPIC programs in Chile was about to be issued. There would have to be some resolution of the Letelier case for the arms embargo to be lifted, with approval by the Chilean congress for compensation and recognition by the U.S. Congress that such steps were being taken. The Aylwin administration had agreed that Chile would pay compensation to the Letelier family and to the family of his coworker Ronni Moffitt, though their efforts to proceed with a criminal case against the security agents involved were being blocked by the former military prosecutor. They discussed beginning negotiations for a bilateral free trade agreement, and Bush told Aylwin there was excitement in Washington over Chile's new democracy. Then Aylwin raised a political problem he faced: "The Pinochet opposition is aggressive—small, but very aggressive," he said. "At present my government is seen as being very friendly and subservient to the United States, but it doesn't seem to get anything out of this new relationship and this is beginning to affect public opinion. I need a card to show that democracy in Chile is of direct benefit, that democracy means our friends give us better bilateral treatment." Bush responded by promising to search for ways to support Chilean democracy and noted that "under previous conditions the President of the United States would not go to Chile."[23]

This visit, which took place that December, was the first by a U.S. president to Chile in thirty years. In Santiago Bush announced that eligible Chilean exports would be reinstated in the GSP, but this measure was not immediately implemented. This bureaucratic delay irritated many in the Chilean congress, and the president of the senate traveled to Washington in January to investigate. Bush finally signed the official decree on February 5, 1991.[24]

VI

Just ten days after Aylwin's inauguration, two gunmen walked into an office building in eastern Santiago and proceeded to the real estate business of former air force commander General Gustavo Leigh. The retired general had been one of the original junta members but had been forced out of the regime in 1978 by Pinochet after publicly urging a return to civilian rule. This made Leigh a hero to some, but many Chileans who had been arrested after the coup had reason to hate him.

The air force had organized its own secret intelligence unit, the Comando Conjunto, partly as a counterweight to the DINA, which was greatly feared. Leigh resented the growing power of DINA chief Manuel Contreras, who reported exclusively to Pinochet and who also kept tabs on any potentially disloyal officials within the regime. While Contreras's DINA targeted members of the MIR, smaller left-wing groups, and, occasionally, the Christian Democrat Party, Leigh's Comando Conjunto dedicated its efforts to eradicating the Chilean Communist Party. The gunmen ordered the office secretary and another employee to lie on the floor before firing several shots directly at Leigh and his associate, another air force general.[25]

The attack unnerved the new government, for just days earlier Aylwin had issued pardons for forty-six political prisoners and had proposed legislation to amend laws the Pinochet regime had used to quell dissent: the terrorism law, the state security law, the code of military justice, the arms control law, and the criminal code. None of the pardoned detainees had been charged with anything other than nonviolent political offenses, and there was nothing to link them to any crimes, but the attack rekindled the age-old debate about individual rights versus public security. Leigh lost an eye in the attack but within hours was reported to be sitting up in his hospital bed, alert and receiving visits from Aylwin, Santiago's Catholic archbishop, the presidents of the senate and chamber of deputies, and other Chilean leaders.

Some Chileans speculated that the attack could have been the work of Far-Right extremists linked to the military regime's security forces who were seeking to cause panic among political conservatives and undermine the Aylwin government. The circumstances of the shooting were not typical of other operations carried out by armed leftist groups in Chile, and the fact that the gunmen were able to make their getaway by nonchalantly boarding a bus in an affluent part of eastern Santiago suggested some collusion with the security forces. The timing of the attack, so soon after Aylwin's inauguration, was also suspicious, for Leigh had worked in that office building for several years and had no bodyguards—a revenge attack could just as easily have been carried out long before Aylwin took office. There was also considerable enmity between Pinochet and the former air force commander, as Leigh had been vocal in his criticism of the regime after leaving the junta.

The Manuel Rodriguez Patriotic Front (FPMR) was founded in 1983 as an armed wing of the Chilean Communist Party. Named after one of the country's independence heroes, it claimed responsibility for regularly blowing up electricity pylons and causing massive power cuts in Santiago and other parts of the country.[26] Many of its members had spent time as exiles in Cuba, where they received militia training, though their Cuban benefactors seem to have overestimated the organization's capabilities and the amount of support they could claim from the Chilean public.

In 1986 Pinochet regime security forces found a cache of three hundred twenty-four assault rifles hidden near a small fishing village in northern Chile and made several arrests at the site. The detainees confessed to being FPMR militants, and their interrogation and subsequent arrests led the authorities to seven other sites, whose contents amounted to "the most ordnance ever found at one time in the possession of Latin American terrorists."[27] The arms caches, which included antitank weapons, rocket launchers, nearly two thousand hand grenades, and over three thousand kilograms of explosives, had been sent by freighter to a site off the north coast of Chile and delivered to fishing boats owned by the FPMR. Although the FPMR's membership had never numbered more than a few hundred, the weapons caches could have armed several thousand insurgents, but they may have been intended for a future conflict.[28]

The group had also attempted to assassinate Pinochet by ambushing his motorcade that year, killing five of his bodyguards. The regime security forces reacted by killing three Chilean left-wing activists—who had no ties to the FPMR—and arresting several other opposition political figures. But for all the regime's repressive apparatus, it never succeeded in completely eliminating armed leftist groups. And shortly before Pinochet was due to leave office, the regime would face another security failure when forty-nine FPMR members staged a spectacular escape from Santiago's public jail. Using rudimentary tools, they managed to dig a three-hundred-foot tunnel and ventilate it with plastic soft drink bottles and motors extracted from small appliances. The escapees included eighteen men accused of participating in the 1986 assassination attempt of Pinochet.[29]

By the time Aylwin had taken office, the group had split into two factions—one that advocating working with the political system, the other, a dissident group that continued its violent, score-settling attacks. "It was a serious matter for a new government," air force commander Fernando Matthei later said of the attack on his former chief.[30] Matthei issued a communiqué condemning the assassination attempt while also affirming the Chilean air force's unequivocal support for the democratic process. The Chilean Communist Party and the MIR also condemned the attack, saying it "only served the purposes of the nostalgic sectors of the dictatorship."[31]

Pinochet, meanwhile, was quoted in the Chilean press as saying the attack on Leigh would be the first of many such terrorist attempts. The army public relations office quickly issued a disclaimer, but Aylwin and other government officials took Pinochet to task, challenging him to come forth with any information that might assist the authorities. Regardless of what Pinochet did or did not say, the prediction turned out to be true: over the next twelve months there would be nearly two dozen similar attacks in Chile. The targets were almost all police and army officials linked to the security forces, including a military doctor accused of helping keep tortured prisoners alive during interrogation sessions.

Then, on April 1, 1991, a Chilean whom no one had ever accused of human rights abuses was shot and killed. Senator Jaime Guzmán had been a political advisor to Pinochet, one of the authors of the regime's 1980 constitution, and a founder of the rightist Unión Democrática Independiente party. A caller identifying himself as a spokesman for the FPMR told a radio station that Guzmán had been killed for his "service to the previous government."[32] The killing was condemned by figures across Chile's broad political spectrum, but rightist opposition leaders challenged the Aylwin government to take tougher actions. A few days before Guzmán's murder, members of the FPMR had paraded openly in a poor neighborhood of Santiago, though it was unclear which faction the demonstrators represented—violent or merely political. According to a declassified CIA report, the Aylwin government had instructed the carabinero police to prevent the demonstration. "The carabineros, however, permitted the demonstration to occur and made few arrests," the report said.[33] Some critics called for the resignation of Aylwin's interior minister for failing to contain terrorism. At the memorial service for the slain, rightist political passions ran high, with some mourners shouting that Aylwin was responsible for Guzmán's death.

"We had a real problem," said Jorge Burgos, Aylwin's cabinet chief and legal counselor to the Interior Ministry. "We imagined that when the new government took over the ultraleft was going to lay down its arms. This was a mistake."[34] The authorities were hamstrung by a lack of intelligence on the FPMR and other fringe groups, which the CNI had monitored. Regime officials claimed to have destroyed the CNI's files as the agency was incorporated into the army intelligence department shortly before the Aylwin government came to power. If the army had any information, it was not sharing, and Aylwin was determined to limit the military's role in internal security matters. "We had no files, the CNI left us with no data," Burgos said. Other law enforcement agencies were not yet prepared to take on an antiterrorist role: the Investigaciónes were distrusted as corrupt, and the new director was in the midst of trying to reorganize the institution and to purge the worst offenders. And the carabineros had little experience in counterterrorism and intelligence gathering.

The Aylwin government declared two days of mourning and announced the appointment of a special investigator in the case as well as the creation of a new antiterrorist unit made up of carabineros and Investigaciónes detectives. But the attacks continued: later that month another right-wing senator received death threats and was given police protection while a third was the object of a failed attack in which a bomb placed outside his home exploded prematurely, killing the two perpetrators.

How and why this splinter faction of the FPMR continued to operate during the Aylwin government is unclear. A declassified CIA report noted, "There is no intelligence indicating continued foreign support for terrorist groups since Aylwin took office. Both Cuba and the Soviet Union are actively wooing the Aylwin government and seem unlikely to risk relations or the prospect of promoting terrorism."[35] U.S. interests had been the object of some low-level violence, such as Molotov cocktails or spray paint on Mormon churches, American banks, and fast-food restaurants. The worst incident was a bombing during a softball game in which a Canadian citizen was killed. But the sheer number of incidents brought Chile to the top of the U.S. State Department's annual report on terrorism, much to the consternation of the Aylwin administration.

Chile's deputy foreign minister summoned the U.S. embassy chargé d'affaires to protest the report, noting that it contained some positive material but that the statement that terrorism in Chile had increased "notably since the March inauguration of the country's first democratically-elected government" was particularly offensive. How, he asked, could the United States do something so unhelpful to Chile's democracy? In Washington, D.C., the Chilean embassy political counselor delivered the same message to State Department officials. He also said, "The Aylwin administration had originally underestimated the strength and determination of these radical groups to perpetuate such violence, but that since the Guzmán assassination the government had stiffened its position on terrorism."[36]

In fact, Chilean police were improving their intelligence capabilities and had managed to locate and arrest some of the terrorist suspects, including two men linked to the Guzmán assassination. Over the next few years the remnants of Chile's extreme Left declined further as the authorities made more arrests and membership in parties such as the FPMR declined.[37]

VII

Less than a fortnight before Christmas 1991, the Aylwin government was faced with a very different kind of foreign policy dilemma. Erich

Honecker, the longtime Communist leader of East Germany and builder of the Berlin wall, arrived at the Chilean embassy in Moscow. He had been forced to resign during the unrest leading up to the dissolution of the German Democratic Republic and later fled to Moscow. Now the Soviet Union was collapsing, and Honecker was wanted by German prosecutors for embezzlement and for the murder 192 people, who were shot by guards on his orders as they attempted escape over the Berlin wall.

The Chilean ambassador Clodomiro Almeyda had been living in exile in East Germany during the military regime, along with some four thousand other Chileans (including the future president Michelle Bachelet and her mother, Angela Jeria). Almeyda and his wife had become good friends with Honecker and his wife, and Honecker's daughter had married a Chilean exile and now resided in Chile. Over the next seven months the Aylwin government found itself embroiled in a diplomatic and political quandary as it negotiated with the Soviet Union and German authorities while Chilean political leaders debated whether Honecker should be offered asylum.

Within the government's Center-Left coalition, opinions varied. Aylwin's cabinet chief, another former exile who had lived in East Germany, was strongly in favor of granting Honecker refuge, whereas others were afraid of what such a move would mean for Chile's image if it were to protect a notorious human rights violator. The debate was further complicated by the fact that some right-wing Chilean leaders, while having no sympathy for Honecker, did not want to be seen as submissive to Germany. Chancellor Helmut Kohl had visited Chile the previous November and given a speech before congress in which he mentioned human rights abuses during the Pinochet regime. Several right-wing politicians walked out of the chamber in protest.[38]

Ambassador Almeyda arranged for a medical team inside the Chilean embassy to examine Honecker, who appeared to be in poor health. A mobile X-ray had detected lesions, possibly malignant, on his liver. But German officials were making increasingly sharp demands for the former Communist leader's extradition, noting that asylum—which Honecker had not formally requested—was not an issue, as the Communist leader had never been politically persecuted. They rejected Chilean assertions that Honecker was merely a guest at the embassy and insisted that if he were to undergo additional tests at a clinic, there would be no guarantee he would be allowed to return to Almeyda's residence.[39]

German authorities did not issue formal indictments against Honecker until that June. In an eight-hundred-page document, German prosecutors charged Honecker and five other former officials with forty-nine counts of manslaughter. A second indictment charged him with embezzling over $9 million in public funds to pay for his decidedly non-Communist lifestyle. On July 29, 1992, the Chilean embassy allowed Russian security agents to escort Honecker to the airport, where he was flown to Berlin to face trial. At the Berlin airport he was shielded from onlookers, some of whom carried posters calling him a murderer. After his appearance in court, German officials ordered his release on the grounds of his age and illness. He was entitled to a monthly pension of about $500 from his prewar career as a roofer but seemed to have access to far greater funds, and on January 14, 1993, he arrived in Chile.

For a year and a half he lived quietly, sometimes appearing on the streets near his apartment to take morning walks. He made no public statements and gave no interviews. Chilean authorities appreciated Honecker's low profile, and German officials seemed pleased to be rid of him. On May 29, 1994, the former dictator died of cancer. His funeral at Santiago's General Cemetery was attended by hundreds of Chilean Communist Party members and other leftists, many waving red flags as they bid farewell to a leader they considered a friend and supporter. There had been no justice for Honecker's victims, but there had been no politically disruptive revenge, either. And five years later Chileans would recall the Honecker affair when their own former dictator became embroiled in an international extradition case in London.

THREE The Commander

I

A few days after President Aylwin's inauguration, Pinochet had a meeting with the civilian official who in theory would be his new boss: Defense Minister Patricio Rojas, a Christian Democrat. Rojas had known Pinochet since the 1960s, when he had been interior minister during the Frei government and Pinochet had been a division general in the northern city of Iquique. Toward the end of this period, the Frei government faced a short-lived uprising by the Chilean army, which charged that its complaints about low salaries had been ignored.[1]

Rojas recalled that his dealings with Pinochet in those days had been cordial, but this cordiality did not last during the military regime. After leaving the interior ministry he became a professor at the University of Chile, only to be fired for undisclosed political reasons two years after the 1973 coup. "[Pinochet] told me I should be grateful I had to seek work abroad, since that meant I would earn more," Rojas said. "I asked him why I had been fired. He said, 'well, you must have done something wrong.'" He said that Pinochet did refer to the generally amiable contact they had had before the coup, and Rojas, trying to get things off to a fresh start, responded, "Well, general, we will perform even better in our relationship in the future." This hopeful prediction did not come true, for the former dictator bitterly resented having to report to a civilian cabinet minister. Rojas said that his relationship with Chile's air force and navy commanders was good, but that Pinochet seemed bent on making things as difficult as possible. "I probably had the worst job in the transition," Rojas said. "The whole defense ministry was left with just empty boxes, no files at all." What did remain from the Pinochet regime were defense ministry employees who by law could not be fired and whom Rojas suspected were reporting his activities to Pinochet. "My driver, my security staff were all people from the regime," he said. "It was hard, though not impossible, to work under those conditions."[2]

In La Moneda, Aylwin had a similar sense of being watched, and on more than one occasion opted to hold politically sensitive discussions in the open courtyard of the presidential palace rather than in the presidential office itself. A few months after taking office, Aylwin discovered that army officials were indeed listening in on his government. "Some of my phone conversations were being tapped," he said. His interior minister, Enrique Krauss, contracted some electronics specialists from Germany, who found that the presidential phone lines were connected to one of the army's installations. And did Pinochet or any other army officials give any reason for the surveillance? "Enrique judged that the explanations offered were inadequate."[3]

Adding to the new government's worries was the fact that after nearly seventeen years of military rule, the army's younger officer corps had no experience with democratic rule or with operating under civilian authority.[4] In his visits to Chilean army regiments around the country, Rojas was taken aback by the fervent support still given to Pinochet. "In most army barracks you'd find pictures of girls pinned to the walls," he said. "But these guys all had pictures of Pinochet."[5]

Less than six weeks after taking office, the Aylwin government created the National Truth and Reconciliation Commission to document the worst human rights abuses committed during Chile's sixteen and a half years of military rule. The jurists Aylwin appointed included conservatives as well as Pinochet regime opponents, but the mere fact the commission was formed in the first place enraged Pinochet and set the scene for their first confrontation.

The former dictator maintained a military advisory council, made up of four colonels and led by longtime collaborator and confidant General Jorge Ballerino. The council seemed to function as Pinochet's own cabinet, and Ballerino acted as Pinochet's envoy to the new government at times, bypassing the defense minister. Aylwin tolerated this arrangement and occasionally invited Pinochet to his own home for private meetings. The advisory council, consulting other army generals, had prepared a report on its objections to the human rights commission, referring to a 1978 amnesty the Pinochet regime had decreed for crimes committed during its first five years in power. Backed by some right-wing politicians, the council argued that the commission should not investigate this early period of the regime (though there were plenty of abuses after this date).

Pinochet asked to speak directly with Aylwin, and the two met at La Moneda on May 3, 1990. It was the first time Pinochet had gone to the presidential palace since his successor's inauguration, and a jeering crowd quickly formed as he arrived. At the meeting Pinochet complained about the delay in getting the appointment to see Aylwin, who responded that he could have spoken to Defense Minister Rojas days earlier. Pinochet said he did not want to have to go through a mere cabinet official, an *administrativo.* Aylwin picked up a copy of the regime's 1980 constitution and showed Pinochet the article establishing the Chilean Defense Ministry's control over the army. Pinochet then presented Aylwin with the report he and his advisors had written about the Truth and Reconciliation Commission.[6]

The next day was a previously scheduled lunch Aylwin had organized for Pinochet and the other military commanders. Matthei and Admiral Martinez attended, and carabinero commander Rodolfo Stange, who was recovering from an operation, sent his deputy. Pinochet, still seething from the fact he had not gotten his way at the previous day's meeting at La Moneda, boycotted the lunch and sent a general who had been the director of the CNI in his stead.

Later that month Pinochet failed to turn up at Aylwin's state of the union address to congress, sending his deputy instead. Officially, he was on vacation in northern Chile, where he appeared at a naval commemoration in Iquique and visited several army bases. He then returned to Santiago, called a meeting of senior army officers, and sent his deputy to confer with the head of the Truth and Reconciliation Commission. After this meeting, Pinochet's advisory council issued a statement criticizing the commission and questioning its very existence.

Exasperated, Aylwin summoned Pinochet to a meeting, which lasted over an hour. According to an official communiqué read after the meeting, Aylwin had informed Pinochet, "It was not the army's business to discuss or question the convenience or opportunity of decisions taken by the President of the Republic." The statement also said that Pinochet indicated that the army would cooperate with the commission "within the framework of the constitution."[7]

II

The town of Pisagua is located on a lonely stretch of Chile's northernmost coast and can be visited only after a white-knuckle ride down a cliff road that in places seems to descend almost vertically. It was once an important port during the country's nineteenth-century nitrate boom, with a theater and a railway connecting it to the larger port of Iquique, seventy-five miles south. But after the nitrate industry's collapse, Pisagua, which in Spanish means *piss* and *water,* acquired a reputation as awful as its name. The town's remote location made it an ideal site for a penal colony, which would be opened and then abandoned several times during the twentieth century. And any prisoner foolhardy enough to attempt escape on foot would have faced almost certain death. The town borders the Atacama Desert, which is the driest place on earth. A few hundred people still live in the area, eking out a living by fishing, but most of Pisagua's buildings are abandoned.

Pisagua was used by the military regime of General Carlos Ibañez (1927–31) as a detention center for male homosexuals. Chile's first cold war president, Gabriel Gonzalez Videla (1946–52), also utilized Pisagua as a prison during his crackdown on the Chilean Communist Party. And Pinochet, who had been stationed in the region as a young army officer in the 1940s and then as a brigadier general in the late 1960s, made a similar use of Pisagua during his regime.

On June 3, 1990 officials discovered an unmarked grave containing the bodies of five prisoners. The site, near the Pisagua cemetery, had belonged to the Chilean army until recently. Those who buried the dead men had added lime to the soil in an effort to speed up the decomposition, but the dry, saline soil had practically mummified their bodies, preserving their clothes, bonds, blindfolds, and bullet wounds—an undeniable record of what had taken place.

There had been earlier discoveries of unmarked graves filled with victims of the Pinochet regime, but the Pisagua case was certainly one of the most horrifying. The press coverage was unrelenting—and in some cases sensationalist—as investigators found more bodies in the area. Pinochet and his advisors suspected that the discovery had been timed to embarrass the armed forces, and General Ballerino said as much to Aylwin government officials. Aylwin himself was concerned that the public uproar over the Pisagua graves might jeopardize the fragile line of communication his administration had with the military and asked the Chilean news media, "especially the television networks, to avoid inflammatory coverage."[8]

But it was the Catholic Church passing on information it had received that had led authorities to the graves. A statement by the bishops' conference urged Chileans not to fear revelations about the country's recent past: "This could be a moment of grace, offering us the chance to take steps to achieve the peace for which we yearn."[9] The Pisagua discovery was followed by another in southern Chile: eighteen farm workers had been shot to death and buried in two separate sites. There were more discoveries over the next two months in a half-dozen areas around the country, reaching a grisly total of one hundred twenty-five cadavers by September, the month that marks the anniversary of the 1973 coup and Chile's *fiestas patrias.*

At least some army officers were badly shaken by the discoveries, though publicly they insisted the institution was united against any trial of its members. A U.S. military attaché who met with a senior Chilean officer described how the official "became quite emotional as he explained he was not a murderer, even though he participated in the September 11 coup. He repeatedly said how difficult it was to explain to his son that he was no murderer in light of the recent publicity. As a Christian he was upset that the bodies at Pisagua had not been returned to their families. He acknowledged the strong emotional impact of the news photos of the Pisagua bodies." The source then described his role as a junior officer during the coup:

> He said he was shot at in front of his own house and soldiers with him returned fire. He didn't know if anyone was killed, but he was still no murderer. He then told me that his regiment contained reserve officers. One of these officers took prisoners out and shot them without trial. Members of the unit denounced this officer for the act. Source was unclear, however, as to what sanctions if any the reservist received.
>
> Source stressed to me that the army was more united than ever by recent publicity against military. He assured me that army officers would not be brought to trial. He implied that army would use force to prevent this.[10]

Pinochet's advisory council had devised a public relations plan to cast the former regime in the best possible light. On the first of September, full-page advertisements appeared in two of Chile's largest daily newspapers thanking the country's military for making democracy possible ("gracias por la democracia").[11] A book launch was held for the first volume of Pinochet's memoir, *Camino recorrido.* The book covered Pinochet's early life and career up to the 1973 coup; the final chapter is entitled "The Battle of Santiago" and repeated his earlier account of the evening before the military takeover and the coup itself.[12]

While Pinochet and his followers were promoting their version of the coup as a military victory, the Aylwin government was paying its respects to the fallen socialist president. On September 4 Salvador Allende was given a long-delayed state funeral. Allende had been hastily buried after the coup in an unmarked grave in a family plot in Viña del Mar, and for years, cemetery guards discouraged visitors from approaching the site. Now his coffin was being moved to a mausoleum in Santiago's Cementerio General, in a service attended by Aylwin and other Chilean dignitaries, with the all the respect customarily given to a dead president save for the glaring absence of any military honors.

The following day Pinochet took a swipe at the Aylwin government in a speech at a Rotary Club lunch. He was worried, he said, about some of the changes the new government was attempting to impose on the Chilean army, making it similar to that of Germany, "which is made up of potheads, drug addicts, long haired men, homosexuals and trade unionists." German officials responded by withdrawing an earlier invitation for Chilean army officers to visit the country, stating that Pinochet's remark "clearly attacks the honor of thousands of German soldiers."[13] Chile's ambassador in Bonn was summoned and handed a formal protest. German officials were not mollified by Pinochet's subsequent letter that stated his comments had been misinterpreted and that the Chilean army greatly admired its German counterpart.[14] The chamber of deputies passed a resolution, fifty-eight votes to forty-three, reprimanding Pinochet for his comments.

The next tension-filled date was the eleventh, the anniversary of the 1973 coup, which had been made a holiday during the military regime. General Fernando Matthei offered Aylwin a way to avoid further confrontation with the army by arranging a presidential visit to the Chilean air force base in Antarctica.[15] Pinochet, meanwhile, said publicly that he "would not hesitate for a moment" to lead a new coup should the country find itself in the same conditions it faced in 1973.[16] Back in Santiago for Chile's two-day independence holiday, Aylwin and other officials received treatment that was less than respectful. When Defense Minister Patricio Rojas visited the rehearsal for the annual military parade, he was jeered by many of those present. At the special Te Deum Mass on the eighteenth, Aylwin and other officials were confronted by pro-Pinochet demonstrators in the plaza outside the Santiago cathedral. At the military parade the next day, the new president and first lady were booed as they entered. A cavalry officer leading the marching soldiers pointedly failed to make the traditional request to the president for permission to begin the procession. After the parade, Pinochet attempted to leave before Aylwin and reacted angrily when stopped and informed that the president, the defense minister, and the president of the Chilean senate would be the first to exit, according to protocol.[17]

Once again Aylwin summoned Pinochet to La Moneda for a meeting, citing as a reason his statements about the German army and the actions by pro-regime demonstrators during the independence celebrations. These events suggest that the Chilean army had still not returned to its proper institutional role, Aylwin said. Pinochet claimed that the incidents at the military parade had not been premeditated and that he had already made his apologies to the German government. He said the Chilean army felt aggrieved by negative press coverage and the renewed interest in the 1976 Letelier assassination case. The meeting did not produce much resolution, and a few months later, Aylwin vetoed some of Pinochet's choices for promotion, including the army officer who had failed to show him deference at the military parade.[18]

The army's annual round of promotions, retirements, and postings that year included some unexpected changes. The director of the army's intelligence department and a former director of the CNI were among six high-ranking officers leaving the service in the midst of a scandal involving an illegal financial operation run by former security agents. The finance company, known as La Cutufa, had attracted investors by offering interest rates that were double the normal level. There were suspicions that La Cutufa, which was also involved in real estate and automobile sales, was actually a money-laundering operation backed by drug traffickers. What is certain is that La Cutufa's management operated like gangsters: one former CNI official who had invested over half a million dollars in La Cutufa was shot dead after he demanded his money back.

Pinochet insisted that the officers' departure from the army had been voluntary and that the institution was investigating whether public funds had been used in La Cutufa's operations. But a civilian judge assigned to the case also met a violent death after she ordered the arrest of an army captain. Her remains were discovered in her burnt-out car on the outskirts of Santiago, near the very site where the former CNI officer had been shot.[19]

III

The offspring of heads of state often encounter career opportunities and business ventures they might not otherwise have enjoyed. During the regime Pinochet's eldest daughter, Lucia, earned substantial commissions from the state insurance company, the Instituto de Seguros del Estado. Her sister Veronica's husband had been a director of the state development corporation CORFO, which managed the regime's privatization of state-owned companies. He later acquired 230,000 acres of nitrate fields previously controlled by a state enterprise, eventually converting these assets into a lucrative business. Pinochet's eldest son, Augusto Osvaldo, had had a checkered employment history, struggling through a short career in the army and several failed business ventures before his father sent him to live in the United States in 1980. The regime arranged for a false identity, that of Augusto Del Pino, and a vague job title of "economic counselor" at the Chilean consulate in Los Angeles. Pinochet did not trust his son's ability to manage money and arranged for a monthly payment of $3,000 to be sent to the Chilean consul, who then turned the funds directly over to the younger Pinochet's wife.[20]

Augusto Osvaldo Pinochet eventually returned to Santiago and in 1987 applied for a line of credit from Chile's state bank, the Banco del Estado, to purchase shares in a private rifle and munitions company. According to bank records obtained during a subsequent court inquiry, the former dictator's son presented no collateral or other guarantees during the loan application, just his signature. This may not have been prudent or even legal, and it certainly was contrary to the usual procedures of the Banco del Estado, which had a reputation as one of the country's more upright financial institutions and usually demanded documentation and a sizeable amount of paperwork before granting any loans to small- and medium-sized business borrowers. That same year Pinochet's son also and received a loan from CORFO in what may have been the first time the state development corporation had become involved in the arms trade. Together these two state loans totaled US$9 million, a rather large sum for the agencies to grant an individual borrower.[21]

Then, a year before Aylwin took office, the Chilean army's munitions company, Fábricas y Maestranzas del Ejército (FAMAE), paid approximately $3 million to Augusto Osvaldo Pinochet for reasons that seem murky at best. His munitions company was being taken over by the army via a complicated transaction in which the earlier $9 million debt he'd acquired from government agencies was canceled. An additional $3 million in payments was made with three separate checks drawn from the Banco del Estado, and, rather than cash them in Chile, the dictator's son deposited them in a U.S. account under his wife's name. FAMAE's then-director later told investigators that the younger Pinochet had appeared at his office to collect the checks, but that the director had insisted upon checking first with General Pinochet, who approved the payment.[22]

Aylwin had been president for barely five months when he received a confidential folder containing photocopies of the three checks, discovered by the new government's officials at the Banco del Estado. The "Pinochecks" were discussed at a meeting of cabinet ministers, who debated what to do with this potentially explosive material. Simply asking Pinochet for an explanation was ruled out, for it seemed unlikely that he would offer any satisfactory answer, and the Aylwin government, trying to be selective about which battles to fight, did not want yet another showdown with the former dictator. The photocopies were turned over to Defense Minister Patricio Rojas, who later showed them to selected members of the chamber of deputies.[23]

More copies of checks began circulating, some appearing in the press. Some Concertación politicians were hoping the scandal might force Pinochet into early retirement, while conservative members of congress were more skeptical, meeting with Pinochet's advisory council to hear the army's side of the story. And Chile's new congress began its first official investigation, summoning former regime officials—but not Pinochet—

to give testimony. "It was obvious some of the officers were not telling the truth," said Senator Alberto Espina of the Center-Right Renovación Nacional Party. He later had a private conversation with Pinochet, who appears to have played the role of the disappointed parent, asking the senator if he, too, had children. Espina, one of the new generation of moderate conservatives, said he was "absolutely convinced" that Pinochet had no involvement in, or even knowledge of, his son's financial dealings.[24] Other Chilean officials scoffed at this assertion and noted that some parliamentarians were nervous about undertaking an investigation into the Pinochet family's finances at such an early, fragile stage in the country's recently restored democracy. "It was a mixture. Some members of congress took up the investigation enthusiastically, including some on the Right who viewed the case as a sacrilege against a beloved institution—the Chilean army," said José Antonio Viera Gallo, who was president of the chamber of deputies at the time. "But the military pressures were considerable."[25]

There were meetings between Aylwin government officials and General Ballerino. At one point Ballerino hinted that Pinochet might be willing to consider suggestions that he take early retirement, if officials would show restraint during investigations into charges of corruption and human rights abuses. It would be a disaster if Pinochet were indicted, and the army wanted to avoid this at all cost.[26]

On December 19, 1990, Aylwin invited Pinochet and other senior army officers to a luncheon for that year's military academy graduating class. The officers' wives were also invited, and Aylwin recalled that this was the only occasion in which he and his wife ate at the same table with Pinochet and his wife, Lucía Hiriart. The ambience was very formal, the conversation somewhat insipid: Aylwin and Pinochet's wife had both grown up in San Bernardo, a small town south of Santiago, and this was one of the few topics they could discuss comfortably. At one point Pinochet did mention that he had read in the newspaper that his son would be called to testify before Congress in the case of the three checks. Aside from this, the lunch seemed free of tension.[27]

That afternoon General Ballerino had a telephone conversation with Defense Minister Rojas, telling Ballerino that Pinochet had to resign no later than mid-April of the following year. Upon hearing this news, Pinochet put the army on grade one alert, requiring all soldiers and officers to report to their units and to await further orders.

Aylwin and Rojas were attending graduation ceremonies at the carabinero police academy that evening when word of the army alert reached them. In La Moneda the telephone system had mysteriously failed, and officials were forced to use cellular phones—whose frequencies could be easily monitored—to communicate. There were fears that Aylwin might be taken hostage, but the carabineros, along with the air force and navy, were not joining Pinochet's saber-rattling exercise. After the graduation ceremony Aylwin held an emergency cabinet meeting at his own residence. The meeting lasted until the early hours of the morning, when they learned that the army had ended its alert.

"This was definitely a move toward a coup," Rojas said. "Pinochet wanted to scare the government with his power and to show that we could be scared."[28] Publicly, however, Rojas announced that the army alert was in reality just a "security, readiness and liaison" exercise. The government issued a short communiqué stating that Pinochet had been called to La Moneda for an explanation. The army also issued a statement calling the exercise a success "for having achieved the objectives pursued."[29]

According to a partially declassified CIA report, the Chilean army might not have lent its full support to a stronger show of force at that time. "Officers, however, were concerned how their troops would react if deployed due to a belief that conscripts, non-commissioned officers and younger officers would not support any effort to intimidate the civilian government," the report said. "Field grade officers themselves, while supportive of the CINC's [Commander-in-Chief's] resistance to any government attempts to oust him, also did not believe that national circumstances warranted military intervention."[30]

Civilian leaders, however, were taking no chances. Chile's congress passed a resolution backing democracy by a vote of seventy-four to five with two abstentions. A somewhat halfhearted parliamentary investigation into the $3 million army checks resumed after the start of the new year, and Augusto Osvaldo Pinochet appeared to testify. He insisted he had never discussed his business affairs with his father. The final congressional report cited administrative irregularities in the management of his munitions company, but no criminal charges were made. The matter was sent to Chile's state defense council, an entity similar to the U.S. attorney general, and there was a tacit agreement between the government and the army to tamp down the publicity surrounding the case.

The congressional report ended with an enigmatic phrase dictated by chamber president José Antonio Viera Gallo: "The investigation cannot determine if General Pinochet was involved. Nor can it conclude that he was not involved." Viera Gallo, a Socialist, said he believed Pinochet was in fact very much involved. "We knew he had been stealing but nobody knew how much." Then why wasn't congress more aggressive in investigating the matter? "Why do you think?" he sighed. "Because there would have been a coup."[31]

IV

It was important to direct the Chilean military's attention away from internal security and toward external defense. To this end, the Aylwin government sought to improve ties with the armed forces of other countries, particularly the United States. Just two months after Aylwin took office, air force commander Matthei visited Washington, where he was awarded the Legion of Merit and met with National Security Advisor Brent Scowcroft, among other officials. The U.S. finally lifted the fourteen-year-old arms embargo on December 1, 1990, and Defense Minister Rojas was flying to Washington for a Pentagon visit and a meeting with Defense Secretary Dick Cheney. U.S. ambassador Charles Gillespie warned Pentagon officials, "We must take care not to build new strain into this delicate and evolving relationship with reluctant military institutions not yet prepared to accept civilian authority."[32]

"The Kennedy amendment affected our defense capabilities," Rojas said. "We were forced to look for foreign improvisers for all kinds of things, such as system parts, at higher prices. We were able to get what we needed but it cost much more money."[33] The Chilean army wanted training and contacts with U.S. defense colleagues but was not seeking any equipment at that point. The navy wanted maritime surveillance aircraft, while the air force wanted to reopen logistical lines of support and acquire one or two C-130 aircraft. The arms embargo left the Chilean military with ambivalent feelings toward the United States, and Rojas told his American hosts that he wanted to make a fresh start.

Pinochet received an invitation to attend a hemisphere-wide conference of army commanders to be held in Washington, D.C., that November. He was somewhat leery of traveling to the United States, fearing that he might be dragged into the recent trial of one of the codefendants in the Letelier case. General Ballerino was dispatched to the U.S. embassy in Santiago to make discreet enquiries. He said Pinochet would remain in the United States no more than thirty-six hours (though the conference was five days long) and that a Washington law firm had advised him that as head of the Chilean delegation he would be eligible for a diplomatic visa, giving him immunity from any prosecution. Pinochet was aware that there might be demonstrations against him and was willing to deal with that contingency, but he wanted some guarantee that he would not end up in an American court.

However, embassy officials told Ballerino that although there were no criminal charges against Pinochet at the time, it was possible that the federal law enforcement authorities might want to question him in connection with the Letelier case. He was not entitled to diplomatic immunity in the United States, which could only be extended to current heads of state. It was possible that the FBI might request a voluntary interview with him or seek a material witness arrest warrant on the grounds that he might flee if he was not taken into custody. In short, the U.S. executive branch would issue no guarantees that Pinochet would be shielded from either the Department of Justice or private civil actions.[34]

Pinochet eventually opted not to risk the U.S. visit, though he had recently taken a two-week trip to Brazil, Portugal, and the United Kingdom and seemed to be acquiring a taste for foreign travel. He left Chile in a military plane on May 11, 1991, with government authorization to travel until June 3. According to vague statements from the army, Pinochet would visit countries that had supplied arms to Chile or else had dealings with the army munitions company FAMAE. But none of the countries he planned to visit had officially invited him.

His first stop was in Rio de Janeiro, where he paid a courtesy call on the commander of Brazil's eastern military region and was followed by the press during his excursions to the beach and local stores. He commented that Peru's Shining Path guerrillas had killed more than ten thousand people, compared to "only" three thousand dead during his regime. When asked about the situation in Chile, he responded that he was not a politician but a military man. When a reporter noted that he had ruled his country for many years, Pinochet's response was almost comical: "Yes, but I did not learn anything. I was a bad student."[35]

From Brazil, Pinochet and his entourage flew to Portugal, where his itinerary continued to be front-page news in Chile. He commented that he would return to politics in the event of "chaos and preparation for civil war" in Chile. He was photographed at the shrine of Our Lady of Fatima and at an outdoor party wearing casual dress and dancing with a female guest. He visited a private arms company, but Portuguese authorities kept him away from government-owned arms factories. He also met with representatives of a French arms consortium while in Portugal, as he had been informed he would not be welcome in Paris.[36]

Pinochet also made a secretive, seven-hour stop in the United Kingdom, where FAMAE had a joint project with Royal Ordnance, a British arms manufacturer, to develop a short-range rocket. The British defense ministry said it had not invited Pinochet, but according to some reports the Chilean army had asked Royal Ordnance for an invitation to visit its installations. British authorities appeared embarrassed by the dictator's presence in their country, but the outcry from some Labour parliamentarians seems to have provoked a nationalistic reaction from at least some Chilean officials. Pinochet would make subsequent visits to the United Kingdom during the 1990s, ostensibly as a guest of Royal Ordnance.

Pinochet had considered visiting Switzerland, South Africa, and Israel during this trip, countries that had also supplied arms to his regime, but the reaction in all three countries was overwhelmingly negative. The day after his flight left Santiago, Israeli officials said Pinochet would not be allowed to visit. In Geneva Chilean exiles pressured the government not to let him into Switzerland, while officials said that although they had not invited him, they would allow a private visit. In South Africa political groups threatened demonstrations, and a Pretoria newspaper editorialized that "surely South Africa is not that desperate that it should allow such an unsavory character as former Chilean president Augusto Pinochet into the country."[37]

Pinochet cut his trip short and returned to Santiago. He later spoke to a Chilean news magazine, giving his version of events surrounding the trip. He had not gone to South Africa, he maintained, because of the country's internal conflicts and that officials there "could not guarantee [his] safety."[38] South African diplomats in Santiago denied there had been any security problems; the real reason seemed to be that the weapons company Pinochet planned to visit had withdrawn its invitation. But by the time he returned to Santiago on May 24, he had demonstrated his ability to maintain a high political profile. Aylwin government officials may have hoped the international rejection their commander had faced would finally cause the Chilean army to see Pinochet as a liability—but it would take many more years for such an opinion shift to take place.

V

A few weeks before Christmas Aylwin received a phone call from U.S. ambassador Charles Gillespie about a surprising discovery made on the other side of the world. An eleven-ton cargo of weapons, originating in Chile, had been intercepted on its way to Zagreb. The shipment was in violation of a United Nations ban on weapons sales to Croatia and included more than three hundred rifles and bayonets, twenty antitank rockets and launchers, plus mines, cartridges, and ammunition.

The ensuing investigation revealed that within a month of the UN prohibition, a representative of Ivi Finance and Management, a Panama-based arms dealer, visited Santiago and met with FAMAE officials. A deal was made for $6 million worth of weapons, of which the intercepted shipment—worth about $203,000—was to be the first. The cargo, labeled "humanitarian aid" from the Chilean military hospital, left Santiago

November 30, 1991. Gillespie informed Aylwin that the CIA had learned of the shipment when the arms dealers tried to arrange air transport for future deliveries in Miami.[39]

Rojas said the government had in fact authorized a FAMAE arms sale—to Sri Lanka, not Croatia—and that afterward FAMAE had changed the documents. The Chilean munitions company manufactured some of the weapons and collected others from army regiments around the country, including at least ten U.S.-made rocket launchers. The arms export had to be approved by both the Defense and Foreign Ministries, he said, but their controls were not sufficiently rigorous. "In those days such matters were light," he said. "We called the foreign ministry and asked, 'Do we have any problems with Sri Lanka? No? Ok.' Its government was recognized by ours."[40]

Rojas telephoned FAMAE's director, an army general who claimed not to know that the arms shipment had been destined for Croatia and asked for proof of this. He was forced to resign, and two midlevel officers—whom the army claimed had acted on their own—were blamed for the illegal Croatia shipment. But investigators suspected several high-ranking generals were involved, and it would have been almost impossible for Pinochet not to have been aware of these and other questionable arms deals.

As the investigation continued, witnesses began to vanish. On February 20, 1992, the body of Colonel Gerardo Huber was found on the bank of a river outside Santiago with his skull smashed. Huber, the army's director of logistics, had disappeared a few weeks earlier, shortly before he was due to testify before a Chilean judge investigating the Croatia arms case. Huber had joined the Pinochet regime's security forces in 1974, traveling to Argentina to spy on Chilean leftists residing in that country following the coup. He later served a term as a provincial governor before taking the logistics post, which involved the purchase of weapons and other supplies and would have brought him into regular contact with customs agents. According to his widow, Huber had uncovered suspicious information in army records months before the bungled Croatia deal and reported his findings to Pinochet. Her husband told her that Pinochet became enraged with him. "'You're crazy,' Pinochet told him. 'You need to go to the fifth floor' [of the military hospital, where mental patients are interned] 'and see a psychiatrist.'" At that moment, she said, her husband probably signed his own death warrant.[41]

Huber disappeared during a visit to the Andean foothills outside of Santiago. A short time later three army officers appeared at the home of Huber's sister-in-law and attempted to take the missing colonel's six-year-old son, claiming they wanted to question the boy about his father's possible whereabouts. The sister-in-law refused to surrender the child, suspecting the officers—two army intelligence officials and a longtime friend and confidant of the colonel—wanted to use her nephew to pressure Huber. She later told investigators that the three men threatened her and said the missing colonel had committed suicide.

Huber's body, however, was not found until three weeks later. The police report listed "suicide" as the cause of death, which concurred with the three military officers' initial claim. Chilean officials reopened the case in 2003, eventually concluding that Huber had been killed to cover up illegal arms trafficking and other irregular operations within the army. The investigating judge discovered that Huber had been taken to a secret army intelligence installation between the time of his disappearance and the discovery of his corpse. Six high-ranking officers, including the three who had tried to seize Huber's son, were arrested and charged with conspiracy.

The judge in charge of the case also began investigating the death of Huber's former chauffeur, who reportedly committed suicide inside his car. His death was unexpected, and friends and family said he had shown no signs of depression or personal problems. The gun that killed the chauffeur was found on the passenger seat to his right—but friends said he was left-handed and would have been unlikely to use his right hand to commit suicide.

The arms trafficking provided Pinochet and his associates the means to accumulate an illicit fortune that would come to light only years later after a U.S. Senate investigation into money laundering and foreign corruption.[42] Pinochet acknowledged receiving "commissions, fees and honorarium for work on special projects outside of Chile," but the amount of money—at least $27 million—greatly exceeds what a man who spent his entire career in the Chilean army could ever have acquired legally. Chilean prosecutors would detect a number of deposits into Pinochet's accounts by arms manufacturing companies, along with evidence of government funds used for personal benefit and "money related to important commercial operations made by the army."[43]

FOUR Truth and Reconciliation

I

It was a visit she had been dreading for several months. One of her children had said that two men had arrived at the family home, wanting to speak with her. In the days that followed, her old insomnia returned and her health began to suffer. But she had already decided to tell everything she knew, and when the men returned, she made sure to open the door herself. "My heart started beating faster when I saw them. There were two people in front of me, and one of them said, 'Mrs. Luz Arce?'"[1] Luz Arce had been a member of Salvador Allende's paramilitary bodyguards, the Grupo de Amigos Personales. Six months after the coup, she was arrested by the DINA and subjected to a horrific barrage of torture, beatings, and gang rape. Other former prisoners had similar experiences, but what made Arce's testimony of special interest was her insider's knowledge of DINA operations: she was one of three former prisoners known to have been brainwashed and coerced into collaborating with the security forces.

Arce spent several days recounting her experiences to the Aylwin government's Truth and Reconciliation Commission. She had listened to DINA officials describing the murder of a Spanish diplomat who had helped Chileans fleeing political persecution find asylum in foreign embassies. The diplomat, Carmelo Soria, worked for the United Nations Economic Commission for Latin America, headquartered in Santiago; DINA agents kidnapped, interrogated, and poisoned him before dousing him with liquor, putting him behind the wheel of a car, and staging a crash.[2] She had conferred with DINA officials and observed how the security agency expanded into new departments and brigades, including one called the Vampire Group that was specifically created to give an inept lieutenant a second career chance. The bumbling Lieutenant Fernando Lauriani was known as Inspector Clouseau to his fellow DINA agents after such missteps as having his vehicle stolen with his unit's weapons inside while setting up a trap and, on another occasion, commandeering a public bus when he couldn't locate his own car. He had used his DINA identification to force out the driver and passengers, then used the bus to transport prisoners to one of the regime's detention centers. Lauriani had poured out his troubles to Arce at one point, then grabbed his gun and threatened to commit suicide. She persuaded him to take his problems to a senior DINA official, who responded by setting up the new unit and assigning some of the most experienced DINA agents to work with Lauriani. She had witnessed the comings and goings of Michael Townley, the American-born DINA agent who helped organize the Letelier car bomb assassination in Washington, D.C. She had been sent on missions to Uruguay, one of several Southern Cone countries participating in joint antisubversive operations with the DINA. She had remained with the security agency during its changeover in 1977, when it was renamed the Central Nacional de Informaciones (CNI), and observed the resulting power struggle between the DINA's director, Manuel Contreras, and the new security chief, General Odlanier Mena.

Much of Arce's rich store of information did not appear in the commission's final report, for the panel's brief was to identify the victims rather than prosecute the guilty. The commission consisted of eight members, including a conservative historian who had once served as education minister under Pinochet, a regime-designated senator, a social worker who had led a voter registration drive for the 1988 plebiscite, and a Chilean lawyer who had been president of Amnesty International. The group was given just six months (plus the option of an extension of no more than three months) to complete its investigation and prepare a report. The presidential decree convening the commission acknowledged that time was short, which would limit the investigation to the worst abuses, that is, killings.[3] The commission was given no authority to subpoena witnesses and was specifically instructed not to act as a court or to take any actions that might interfere with cases already in the courts. The Aylwin government, mindful that the Chilean Supreme Court and the constitutional court were filled with Pinochet loyalists, did not want to give either judicial body a pretext for challenging the commission's report. And although Chilean human rights groups knew the identities of some of most notorious abusers, there were to be no names given. Some of the younger commission members did not agree with this.

According to Laura Novoa, a lawyer employed by one of Santiago's most conservative legal offices, she and other younger members believed that naming names in no way intruded upon the Chilean courts' jurisdiction and could even pressure them into conducting more-thorough investigations. As the commission sought to gain recognition in Chilean society and avoid open confrontations with the military, the more politically minded members prevailed.[4]

Even with these restraints in place, the Truth and Reconciliation Commission's work was far-reaching. The eight panel members, who received no payment for their work, were joined by a team of seventeen lawyers, eighteen law students and recent law graduates, plus another two dozen social workers, secretaries, computer specialists, and other support staff whose salaries were paid by the Chilean justice ministry. According to the commission's report, no more than 10 percent of its staff had any prior experience with human rights work, as the commission wanted a team that could "take a fresh look at the cases it was to examine and report upon."[5]

The commission set up offices in Santiago and in regional government buildings around the country, and Chilean embassies abroad were also empowered to receive information. Notices were placed in the news inviting families of victims to contact the commission, which also sent formal queries to Chile's political parties, human rights groups, and labor, business, and various other civic organizations. The three branches of the armed forces and the police were also invited to share information on their victims, for the commission wanted to include all those killed for political reasons—whether by the security forces or extremist groups.

II

Just over 3,400 cases were investigated, and investigations almost always began with the commission seeking copies of individuals' birth and death certificates from the Chilean civil registry and checking with immigration police to determine whether the person in question had left the country without informing friends and family (the commission found only a handful of such cases). The commission was given the power to request such documents and reported that officials in these government agencies were usually helpful, though it was not always possible to locate documentation for autopsies performed in rural areas.

The commission also sought copies of any judicial records in previously investigated cases and records of medical treatments or hospitalizations known to have occurred. There were two thousand of these requests, with a response rate of about 80 percent. Then came the more contentious phase of the investigation—obtaining copies of police and military records. Many of these seemed to have been deliberately destroyed.

The Chilean army responded to two-thirds of these requests, but most of these replies stated, "The evidence on such events that might have existed had been burned or destroyed when the legal period [against] doing so had passed." The carabineros responded in a similar fashion, while the Chilean air force "sometimes provided the evidence requested." The Chilean navy replied to all the commission's requests and "sent material that proved very useful for the investigations," though it did not always have any documents on the cases in question. When the commission asked for documents from the military intelligence services, the army, navy, and air force responded by saying they were legally prohibited from giving information on intelligence activities.[6]

Bit by bit the commission members pieced together a history of political repression during the regime. The commission sought interviews with 160 members of the armed forces and police who had been named in discussions with victims' families or had appeared in documents obtained during their investigations. Despite assurances of confidentiality, the military almost always refused these requests, with the exception of one air force official and several carabinero police who agreed to answer questions in writing. The commission did not even attempt to interview the most obvious witness—Pinochet—during the investigation, and commission president Raul Rettig expressed surprise when an interviewer asked why. "No. That of course would not have been possible."[7]

The report the commission delivered to President Aylwin was divided into four parts. The first described the commission's work, defined the terms employed in the report, and outlined how information was gathered. The second part discussed the events leading to the 1973 coup and the effect of increasing polarization against the background of the cold war and the violent language employed by Chilean political leaders and much of the media. As a consequence, the report said, "the moral dykes of society gave way and the path was opened to further and greater excesses."[8]

The report criticized the shortcomings of Chilean judiciary during the Pinochet regime, pointing out that the regime had not dissolved the judiciary, as it had done to the Chilean congress and the presidency, and that a decree issued by the junta on the very day of the coup said the powers of the judiciary would remain in full force. But despite this apparent backing, the Chilean judiciary was "glaringly insufficient" in protecting the legal rights of individuals during this period.

The report said habeas corpus, which is the right of a detainee to be brought before a court, was "completely ineffective" during this period, even though a variety of individuals and organizations—churches, lawyers, the victims' families, and international human rights groups—were furnishing the courts with detailed information on arrests and disappearances. But many senior judges seemed willfully oblivious to such abuses, and the report cited a speech by Chile's Supreme Court president at the start of the 1975 judicial year: "Contrary to what unworthy Chileans or foreigners operating with a peculiar political aim have said, Chile is not a land of barbarians. It has striven to give strict attention to these rights. With regard to torture and other atrocities, I can state that here we have neither firing squads or iron curtains, and any statement to the contrary is the product of a press that is trying to propagate ideas that could not and will not prosper in our country."[9] The Supreme Court president went on to deny that people had disappeared after arrest and complained about Chilean courts being overwhelmed by habeas corpus actions filed on behalf of the detained and the missing, which he said were preventing them from dealing with "serious" cases.

The courts' failure to act in these cases encouraged those responsible to believe they could continue to act with impunity. The report said the courts had to have been aware of notorious places of detention such as the National Stadium but did nothing to address such unlawful situations. The report acknowledged "parallel reasons" for the judiciary's ineffectiveness—the lack of police cooperation and the executive branch's claims that no such arrests had taken place. But the courts' unquestioning acceptance of the official version of events was remarkable: one case described a housekeeper working at a Catholic convent who was killed during an operation by DINA agents. The court did not even interview the agents, even though they had opened fire and no return shots came from the building housing the religious order.

The third part deals with the victims themselves, dividing their cases into three separate periods: from the coup to December 1973, from January 1974 to August 1977, and from then until March 1990 when Aylwin took office. The report said the armed forces quickly gained control of the country and that leftist armed resistance was minimal, uncoordinated, random, and "without the slightest chance of success, even locally." During the second period, the DINA was responsible for the majority of abuses, and the organization is estimated to have had several thousand employees and many more collaborators and informants, including some individuals in "the media, both in Chile and among the press attachés in Chilean embassies in other countries."[10] The commission also listed seven officials—two policemen, two army officers, a soldier, and two civilian detectives—killed by armed left-wing groups in this three-year period. The last period mentioned covers the time from 1977, when the DINA was replaced by the CNI, to the end of the regime in 1990. The report said that armed left-wing activity increased during this time but that the CNI was more selective in choosing its targets than the DINA had been. "During this period the official explanation for the death of left activists was continually that they had been killed in gun battles with members of the security agencies, primarily the CNI," the report said. "This commission has nonetheless been able to determine that a very large number of these gun battles never took place."[11]

The fourth and final section discusses ways to help the victims' families, who had suffered not only the loss of loved ones but official harassment and social ostracism as well. The report ends by proposing ways to prevent abuses in the future and by urging Chileans to seek reconciliation rather than revenge. The commission was able to reach conclusions for about 2,279 cases of political execution and disappearance, and there were another 641 cases on which it was not been able to reach conclusions due to insufficient evidence (but it recommended that the cases continue to be investigated). The report listed the political affiliations of the victims, with the Socialist and Communist Parties and the Movement of the Revolutionary Left (MIR) accounting for about 40 percent of those killed. Members of other parties accounted for 124 victims, but the remaining majority of those killed were described as "sin militancia," or without any known political affiliation.

The commission also listed "serious obstacles" to its investigation, including time constraints, its inability to subpoena witnesses, the difficulty of locating relevant witnesses after so many years, and the fear or unwillingness to testify of potential witnesses who were located.

Crucial testimony was sometimes unavailable because many Chileans "preferred to avoid subjecting mothers, fathers, wives, partners or children who had witnessed what had happened to the trauma of giving testimony and thus having to relive enormous suffering."[12] In view of these limitations, it was inevitable that the commission's report was an understatement of repression and abuses during the military regime, but its impact would still be substantial.

III

On March 4, 1991, President Aylwin appeared on national television to present the human rights report to the nation. His speech, about thirty minutes long, began with the report's contents and then moved to a discussion of actions to be taken. He said that human rights cases occurring before the 1978 amnesty law should continue to be investigated before any pardons are granted under this law. He spoke of the need to end the suffering of families of the disappeared, proposing immunity for those who provided information and sanctions for those who deliberately withheld information. He ended the speech with a plea for "understanding instead of confrontation." His voice breaking with emotion, Aylwin said, "Pardon requires repentance on the one hand, and on the other, generosity." On behalf of the country, he asked for forgiveness from the families of the victims.[13]

There was a small demonstration outside La Moneda during the televised speech, which police later dispersed with water cannons when youths in the crowd began to throw bottles. But most of the reaction from Chilean political groups—from the Communist Party to the Far Right Union Democrática Independiente—was favorable. The report, which Chilean newspapers were printing as a supplement, simply could not be ignored.

The military reaction, not surprisingly, was a different story, but each branch issued its own response. Air Force commander Fernando Matthei was the first to respond, stating that the commission's report should be understood in the context of the civil and political strife that gave way to the 1973 coup, but that the Chilean air force "regrets all loss of life." He expressed his support for the Aylwin government's efforts toward reconciliation and urged Chileans to "accept the past with all its consequences but not dwell on it."[14]

The navy commander, Admiral Jorge Martinez, read a twenty-two-page statement to the press criticizing the commission's report for faulty historical analysis and its politicized and biased view of human rights cases. He refuted the report's conclusion that there had not been any state of internal war in the country in 1973 and pointed to terrorist acts committed throughout the regime. But Martinez's demeanor was somber, and he said that the navy fully shared Aylwin's call for reconciliation.

Pinochet gave an emotional speech at Chile's military academy before an audience of several hundred army officials that was carried live by one television station. The army wanted to express its "fundamental discrepancy" with the report, he said, charging that some commission members lacked impartiality. The army would not be put on trial for "saving Chile," and there was no need for the army to ask for forgiveness. He rejected the proposal for compensation for victims' families (especially a provision exempting the sons of victims from military service). "The legitimate use of force can result in loss of life and physical harm," he said. He accused the commission of sparking violence and creating a climate of hate. The only positive statement was a pledge that the army would be an "enthusiastic participant" in the effort toward reconciliation.[15]

IV

Both the military and the Aylwin government might have hoped that the issue of human rights would be laid to rest or at least be temporarily put aside, in the wake of the commission's report. But matters were soon to become more complicated. Two weeks after Aylwin's speech, three Chilean weekly magazines hit the newsstands with the text of former DINA prisoner-turned-collaborator Luz Arce's testimony to the commission.[16] Arce's graphic account linked specific individuals—mostly

DINA agents and collaborators—to specific crimes, and although she had authorized the commission to turn her testimony over to the courts for use in their investigations, she had not authorized its release to the media. Fearing retribution from former security agents or from the former leftist activists whose names she had revealed under duress, Arce had left the country.

No one believed any of the commission members or staff were responsible for the leak, but an employee of the Catholic Church's human rights department, the Vicariate of Solidarity, was suspected. Concerned that publication of Arce's testimony would undermine the organization's reputation for confidentiality and discourage others from coming forward with information about abuses, the Vicariate tried to block its publication. The Aylwin government declined to intervene, not wanting to appear to endorse censorship. The Vicariate then obtained a court order banning publication of Arce's testimony on March 16, but the magazines said they had received no notice until two days later, when the periodicals had already been printed and distributed. An attempt to confiscate the magazines met with limited success.

A week later former DINA chief General Manuel Contreras gave his version of events in a rare extended interview on Chilean television. He said the human rights commission did not take anything into account except Marxist statements and that no Chileans had disappeared following their arrest by security forces. "There are no detained/disappeared in a subversive war, and this was a subversive war," he said. The interviewer asked him about the car bomb assassinations of Orlando Letelier and his colleague in Washington and former army commander Carlos Prats and his wife in Buenos Aires. Contreras admitted that there were similarities in the cases but claimed that Michael Townley, the American-born agent who had helped organize both attacks, had never been either a DINA agent or informer.

It was impossible to tell whether Contreras actually believed what he was telling his interviewer, and at times the question-and-answer session seemed farcical. At one point Contreras was asked if he were a Catholic.

"A practicing Catholic."

"That is to say, you swear that neither the DINA nor yourself had anything to do with the Letelier case?"

"I swear it."

Asked about the bodies found in unmarked graves in Pisagua, Contreras said the dead had been buried in "battlefield cemeteries" and that all their families had been notified. He said he informed Pinochet of "everything that DINA did." There was no torture, he said, and attributed such accusations to Marxist principles in which "all prisoners once free must say that they were tortured." As for Luz Arce's testimony, Contreras said she had voluntarily opted to work for the DINA and that she was "an excellent medium" who could hypnotize prisoners into providing information. A large number of detainees collaborated with the DINA, he said, and their subsequent disappearances were probably the work of the Far Left. He quoted Che Guevara as saying that "informants and traitors must not be shown any mercy." Contreras also claimed that several high-ranking officials in the Aylwin government were former DINA informants.[17]

Contreras may have wanted to argue that responsibility for DINA's actions was not his alone, but the response to the interview was swift and overwhelmingly negative. Even the right-wing Union Democratica Independiente called Contreras's version of events "extreme," and leaders of Center-Left parties accused him of creating a climate of hate.[18]

V

The Truth and Justice Commission's report was, by its own admission, a limited accounting of human rights abuses. Among those disappointed by the commission's report was Olga Weisfeiler, a Russian-born microbiologist and medical researcher in Massachusetts whose brother Boris had disappeared during a trip to southern Chile in 1985. The commission's report listed Weisfeiler's as among several hundred cases it had not been able to resolve. He became one of the last of the unaccounted-for missing, the only American among the country's *desaparecidos*. The case would remain a contentious issue in U.S.-Chile relations.

Boris Weisfeiler had immigrated to the United States ten years earlier. He became a U.S. citizen in 1981 and was a respected member of the Pennsylvania State University Mathematics Department. He was a veteran backcountry trekker and had made solo hiking trips in remote areas of Alaska, Canada, Uzbekistan, China, Spain, and Peru as well as his native Russia. Olga Weisfeiler recalls that he was a good linguist; he had studied Dutch, Italian, German, and Chinese in addition to Spanish and "always learned the language of the country where he was going to travel."[19]

Prior to his trip, Weisfeiler told his sister that he wanted a break from the harsh Pennsylvania winter and that it was warm in Chile in December. He arrived in Santiago on Christmas day 1994, carrying the same Soviet-made backpack he had used on his previous trips, and proceeded south to Los Angeles, a small city reached by an eight-hour bus ride from Santiago. The region is known for its thermal springs and waterfalls, and after spending the night at a local hotel, he began his fateful hike in the Andean foothills.

On January 3 Weisfeiler met a farmer who invited him to spend the night at his home and the next day helped him cross the Nuble River on horseback. The farmer later told investigators that Weisfeiler seemed experienced at crossing rivers. The mathematics professor then continued hiking northward, passing the farmer's brother, who lived in the vicinity. Such was the climate of fear and suspicion that the farmer's brother went to the police to report that a lone foreigner was in the area. The police set off on horseback to look for Weisfeiler, as did a Chilean army patrol, but reportedly they found only a set of boot prints near the bank of another local river, Los Sauces.

The official report was that Weisfeiler drowned while trying to cross the river. Police later produced his backpack, claiming a local fisherman had pulled it from the water. Missing were the mathematician's passport, his return ticket, his camera, and some money, along with his diary. According to Olga Weisfeiler, her brother always kept a journal of his hikes, detailing the sights, the people he met, the food he ate, and any interesting events.[20]

Weisfeiler's friends in academia hired a private detective in Chile to investigate, but the report he prepared only reiterated the official police version of events. The investigator was not able to interview the carabineros stationed in the area at the time, as they had all been transferred and officials refused to reveal their new postings. Somewhat belatedly, the U.S. embassy in Santiago began an investigation of its own, sending officials to make two separate visits to the area, interviewing the farmer and his brother. When the American officials arranged meetings with two senior police officers in the town where Weisfeiler was last seen, neither kept the appointment. According to a declassified State Department cable on the case, other carabinero police officers appeared at the hotel where the American consular official was staying, saying they had been sent to protect her vehicle. "They were concerned both that night and the following morning with Conoff's itinerary, her length of stay in the area and when she planned to return to Santiago. Conoff had distinct impression that the officials were keeping close track of her whereabouts from the time she arrived until the time she departed," the cable said. "They stated considerable concern for her safety and displayed anxiety over her activities in the area."[21]

The cable also describes a conversation with a Chilean official (name redacted) who suspected that the police, "paranoid about foreign leftist extremists," might have killed Weisfeiler on this assumption, realized their mistake too late, and then tried to cover up their actions by planting his backpack on the riverbank. Such efforts to cover up the killing may have expanded to eliminating witnesses. The following year the farmer's brother who reported Weisfeiler to the police was found hanging from a bridge over the river.

What Weisfeiler did not know was that his hike was taking him near Colonia Dignidad, a secretive German enclave that had operated in the area since 1961. The community, whose full name was the Dignity Charitable and Educational Society, has a history that reads like the script of a horror film. It was founded by a former German army medic, Paul Schafer, who had started a social-religious organization in postwar Germany and fled when he was charged with abusing two children enrolled in the program. Accompanied by some of his followers, Schafer set up Colonia Dignidad, which eventually grew to three hundred

German and Chilean members and included a farm, a school, a hospital, two airstrips, and even a power station. The community was surrounded by barbed wire fences and contained a watchtower and searchlights.

A few defectors who had managed to leave the community told of a harsh and repressive existence in which residents were obliged to wear Bavarian peasant clothing, though Schafer, whom they referred to as the "Permanent Uncle," usually wore more contemporary apparel as a sign of his status. Television, telephones, and sex were banned, and a strict segregation of the sexes was enforced. Some residents were allowed to marry, though their spouses were usually selected by Schafer himself and any offspring were immediately separated from their parents. Children born at Colonia Dignidad spent their first few years at the compound's hospital, later moving into dormitories with others of their age group. Physical punishment (including torture) was commonplace, and Schafer often preached that corporal punishment was spiritually uplifting. Residents were encouraged to confess their sins, real or imagined, to Schafer as well as to denounce the sins of others.

There is no clear evidence to suggest Colonia Dignidad ever sheltered old Nazis, as many suspected, but its ties to the Pinochet regime's security forces were an open secret.[22] Luis Peebles, a former prisoner who had been held and tortured at the settlement, told of being transferred from a site at the Chilean naval base in Talcahuano. Bound and blindfolded, he rode for several hours in a truck that turned from the highway down a dirt road to a location that smelled of farm manure. He was subjected to more interrogation, beatings, and torture, but at times there were no questions, only physical cruelty. During these intervals he heard a German-accented voice instructing his tormentors on ways to increase his suffering.

Peebles was eventually released and fled into exile in Europe, later recounting his experiences to Amnesty International's office in Germany. Using his testimony, that of two other Chileans held at Colonia Dignidad, and a former DINA official, Amnesty International produced a report in March of 1977 entitled *Colonia Dignidad: A Torture Camp of the DINA*. But lawyers for the colony filed a legal injunction in Germany that blocked publication of the report.[23]

Luz Arce told the Truth and Reconciliation Commission she had heard DINA officials discuss the transfer of prisoners to Colonia Dignidad. The commission's report noted the long-standing allegations and conducted its own investigation, drawing upon court cases filed in Germany on behalf of residents whose relatives feared for their safety as well as testimony provided in Chile. (A formal request to visit Colonia Dignidad was rejected.) The report noted that the numerous accounts by former detainees were "so detailed and consistent, that when taken with other evidence, including statements by former DINA agents and even former members of Colonia Dignidad, they cannot honestly be doubted." The commission concluded that the settlement had various ties with the DINA, which used Colonia Dignidad as both a training and detention center, and that torture on the premises was carried out not only by DINA agents but by some of community's residents as well.[24]

A U.S. embassy cable, dated July 23, 1987, tells of a Chilean army officer who informs American officials that Weisfeiler was alive and being held in Colonia Dignidad. The officer, who refused to give his name, said he had been in the army patrol that detained Weisfeiler and that there had been a standing order to deliver any strangers found in the area to the settlement. The army regularly patrolled the perimeter of Colonia Dignidad, which the regime considered to be "a good ally." The unnamed officer insisted on meeting in the offices of the Catholic Church's human rights department, the Vicariate of Solidarity, and the story he offered contained so many details that fit Weisfeiler's particulars that "there appears to be virtually no possibility that it could be some unknown third person." The Chilean officer described how Weisfeiler was accused of being a Russian spy, a CIA spy, and then a Jewish spy by the army patrol's commander and Colonia Dignidad's security chief. The officer said he saw Weisfeiler from a distance on a later visit to the settlement, making bricks. He entered Colonia Dignidad on two subsequent occasions and spoke to a young Chilean guard who had told him he was distressed by the torture inflicted on Weisfeiler and his appalling living conditions. The army officer said this Chilean guard sometimes appeared drugged; he was the nephew of a local carabinero police official who had been trying, without success, to remove him from Colonia Dignidad.[25]

The army officer and other patrol members were later transferred out of the region, but in June 1987 the army officer encountered one of these soldiers, who had been reassigned to the area. This official said he had recently been inside Colonia Dignidad, had seen Weisfeiler alive, and that he and his colleagues had received orders to "clean out" an underground bunker area where prisoners were kept. The army officer said prisoners were often kept for a time at Colonia Dignidad and were then moved to other parts of the country for staged shootouts with the security forces. It was not clear whether Weisfeiler was part of this "clean out."

This was the last tantalizing bit of information to surface about Weisfeiler's possible fate. The army officer did not keep a subsequent appointment with embassy officials. The July 23 cable then describes how the U.S. embassy contacted the German embassy, only to learn that German officials did not have any contacts inside Colonia Dignidad either and that several German citizens were trying to extricate relatives from the settlement. "If Weisfeiler is in fact alive and a prisoner in the Colonia or anywhere else in Chile with the knowledge of the GOC [government of Chile], any investigation we undertake runs the risk of his being killed to cover up the affair," the cable said. "On the other hand, to take no action could be equivalent to abandoning an American citizen trapped in the hands of persons for whom paranoid is one of the kinder adjectives." That same year a West German commission was sent to Chile to investigate possible links between Colonia Dignidad and the disappearance of more than thirty children from Bonn and Cologne. The settlement's leaders obtained an order from a local court blocking access to their compound, and the commission returned to Germany a few days later.

A few weeks after taking office President Aylwin ordered an investigation into Colonia Dignidad, which lasted nine months. The settlement's legal status had been that of a charity, and it operated a number of apparently profitable businesses as well—its holdings included several mills and factories. Nevertheless, investigators could find no tax returns, customs forms, or other documentation. On January 31, 1991, Aylwin issued a supreme decree revoking the settlement's charity status.[26]

A government spokesman said Colonia Dignidad had incurred multiple violations of health, labor, recruitment, educational, and tax codes.

Officials ordered the transfer of the colony's assets to the Methodist Church and forwarded the information investigators had collected to the solicitor general's office for further legal action. Colonia Dignidad's leaders filed an appeal to this measure, transferred some of the settlement's financial assets, and managed to reorganize in such a way as to forestall its closure for another decade and a half.

VI

In the wake of the Truth and Reconciliation Commission's findings, the Aylwin government created an official department to allocate reparations to victims' families. And Chilean courts were beginning to act on some of the commission's findings, with some intrepid judges even daring to summon past and present military and security officials. There were two legal obstacles in their way: the regime's amnesty law, which sought to absolve officials of any charges occurring before 1978, and the continuing jurisdiction of military courts over crimes committed by the armed forces. Aylwin had urged the courts to investigate as thoroughly as possible to establish the facts in the cases, even if it would not be possible to prosecute the guilty parties.

Witness intimidation was also a factor. Marcia Alejandra Merino was another former political prisoner coerced into collaborating with the DINA. She had been arrested in 1974, apparently betrayed by another detained member of the MIR. Under torture she did likewise, and she later recounted how her captors would drive her through Santiago neighborhoods and terrorize her into pointing out fellow MIR members. Merino gave the Truth and Reconciliation Commission a list of forty-eight people she had seen at DINA detention sites and was later asked to testify in the court investigation into the disappearance of a French-Chilean student leader.

It was a heartbreaking case. The missing student, Alfonso Chanfreau, was one of the MIR members whose name had been wrenched from Merino under torture. The DINA then arrested and tortured Chanfreau, and when these sessions failed to produce the information the security agents were seeking, they arrested Chanfreau's wife and tortured her in his presence. She was later released, but Chanfreau was never seen again.

Before Merino was scheduled to testify in court, she was contacted by an attorney who in the past had represented the DINA's successor security agency, the CNI. He told her that the Chilean army's intelligence department, which had absorbed most of the regime's security apparatus, had informants throughout the court system and would know if she named any security agents in her testimony. The not-so-subtle threat worked: Merino did testify in the case but, "out of terror," did not give the names of any DINA agents.[27]

By early 1993 Chile's courts had reopened roughly thirty cases covered by the Pinochet regime's 1978 amnesty law, and the Aylwin government had successfully sought the extradition of a former DINA agent, Osvaldo Romo, who fled to Brazil when Pinochet left office. Romo was to be a witness in the Alfonso Chanfreau case, but the Chilean Supreme Court handed the case over to the military courts before he could testify. This prompted the Chilean congress to pass an impeachment motion against three Supreme Court justices and the army judge involved in the decision for "gross abandonment of duty" and for denying the right to justice.[28] Chile's senate upheld the charges against one of the judges, who was expelled from the judiciary.

Weeding out former torturers from the Chilean army was a jittery but not impossible undertaking. A number of former security agents, sensing political changes about to take place, had already left the service prior to the CNI's incorporation into the army.[29] According to former defense minister Patricio Rojas, taking immediate steps to "cut off and cut out" former CNI agents would not have been a workable plan and might have sparked a rebellion. So he opted for a more gradual culling, timed with each year's military promotions and staffing changes. "I decided to cut them out in four tranches, on an annual basis," he said. "It was hard to explain to Congress."[30] By 1994 most of the identifiable former CNI officials had been nudged out of the Chilean army, and fears that the regime's former security forces might regroup into a large, mafia-like organization did not come true.

VII

The slow pace of justice infuriated many Chileans, especially those who had fled the country as political refugees during the military regime. On a visit to Scandinavia in May 1993, Aylwin's entourage was met with demonstrations by expatriate Chileans outraged over Pinochet's continuing command of the army and the significant backlog of unsolved human rights crimes. In Sweden, home to over thirty thousand Chilean exiles, an angry group of protestors hurled eggs at the Chilean officials. At a press conference Aylwin explained that although Pinochet was still army commander, his presence "did not disturb the functioning of democracy in Chile."[31]

Back in Santiago, however, events were unfolding in such a way as to suggest quite the opposite. On May 28, 1993, Pinochet was infuriated by the front-page headline in the government newspaper, *La Nación:* a criminal court judge was reopening the "Pinochecks" case involving the army's $3 million payments to his eldest son. He ordered the army to be placed on full alert and convened an emergency meeting of generals in Santiago. Heavily armed soldiers in camouflage gear, some carrying bazookas, appeared outside the army headquarters and kept up this intimidating display for five days. At one point, photographers covering the troop movements were attacked and their cameras destroyed.

Aylwin decided not to cut short his trip and return to Santiago, for doing so might create an impression of panic, and instructed his cabinet to maintain a public air of authority. The army contacted the editorial offices of *La Nación,* demanding that the paper publish its version of events, including a headline that it had drafted.[32] The newspaper refused and opted for an unusual front page for the next day's edition, with no headline referring to the army alert, just a close-up photo of one of the fiercer-looking soldiers.

Between May 28 and June 22, Chile's interior and defense ministers held a series of meetings with Pinochet and his deputy. Among Pinochet's demands were the resignation of Defense Minister Patricio Rojas, a new amnesty law that would effectively end judicial investigations of the military's role in human rights cases, and a halt to the inquiry into his son's business dealings. According to Rojas, Pinochet was convinced that there was a conspiracy against him and his family and that the judge in the Pinochecks case was a leftist enemy. "Pinochet had the idea the courts were controlled by the government," he recalled. "He thought you could call the judge and give him an order, that there was a chain of command like in the army."[33] The government refused to remove Rojas but agreed to negotiate a transfer of the Pinochecks case to a different court judge.

The public reaction to the former dictator's belligerence was mostly negative, with 57.8 percent of those polled describing Pinochet as having acted "very badly" or "inadequately." Another 26 percent either had no opinion or gave neutral responses, while 15.9 percent said the general had acted either "appropriately" or "very well." When asked about the Chilean army, 63.3 percent responded that the military had acted "in an inadequate way" during the conflict.[34]

A civilian-military committee was formed to study the judicial status of human rights cases around the country. The committee included Aylwin's justice minister and the army's chief prosecutor. Aylwin, still hoping to somehow bring closure to the wounds of the past, held a series of meetings with military, political, and human rights leaders and drew up a bill that sought to speed up the trials. The bill's provisions included the appointment of special judges who would work exclusively on human rights cases. Military officers would be allowed to give evidence in secret, and their names would not be revealed. Witness testimony "which contributes to the clarification of the crime and its circumstances" could be kept off the public legal record. Any lawyers or court officials who violated this confidentiality would face imprisonment.

The proposal was presented to the Chilean congress on August 4, 1993, and immediately sparked heated debate—within the government's own political coalition. Critics of the bill pointed out that the increased secrecy would mean even less accountability, and a group of relatives of the disappeared began a public hunger strike in protest. After a month of stormy debate, the bill was withdrawn.

That September marked the twentieth anniversary of the military coup, and Pinochet was showing no regrets for the crimes committed.

On September 7 he gave a speech at Santiago's Union Club, the same venue where, two years earlier, he had proclaimed that the German army was full of potheads and homosexuals. This time Pinochet's discourse was equally provocative: he suggested that there had been no *desaparecidos* and that claims to the contrary were pure propaganda. The Chilean Left "hid their casualties," he said. "There were never any injured on the other side. They injured our people but the other side had no injured, curiously, though there were bloodstains. So we became convinced that they used to carry away the injured or the dead, in order to leave no traces." He said that on the day of the coup the Chilean army was confronted with "15,000 Cuban-trained guerrillas."[35] Pinochet also criticized the United Nations officials who had investigated his regime's human rights record and even the Truth and Reconciliation Commission itself.

A government spokesman said the Aylwin administration had been "deeply disgusted" by Pinochet's statements, but the general continued to promote his version of events.[36] Two days after his speech, the afternoon tabloid *La Segunda* published excerpts from the third volume of his memoirs, *Camino recorrido,* in which Pinochet defended the practices of his security forces: "In these tasks there are inexcusable methods, which everyone uses, though they may be disagreeable. Use is made of confidential agents and informers. It is frequent to use turncoats and even double agents." Pinochet then seemed to contradict himself, suggesting that allegations of abusive treatment were lies concocted by his enemies: "Without the least shame they handed over their Marxist comrades to our intelligence chiefs. Then, in order to collect another reward, they presented themselves as 'victims' of torture and ill-treatment. With such 'testimonies' several court actions for 'violations of human rights' were fabricated."[37]

The book also contained a five-page section on foreign intervention in Chile, most of which was about the United States and the Reagan administration. Pinochet wrote that former secretary of state George Schultz colluded with the U.S. Congress in a campaign against Chile, and even Reagan himself joined in the "interventionist escalation" when he said that he wanted to see democratic governments in Chile and Paraguay.

Pinochet also decried the "nefarious influence of some high dignitaries of the Catholic Church."[38]

Chile's state television station broadcast a documentary on the coup and Salvador Allende's death, giving younger Chileans their first glimpse of the bombardment of La Moneda The day of the coup's anniversary, September 11, produced the worst street violence seen during Aylwin's presidency. Police used teargas and water cannons to break up demonstrators trying to get through the barriers around the presidential palace. Some youths began hurling rocks and breaking windows. During clashes lasting two hours, a policeman lost an eye after being struck by a rock, and an elderly employee from the ministry of agriculture died after being run over by a riot control vehicle. There was more violence in Santiago's General Cemetery, where witnesses accused police of attacking an authorized group of demonstrators with rubber bullets and tear gas. A nineteen-year-old in the crowd was shot in the neck by a police bullet and killed.[39] The day's arrests totaled 215. Aylwin's interior minister defended the police actions, though there was a subsequent inquiry into some of the day's violent incidents.

Figure 1. General Augusto Pinochet, who ruled from 1973 to 1990 and remained commander of the Chilean army until 1998. Photo by Marcelo Montecino.

Figure 2. Young campaigners for a "no" vote against Pinochet in the 1988 plebiscite. Chilean voters were asked to cast "yes" or "no" ballots on a measure to prolong Pinochet's rule for another eight years. Photo by Marcelo Montecino.

Figure 3. The junta, which served as Pinochet's legislature. From the left: the army's representative, General Humberto Gordon; air force commander General Fernando Matthei; navy commander Admiral José Toribio Merino; and carabinero commander General Rodolfo Stange. Photo by Marcelo Montecino.

Figure 4. Patricio Aylwin addresses supporters after winning the 1989 presidential election. Photo by Marcelo Montecino.

Figure 5. Patricio Aylwin, a Christian Democrat who presided over the first post-Pinochet government from 1990 to 1994. Photo by Marcelo Montecino.

Figure 6. A protestor holds a picture of Orlando Letelier, a Chilean exile who lived in Washington, D.C., and was killed by a car bomb set by the Pinochet regime's secret police in 1976. Also killed was Letelier's American colleague, Ronni Moffitt. Photo by Marcelo Montecino.

Figure 7. Olga Weisfeiler, the sister of missing Pennsylvania State professor Boris Weisfeiler, and Ambassador Craig Kelly at a 2006 press conference at the U.S. embassy in Santiago. The two background photos show Weisfeiler at the time of disappearance and how he might look now. Photo courtesy of the U.S. embassy in Santiago.

Figure 8. Barbed wire at the entrance to Colonia Dignidad, renamed Villa Baviera, a former detention site under the military regime. Photo by Anna Weisfeiler.

Riggs Bank Miami

Riggs Bank London

Citibank New York

Figure 9. The passports show some of the identities Pinochet used to open bank accounts abroad. A U.S. Senate investigation found he used at least ten different aliases. Prepared by the Senate Permanent Subcommittee on Investigations.

Figure 10. *The Black Book of Chilean Justice,* by Alejandra Matus, was a critical exposé of the state of the Chilean judiciary. When it was published in 1999, a Chilean court issued an injunction against the author, who was forced to seek temporary asylum in the United States. Photo by Mary Helen Spooner.

Figure 11. Ricardo Lagos, a Socialist and economist who was briefly imprisoned under Pinochet, was Chile's president from 2000 to 2006. Photo by Marcelo Montecino.

Figure 12. Michelle Bachelet receives the presidential sash from Ricardo Lagos; senate president Eduardo Frei looks on. Photo courtesy of the Chilean government.

Figure 13. Michelle Bachelet and her mother, Angela Jeria, visit Villa Grimaldi, a former detention center where they were both imprisoned during the military regime. The site is now a peace park and museum. Photo courtesy of the Chilean government.

Figure 14. Michelle Bachelet stands before a memorial to those killed during the Pinochet regime. Photo courtesy of the Chilean government.

Figure 15. Michelle Bachelet signs the charter creating the Institute for Human Rights. Photo courtesy of the Chilean government.

PART TWO Building Democracy

FIVE Elections and the Military

I

As Chile approached its first presidential election since Pinochet left office, the general mood was unmistakably optimistic, as if the country wanted to leave its polarized political past behind. An opinion poll published in March 1993 by the conservative Centro de Estudios Públicos (CEP) showed that 68.5 percent of respondents thought the country was progressing and that just over half felt their own economic circumstances would be better or much better in the future. Out of a list of thirteen issues, crime, health, and poverty were listed as voters' chief concerns, with human rights ranked sixth and terrorism, environmental issues, and corruption at the bottom of the list.

The same poll showed respondents giving the Aylwin government an above-average approval rating of 4.8 on a 7-point scale, and Aylwin's personal approval rating was 72.6 percent.[1] The country's economic growth was averaging 6 percent annually, and the number of those living in poverty, which had been 40 percent when Aylwin took office, had dropped to 33 percent, supported by the 36 percent increase in the minimum wage. Inflation had also been reduced from 26 percent in 1989 to 12.7 percent.[2]

The Concertación party's candidate was Eduardo Frei Ruiz-Tagle, son of the former president Eduardo Frei Montalva (1964–79), a civil engineer and Christian Democrat who had won his party's presidency after defeating several rival factions. Despite his parentage, the younger Frei was a relative newcomer to Chilean politics, only entering public life following his father's death in early 1982. The circumstances of that death were suspicious: the seventy-one-year old former president had been a formidable Pinochet detractor whom the regime could not dismiss as a Marxist apologist. Frei had checked into one of Santiago's best hospitals for a simple hernia operation, appeared to recover, but then suffered a relapse and returned to the hospital. Following a second operation, Frei died of septicemia.

In 2004 a Chilean court ordered the exhumation of the former president's body, and forensic specialists took samples of tissue, which were sent to the United States for analysis by the FBI. The report that followed said it was unable to detect traces of any toxin such as those concocted in DINA and CNI laboratories. Two years later a doctor who had treated Frei said his death from septicemia was unexpected and that a "foreign chemical substance" was a likely cause of death. A subsequent judicial investigation discovered that the former president and his family had been under constant surveillance by the Pinochet regime's security forces and that the medical team treating Frei had documented links to the DINA and CNI.[3]

Despite the aura of the Frei name, some left-wing Concertación politicians were arguing that it was now the turn of the socialists to lead the next government. They were backing the candidacy of Ricardo Lagos, a popular former education minister during the Aylwin government who had founded the Party for Democracy in 1988, attracting former communists and other leftists as well as independent voters. There were understandable fears that Chile would not be ready for a left-wing presidential candidate and that a Lagos nomination might cause the breakup of the Concertación. But the coalition held itself together, agreed upon Frei as its candidate, and began another successful political campaign.

Frei, buoyed by the Aylwin government's economic successes, easily defeated the right-wing presidential candidate, Arturo Alessandri, a businessman who was the nephew of yet another former Chilean president, Jorge Alessandri (1958–64), Frei's father's predecessor.[4] Frei received 58 percent of the vote to Alessandri's 24 percent, with the remainder going to candidates from smaller political groups and a former Pinochet regime cabinet minister who ran as an independent.

There was relatively little ideological debate during the campaign, despite the fact that Alessandri, who had somewhat belatedly agreed to be a candidate, was a staunch *Pinochetista*. He had even gone so far as to back the former dictator's recent assertion that there had been no Chileans who disappeared during the regime.[5] He was supported by the Center-Right Renovación Nacional and the Far-Right Union Democrática Independiente (UDI). There was visible friction between these two parties, with the UDI suspicious of Renovación Nacional's past deal making with the Concertación leadership. There were times during the campaign that these two right-wing parties conducted themselves "as if they were each other's chief opponent, rather than the governmental alliance," according to Oxford University political scientist Alan Angell.[6]

Frei might have faced a stronger challenge had the Chilean Right's leadership not imploded the previous year. Two rising political stars in Renovación Nacional became embroiled in a scandal that derailed the party's hopes that year of putting forth a presidential candidate who was conservative but did not represent a continuation of the Pinochet regime. Evelyn Matthei was the daughter of the former junta member and air force commander whose popularity had been further enhanced when she became the first deputy in Chilean history to give birth while serving a term in congress. Her rival was Sebastián Piñera, a businessman who had backed a "no" vote against Pinochet in the 1988 plebiscite but who had been campaign manager for the regime's presidential candidate, Hernán Büchi, the following year.

Matthei received a tape recording of a telephone conversation between Piñera and a television journalist who would be interviewing her in a forthcoming panel discussion. In the recording, Piñera told the journalist he should aggressively interrogate Matthei to present her in a bad light and offered detailed suggestions about how to word the questions. The owner of the private television channel where the program was scheduled then went on air and played the tape, claiming that an unknown source had provided him with the recording. The journalist speaking on the tape was fired, and Piñera withdrew from the race. The more obvious question of the tape's origins remained unanswered.

Matthei later admitted that she had provided the tape to the television station, withdrew her candidacy, and left Renovación Nacional.[7] Many Renovación Nacional leaders had long suspected they were under surveillance during the Pinochet regime, but was the Chilean army still spying on politicians under a democratically elected government? A judicial investigation revealed that this was indeed the case. An army captain working in the telecommunications unit had recorded the conversation, using army equipment while on army premises. To make matters more embarrassing for the military, the officer in question had been one of Pinochet's confidants, at times following Pinochet on his rounds to set up secure telephone connections.[8]

The army offered up the captain as a kind of scapegoat, though few believed he had acted alone. A civilian employee of the army's intelligence department also testified in the case and gave an anonymous interview to a Chilean television station in which he speculated that the espionage operation was army payback for Piñera's past opposition to Pinochet. The army continued to insist that it did not routinely spy on Chilean citizens but admitted it monitored all radio communications, including cell phones.

Throughout the so-called Piñeragate scandal, Pinochet kept a relatively low profile, choosing that time to take an extended tour of army installations in southern Chile. He was still away on "routine military duties" when U.S. Army chief of staff Colin Powell visited Santiago that month.[9]

II

The 1993 presidential election featured candidates ..
surnames from Chile's past, and so did the new government lea ..
younger Eduardo Frei. Edmundo Pérez Yoma, the defense minister, was the son of one of Frei's father's cabinet ministers, Edmundo Pérez Zukovic, who was killed by a left-wing group in 1971. Although the Aylwin government may have hoped it would be possible to maneuver Pinochet out of the army command, both the new president and his defense minister seemed resigned to living with Pinochet until 1998, when he was scheduled to retire.

For his part, Pinochet seemed happy to see the back of Pérez Yoma's predecessor, the strong-willed Patricio Rojas. As soon as his appointment was made public, the general paid a surprise visit to Pérez at his home, accompanied by several army officers. "This is a small country and people are familiar with each other," Pérez said. "Pinochet knew of my father's case, for he was army *intendente* in 1971 and a curfew was declared after the killing." Pinochet greeted Pérez Yoma, who felt slightly intimidated by the presence of so many military officials at his door, and said he wanted to pay his respects. He made a sympathetic reference to Pérez Yoma's late father and said he was at his service. "I told him I wanted to be the military's contact for the political world and the political world's contact for the military," Pérez Yoma recalled. He also told Pinochet that he wanted to gain an in-depth understanding of the Chilean army: its strategy, its operations, and how it served the country's defense. "Pinochet responded very well to this and turned to his chief of staff to instruct him to immediately prepare a tour for me of army installations around the country. I hadn't even taken office yet!" he said. "This led to an interesting working relationship that helped reduce political tensions."[10] The relationship would remain interesting, though hardly tension free, for the duration of the Frei administration. Pérez Yoma continued a process begun during the Aylwin government: prying apart the issues of national defense and human rights, turning the latter over to the judicial system for further action.

For many years the Chilean armed forces had been almost a caste apart from the rest of society. The Academia Nacional de Estudios Políticos y Estratégicos (ANEPE), a defense college in Santiago, was one of a very few meeting places where Chilean civilians could mingle with the military. As far back as 1961, ANEPE began offering some of its courses to civilian government employees, but in the wake of the Pinochet regime, it was still an entity largely unknown to the leaders of Chile's newly elected governments.

Francisco Ledantec, a naval captain who joined the faculty in 1989, recalled that the atmosphere at ANEPE following Pinochet's plebiscite defeat the previous year was one of cautious anticipation. "Nobody talked about torture or anything like that," he said. "We were all waiting to see what would happen."[11] ANEPE's directors might have been hoping the academy would play a role in Chile's transition to civilian rule, but instead the Pinochet regime used ANEPE as a political tool during its last few months in power. In November of that year the academy was abruptly notified by regime officials that its premises were to be used for a conference entitled Human Rights: Towards a New Focus in one week's time. The regime also telephoned foreign military attachés and civilian diplomats the same day to invite them to the conference.

The military attachés were asked to attend in uniform, though the others present—including Pinochet's defense minister—were in civilian clothing. Television cameras took extensive footage of those present, and the entire gathering was evidently a contrived media event. A civilian lawyer with close ties to the Pinochet regime told the audience that he represented a new truth committee, one formed in response to attacks on the regime over human rights. He gave a presentation on human rights issues under the Allende government and said Marxist-sponsored terrorism was a source of violations. He attacked both Aylwin and his political coalition and a Washington think tank, ending with a call for national unity. In contrast to most conferences held at the academy, there was no question-and-answer session after the presentation. The regime's defense minister left immediately afterward, avoiding the coffee social that followed.[12]

"ANEPE had been a big mystery to people," Ledantec said, recalling the academy's previous image. "If you dared knock at our gate, you'd be met by a sentry with a gun."[13] But the institution was now under civilian control, welcoming members of Chile's new congress and briefing them on defense issues. With the cold war ending, the emphasis was shifting from war to peacekeeping, and Chilean soldiers would be joining United Nations peacekeeping operations in Haiti, Cyprus, and other countries. Pinochet, he noted, had never liked the idea of sending Chilean troops abroad.

Defense Minister Pérez Yoma gave at least two seminars at ANEPE, and increasing numbers of civilian officials began enrolling in courses. Chief among them was a pediatrician working in the Chilean health ministry, a former political prisoner and torture victim. Michelle Bachelet, daughter of an air force general who died in detention after the 1973 coup, had the highest grades of any of her classmates in the ANEPE course that year.[14] She was rewarded with a scholarship to study at the National War College in Washington, D.C., in 1997 and went on to earn a master's degree at the Chilean army's war college. A few years later she would become the country's first female defense minister and later president.

III

The Frei government may have thought it politically expedient not to challenge Pinochet's position as army commander. However, it did eventually manage to remove a former junta member from his post as police commander. General Rodolfo Stange had headed the carabineros since 1985, replacing a police chief whom judicial investigators accused of covering up the grisly murder of three Chilean leftists. Some Chilean human rights activists had observed improvements in the treatment of prisoners by carabineros under Stange—though reports of serious abuses continued.[15] And in the junta, he had helped shift the balance of power away from Pinochet. But many suspected he knew more about the triple murder than he admitted, and a few weeks after Frei took office, a judge issued indictments against Stange and six retired carabinero officers on charges of obstructing justice.

Frei asked Stange to resign for "moral and ethical reasons," but he refused, insisting that he was innocent of the charges and citing his constitutional right to remain in office until 1998, when Pinochet was due to resign as army commander.[16] The impasse was not resolved for another year, when Stange announced his own resignation at a press conference, saying he was stepping down to show his disapproval of a government reform bill that would allow the president to appoint and remove military commanders and the director of the carabinero police. The reform bill stalled in congress while courts eventually absolved Stange of all charges. The episode was embarrassing to the Frei government and caused a cabinet shake-up, resulting in the removal of Frei's socialist interior minister, a staunch opponent of the former carabinero commander. After leaving his post, Stange joined the UDI party, later winning a seat in the Chilean senate, where he served from 1998 to 2006.

Stange's departure left Pinochet as the only military commander remaining from the days of military rule. Air force commander Fernando Matthei had voluntarily retired at sixty-five, one year into the Aylwin government—though Aylwin invited him to stay on the job.[17] The still-unresolved issue was the president's authority over the Chilean armed forces. Aylwin was able to appoint Matthei's successor, who became the first to serve out a fixed four-year term. When that term expired, Frei appointed his successor.[18] But the Chilean army was still a law unto itself.

In April 1995 the body of Eugenio Berrios, a Chilean chemist who had worked for the Pinochet regime's security forces, was discovered on a beach in Uruguay. Four years earlier a Chilean judge had ordered him to testify as part of the investigation of the 1976 Letelier assassination. Other witnesses in the case had stated that Berrios, a close associate of American DINA agent Michael Townley, had developed poison gas for the secret police that was used in a number of assassinations. But army intelligence agents ushered Berrios out of the country, transporting him first to Chile's southernmost city, Punta Arenas, then across a mountain pass into Argentina. According to officials of the civilian detective agency, Investigaciónes, Chilean army intelligence agents then leaked photos to the press suggesting that Berrios was in Europe. "Some of the papers speculated his disappearance could have been the work of the DEA, or had something to do with drugs," said Nelson Mery, the Investigaciónes director at the time. He recalled that officials were eager to find out what Berrios might be able to tell them about other murder cases in which the Pinochet regime's security forces were implicated. But every time his agents' inquiries led them to an army officer, "there was some kind of distraction created by *Pinochetistas*."[19]

In November 1992 the missing chemist resurfaced at a beach town near Montevideo. He had climbed through a broken window of the bungalow where he was apparently being held and rushed to a neighbor's house, begging for help and saying that he was going to be killed. At a local police station Berrios identified himself and repeated his assertion that he was being held prisoner and about to be killed. He later recanted, saying he was under too much stress, and the police released him to two Uruguayan army officers.

It was the last time Berrios would be seen alive. Investigators learned the chemist had been moved across the border into Brazil. At some point he was returned, either dead or alive, to Uruguay, where his body was discovered. Forensic scientists calculated that he had been killed between January and June of 1993, which meant that his captors kept him alive for at least a few more months after his appearance at the Uruguayan police station.[20]

The case caused a political storm in Chile and Uruguay. Several Uruguayan police and military officials, including the head of the country's military intelligence, were fired. A number of Chilean consular officials who had been aware of Berrios's presence in Uruguay were also sanctioned or fired. But the most troubling aspect of this case was the fact that the old network of illegal and brutal security operations in Chile and other Southern Cone countries was alive and well. Even with a democratically elected government in power, the country's army intelligence had made a mockery of the Chilean justice system, moving Berrios across borders on at least four separate occasions, holding him prisoner for over a year, and then finally killing him.

IV

Some of the more notorious human rights crimes of the past were receiving attention, but there did not appear to be as much concern for establishing safeguards to prevent new abuses. Chilean courts received approximately sixty complaints of torture occurring between March 1990 and October 1994, according to Human Rights Watch, and even though police had new procedures in place for investigating such complaints, they almost never resulted in court prosecutions. A representative from Human Rights Watch met with officials from the Chilean ministries of justice and the interior and representatives of the president's office, but they "failed to provide evidence that any police officers had been convicted of torture since the return to democracy."[21]

Of greater concern to the Frei government was the economy and the prospects for a free trade agreement with the United States. When the North American Free Trade Agreement (NAFTA) went into effect in 1994, U.S. officials and their Mexican and Canadian counterparts announced their intention of bringing other Western hemisphere countries into the club—and Chile would be first in line. The Clinton administration sought congressional approval for fast-track negotiations to expand NAFTA, which would have allowed the measure to be voted on without being subjected to unlimited amendments. Unfortunately for Chile, the view of free trade on Capitol Hill was souring: shortly after the treaty was implemented in 1994, Mexico was forced to devalue the peso, setting off an economic crisis that had required a multibillion-dollar emergency financing effort led by the United States.

While Chile's entry into NAFTA stalled, the Frei government negotiated a bilateral free trade agreement with Canada in 1996. U.S. officials viewed the Chile-Canada pact as "a good interim step" that might help pave the way for the country's eventual entry into NAFTA.[22] And other issues began to emerge, such as a report by the U.S. State Department noting that drug trafficking and money laundering in Chile had grown considerably, due in part to its economic stability and booming exports. The country's shared border with Peru and Bolivia, the leading producers of coca, made it an attractive transit point for drug shipments. The report also noted that some former Chilean exiles had cultivated ties with drug-trafficking groups while living abroad and that construction companies in central Chile and fishing companies in the south had been used to launder money.[23]

U.S. officials said Chile was sincere in its efforts to address the drug problem, which was threatening its entry into NAFTA. It should be pointed out that some influential groups within Chile were less than enthusiastic—labor unions, who feared job losses, and owners of traditional farms, whose interests were represented by conservative members of congress. Chile later opted for bilateral trade agreements, signing a free trade pact with Mexico in 1998, a much-belated agreement with the U.S. in 2003, and eventually an agreement with most Latin American and European countries as well as several Asian nations.

Chile's exports of goods and services grew by an average of 9.5 percent annually during the Frei government, and the growth was qualitative as well as quantitative. According to Central Bank figures, exports of goods involving some level of processing increased from 32.7 percent in 1990 to 40.9 percent in 1997. Chile's fruit and vegetable exports grew by more than 500 percent, making the country the single largest wintertime supplier to northern hemisphere countries. In other words, Chile was not simply mining more copper or cutting down more trees but was diversifying its products and improving productivity.

Shortly before taking office, the Frei government was faced with a harrowing multimillion-dollar loss by the Chilean state copper company. A trader at Codelco, the world's biggest copper company, admitted losing over $200 million in futures contracts between September and January 1993. He told investigators that he lost the money after mistakenly putting several "sell" contracts into the "buy" column of his computer, and his efforts to recover the losses through additional transactions only resulted in more losses.[24] The trader was charged with fraud and tax evasion and sentenced to three years in prison, and the Codelco losses amounted to 0.5 percent of Chile's gross domestic product.

In some ways Codelco's rogue trader seemed emblematic of the country's new economic confidence. Chilean investors were looking beyond their borders, and by 1996 had $8 billion in holdings in neighboring Latin American countries, including majority stakes in pharmaceutical firms, utilities companies, telecommunications systems, textile factories, and supermarkets. And inevitably this business success brought a measure of resentment from other countries. Argentines were outraged over a Chilean power company's decision to cut off electricity to the Buenos Aires airport when officials fell behind on bill payments, and an angry Bolivian crowd vandalized the offices of a Chilean airline in La Paz after Chilean investors acquired a 50 percent share of the country's railroad. "Chileans have always been a kind, humble, hard-working people," an Argentine businessman told the *New York Times*. "But now [that] they've earned a few pennies and learned how to dress, now they think they rule the world."[25] There was sufficient concern about this perception of Chilean business travelers abroad to prompt a series of public service television advertisements warning viewers of the dangers of overconfidence, often featuring a well-dressed executive losing his footing or bumping into a pole.

In their own country, Chileans may not have been bumptious, but there was an undeniable sense that better days were ahead. A poll by the CEP taken in June and July 1996 showed that 60 percent of respondents believed their situation was better than that of their parents a generation earlier, and that 72.3 percent felt that their children would enjoy greater opportunities than they had. The same poll indicated that public perceptions of the level of poverty were less optimistic—only 29.7 percent believed that poverty had decreased, and a similar number responded that the poor were living in better circumstances than they had five years earlier.[26]

Conservative politicians maintained that the Concertación had exaggerated the level of poverty under Pinochet, but according to a measurement used by the regime's own planning ministry, the numbers of poor and indigent were indeed declining. Since 1985 the planning ministry had carried out detailed surveys of Chilean households, setting the poverty line as the minimum per capita income needed to cover basic food and nonfood requirements. Indigence, or extreme poverty, was defined as having less than the minimum income needed to cover basic food needs. The Aylwin and Frei governments continued these household surveys, which revealed that the number of Chileans living in poverty declined from 25.7 percent of the population in 1990 to 17.5 percent in 1996 (and later dropping to 14.9 percent in 2000). The number of indigent Chileans shrank from 12.9 percent in 1990 to 5.7 percent in 1996.[27]

V

Winter is the unhealthiest time to be in Santiago, as heavy smog often obscures the view of the mountains ringing the city. Thermal inversion, a layer of warm air trapping cold air close to the ground, causes smog levels to rise, along with hospital visits for respiratory illnesses. A 1995 World Bank study reported that during the months of July and August the amount of particulate matter in the city's air was among the highest in the world, with a measurable impact on life expectancy.[28] The Frei government unveiled a pollution abatement plan three years later, but its goals were never met.

The Pinochet regime had had no environmental policy to speak of, other than a commission to study the issue of pollution and an underfunded national parks department. In 1994, after two years of difficult negotiations, the Chilean congress finally approved the Environmental Framework law, which required environmental impact statements for new investment projects, both national and foreign. It also established fines for noncompliance, although many companies felt it made more economic sense to pay the fines rather than make changes in their projects. Critics pointed out that there didn't seem to be any incentives for companies to develop practices that were less polluting or more friendly to the environment.[29]

Frei viewed economic growth as the best antidote to his country's bitter political past, but Chile's growing environmental movement was not happy with his administration's gung ho development policies. Chile was also attracting the attention of international environmentalists, including a former California clothing manufacturer–turned-conservationist, Douglas Tompkins. Tompkins first visited Chile on a skiing trip in 1961, when he was seventeen and the country was governed by a Center-Right president. The previous year southern Chile had suffered an almost apocalyptic series of natural disasters: two earthquakes, one with a magnitude of 9.5, the most powerful ever recorded, followed by the eruption of a volcanic fissure that sent ash and steam into the air for several weeks. The Great Valdivia earthquake caused death and devastation across an area of four hundred thousand square kilometers and set off a series of tsunamis with waves up to eighty feet that destroyed communities along Chile's southern Pacific coast and reached as far away as Hawaii, Alaska, and the Philippines. The tremors also set off landslides that blocked a river, causing water levels to rise precipitously, which threatened to burst open a dam that would have flooded the already devastated area.[30]

Earthquakes and volcanic eruptions are a harsh fact of life in Chile and might explain in part why many Chileans have a less-than-benign view of the natural world. But the beauty of its southern forests, lakes, and glaciers have long attracted visitors, and Tompkins would make several return trips over the years as he built his fortune with the North Face and Esprit clothing companies. He helped finance a twelve-hundred-acre nature reserve and ecotourism center, the Santuario Cani, in Chile's southern lake district.[31] Turning his attention farther south, he began buying up land in Patagonia, where Chile's lakes give way to spectacular fjords, for what was to become the biggest privately managed conservation project in the world. By 1995 he had acquired six hundred and seventy thousand acres, with plans to buy another thirty thousand, for what would become the biggest privately managed conservation project in the world. But not everyone was supportive of Tompkins's ambitious projects.

One of the first obstacles came from Fiordo Blanco, a salmon farm operating in an estuary near Tompkins's lands. The environmentalist accused the company of illegally dumping its waste into the area's waters and of shooting a colony of sea lions, a protected species under Chilean law. Tompkins sent letters of complaint to Fiordo Blanco but received no response, and when yet another dead sea lion was discovered, he placed an advertisement in a local newspaper offering a reward for information about the culprits.

Fiordo Blanco's plant manager was a former official in Pinochet's secret police agency, the DINA, and had good contacts with local military officials in the region.[32] For its part, the country's armed forces were suspicious of this eccentric foreigner, whose holdings covered a strategic section of Chilean territory where the mainland contracts to one of its narrowest points between the sea and the Argentine border. Tompkins later won a legal case against the salmon farm, but by then his critics had galvanized a considerable section of Chile's business community and politicians against him—not just right-wing members of congress but several prominent Christian Democrats as well. Wild rumors began to circulate: Tompkins had forced poor Chileans off the land; he was a CIA agent; he was a spy for Argentina; he was an Israeli agent planning a new Jewish homeland. He and his wife received death threats.[33]

Chilean environmentalists came to Tompkins's defense, along with some U.S. officials. Richard Gephardt, then minority leader in the House of Representatives, called on the Clinton administration to monitor the case during the free trade negotiations with Chile. Environmental groups pointed out that the Trillium Company, an American forestry company, had bought up almost as much land as Tompkins had but had encountered no opposition. "If this investment were anywhere else but Chile, Mr. Tompkins would be considered a hero," Adriana Hoffmann of the Defenders of the Chilean Forest told the *New York Times*. "But it happened in Chile, where envy and jealousy and business interests are institutions."[34]

In April 1995 Tompkins petitioned Chile's National Monuments Council for his lands to be designated a nature sanctuary, a move that should have resolved any questions about his intentions. The additional thirty thousand acres that he sought to buy and whose location currently cut his planned park in half were owned by Chile's Universidad Catolica. The university was not initially opposed to selling the land to Tompkins's foundation, but under pressure from the Frei administration, it sold the property to the Spanish electric company ENDESA instead. Two more years of hard bargaining elapsed before the government finally reached an agreement with Tompkins. The agreement allowed him to continue to develop the project as a park but prevented him from purchasing any additional lands until the government passed new legislation.

VI

As the Chilean economy grew, so did the fortunes of the country's former dictator and his family. Pinochet and his wife still lived in the army commander's residence, a house formerly occupied by his predecessors but considerably expanded and improved during his time in office. They also owned a large country estate just outside of Santiago. Lucía Hiriart de Pinochet bought and sold a number of real estate properties, including, in 1994, a site on Chile's central Pacific coast for the construction of another country estate for the family. She did not file any income tax returns during this period, though the properties were listed in her name. She also continued as director of the Centros de Madres (CEMA), an organization with a network of centers for low-income women. CEMA offered handicraft classes and sold the products at its stores throughout the country, at one point opening an outlet in Miami. But for a nonprofit organization, its coffers seemed suspiciously full. A law issued in 1980 decreed that 20 percent of the proceeds of Chile's national lottery go to CEMA, and during the Pinochet regime, CEMA took possession of no less than one hundred ten real estate properties owned or administered by the government.[35] According to women working at CEMA, the crafts were sold at three times the price CEMA paid its artisans.[36]

CEMA's Miami branch was overseen by the Pinochets' eldest daughter, Lucía, who made regular private visits to the United States. Like her mother, the younger Lucía also dealt in real estate, and since the early 1980s had opened a number of foreign bank accounts, including some under the name of Redwing Holdings, an offshore entity based in the British Virgin Islands. With the help of Citigroup, she and her brother Marco Antonio opened twenty-nine accounts and certificates of deposit in the name of Redwing and two other offshore entities. According to a later investigation by the U.S. Senate, Citigroup provided Pinochet family members with "many types of financial services," including over $3 million in loans that were repaid in full.[37]

Their father also held several accounts with Citigroup, with the first opened in 1981 in New York. Documentation retrieved by U.S. Senate investigators shows that the account was opened with a one-page application form and minimal information, though the applicant indicates he holds two other bank accounts in Chile. The identification provided was a Chilean passport in the name of José Ramón Ugarte, with a photograph of the dictator wearing glasses—which he did not normally wear in public. The false passport was most likely provided by the regime's security forces and was one of at least ten multiple identities Pinochet would use to open bank accounts in the United States.

Four years later another account was opened at Citigroup's Miami branch, under the name of José Pinochet Ugarte. The application for this account contained even less information, waiving the requirement for two references, and describes the applicant as a retiree ("empleado jubilado") and "Lucía P. Hirart" as his niece. Citigroup officials later told investigators that the bank managers in both cities had been unaware of the dual sets of accounts as well as the account holder's true identity. The Miami manager said that in the nine years she had handled the accounts, she had never met her client, dealing primarily with Lucía. She had been given the impression that "José Pinochet" was Lucía and Marco Antonio's uncle.

In 1992 she learned from a conversation with Lucía that "José" was in fact General Augusto Pinochet and immediately alerted the head of Citigroup's Florida operations, who did not want to handle accounts for the former Chilean dictator. Citigroup's Miami branch began closing all accounts under the name José Pinochet Ugarte over the next year, but it did not inform the New York branch, where the accounts were held under the name of José Ramón Ugarte. And although the funds held in the various Citigroup accounts reached $3.1 million, there is no indication anyone ever inquired into the source of this wealth.[38]

Marco Antonio, Pinochet's younger son, also used a false identity when dealing with Citigroup, where he opened several joint accounts for himself and his father. He had a reputation for reckless behavior, and following a motorcycle accident, his parents sent him to live for a time in the United States, where he learned English and took flying lessons. Using the name Marco Antonio Hiriart, he described himself on application forms as a diplomat attached to the Chilean embassy. He appeared to have had no official duties during this period but did build up a complex network of business interests in Chile, often with his siblings and other partners. Several of these holdings, such as a set of mining concessions he acquired with his brother Osvaldo Augusto, seemed to be nothing more than speculative investments made with no business plan in mind.

Citigroup later compiled a financial profile of Marco Antonio, at one point estimating his net worth as high as $15 million, derived from multiple businesses in Chile: real estate investments, a clothing store chain, a motorcycle and small boat import business, and an aeronautical equipment advisory firm. The account documents also noted his concern for privacy; one mentions that Marco Antonio "does not want contact from Chilean Citibank employees."[39]

He opened another joint account using false names for himself and his father at the First Tulsa Bank in Oklahoma and a single account at the Riggs Bank in Washington, D.C. If some Miami Citigroup executives did not want his father as a client, the Riggs Bank's senior management had no such qualms and even went to extraordinary lengths to elicit additional business from Pinochet, his family, and the Chilean military.

The Chilean military mission in Washington, D.C., had been a previous client of Riggs Bank but had moved its accounts to Canada in 1976 following the car bomb assassination of Orlando Letelier (which occurred just a few blocks from Riggs's headquarters on Dupont Circle). In July 1994 the accounts were transferred back to Riggs, and a few months later the bank's president and two senior Riggs executives visited Santiago. The purpose of their meeting with Pinochet, according to a November 3, 1994, memorandum, was "to express . . . gratitude for returning the official Chilean Military's accounts from the Bank of Nova Scotia to Riggs." The Riggs officials also offered Pinochet personal banking services, promising to send him the necessary documentation. Curiously, the memoranda from their other meetings during this trip indicate they made no such sales pitch to the commanders of Chile's navy and air force, and the executives' overtures to Pinochet seem to have been motivated by political admiration of the former dictator as well as interest in securing the Chilean army's bank deposits.[40] Riggs president Timothy Coughlin even wrote to Pinochet, saying, "It would be an honor for us to open an account for you and to assist you with any banking services you may require outside of Chile." He ends the letter saying he had "prominently displayed" in his office a medallion Pinochet had given him in Santiago, which he would be pleased to show him should he ever visit Washington.[41] Though Pinochet, still worried he could face legal retribution from the Letelier case, would not risk visiting the United States, his relationship with the Riggs Bank executives would grow even warmer over the next few years.

Coughlin and other senior officials at Riggs Bank may not have been aware of the fact that Pinochet, his family, and associates had been using the institution's financial services since July 1979, when one "Jose Ugarte" opened an account in Washington. Two years later that account was closed and another opened at Riggs's Miami branch under the name of José Ramón Ugarte. In January 1985 "José R. Ugarte" opened another account in Miami, and "Daniel Lopez," another one of the ten identities Pinochet used when banking abroad, opened a new account in Washington. In 1990 "Daniel Lopez" wrote a check for $410,000 to "Augusto P. Ugarte" and "Lucía Hiriart P." to open a trust account for the Pinochet children.

The Daniel Lopez accounts were conduits for Pinochet funds used in multiple complex transactions, according to the 2005 U.S. Senate report on Pinochet's accounts. The report said that several Riggs Bank officials in Miami were very aware of the account holders' true identities, for "even a cursory review of the account statements shows that they were carrying Pinochet funds." In addition, there were eight Riggs accounts opened after 1981 in the names of individual Chilean military officers that channeled funds into Pinochet's accounts, with transfers amounting to more than $1.7 million.[42]

VII

Pinochet turned eighty in 1995 but still seemed in robust health and was showing few signs of slowing down. To mark the occasion, he and his supporters launched the Pinochet Foundation, located in a large, nondescript house in eastern Santiago. According to its Web site, the foundation's purpose is to "cooperate with the development of a free society and the historic patrimony of Chile."[43] Most of the site's contents are a homage to Pinochet, listing his regime's achievements: a new constitution, the construction of hydroelectric projects and other public works, and the creation of a private pension fund system, among others. The foundation distributed college and secondary school scholarships and occasionally held conferences on historical and political topics, such as the 1879 War of the Pacific or Chile's foreign relations during the regime.

The foundation's twelve-member board included Pinochet's wife, his son Marco Antonio, and at least two of his regime's former cabinet ministers. Despite the organization's purported interest in history, there is no presidential library per se at its headquarters, although Pinochet amassed his own private library of over fifty-five thousand books, and these combined with his collection of historical memorabilia are worth at least $2.8 million. The collection included items that ought to have been held by the Biblioteca Nacional, such as a handwritten letter from Chile's independence hero Bernando O'Higgins, a 1646 colonial history of Chile valued at approximately US$6,000, and part of the personal library of former Chilean president José Manuel Balmaceda (1886–91). There were a number of first editions and nine antiquarian books on Napoleon (in French) and a biography of Spain's Francisco Franco, signed and dedicated to Pinochet by the author.[44]

Pinochet once told an interviewer that he read for only fifteen minutes at bedtime and was not known to be conversant on topics other than military matters; nevertheless he was an avid collector of rare and antique books, and for many years he was a regular customer of an antiquarian bookseller in downtown Santiago. Pinochet did donate some of his private library to the Chilean War Academy and a few hundred books to his foundation, but the bulk of the collection remained at his homes.

In 1997 the Riggs Bank made a donation of $5,000 to the Pinochet Foundation after a request by General Ricardo Izurieta, who would later succeed Pinochet as army commander. A memo from Carol Thompson urging the bank to make the donation said the foundation's main purpose is "to develop Chilean culture, art and education" and that "the Chilean armed forces feel it is important to promote and preserve the value of the historical and cultural identity of Chile." The Riggs Bank relationship with the Chilean military is "long-standing, highly valued and one of the largest in Embassy Banking both on an official and personal basis," she wrote. "Total deposits for the relationship are in excess of $50 million and at times have exceeded $100 million."[45]

The previous year Izurieta had relayed an invitation from Pinochet to Riggs Bank chairman Joseph Allbritton to attend a horse race in the resort city of Viña del Mar, on the Chilean coast, in February 1996. Allbritton attended the race and was later received by Pinochet at the Chilean army cavalry school. The Riggs chairman sent Pinochet an effusive thank you letter and told Izurieta that the former dictator had "a standing invitation" to visit his horse farm in Virginia. "I very much enjoyed visiting with General Pinochet and complimented him on making Chile into such a success," Allbritton wrote to the military attaché at the Chilean embassy in Washington.[46]

The $5,000 donation, approved by Allbritton and at least three senior Riggs Bank officials, occurred shortly before their 1997 trip to Santiago. By this time Riggs calculated that the Pinochets' and other Chilean accounts represented more than $65 million in deposits and $600,000 in annual profits for the bank.[47] During their three-day visit, the delegation had two dinners with General Izurieta, held an individual meeting with Pinochet followed by a meeting with President Frei, and then attended a reception hosted by Pinochet and Marco Antonio for Allbritton at the military club, which was located in a mansion originally built as a presidential residence. Pinochet was "very gracious and warm" during this visit, according to Riggs vice president Carol Thompson, who seemed to have noticed nothing untoward in a Chilean army commander's extensive travels abroad: "He briefly touched on his retirement plans in the near future and indicated that he hoped to have the opportunity to visit the U.S. as a civilian. He also commented that he had just returned from an interesting trip to China. He was an official guest of the Chinese Government during the first half of October. General Pinochet complimented Mr. Allbritton on the new Embassy Banking Branch in London. During a recent trip to London, Bob Roane gave General Pinochet a tour of Embassy Banking in London."[48]

Allbritton followed up the visit with another friendly letter to Pinochet, thanking him for his hospitality and praising him for having "rid Chile from the threat of totalitarian government and an archaic economic system based on state-owned property and centralized planning. We in the United States owe you a tremendous debt of gratitude and I am confident your legacy will have been to provide a more prosperous and safer world for your children and grandchildren." Allbritton's wife, Barbara, who served on the Riggs Bank board and accompanied him on the trip, also sent a letter ("My dear General Pinochet") thanking him for the lapis lazuli box he had given the couple and saying she was "excited about the possibility of meeting more of your family and having our friendship develop more." She said she hoped Pinochet and his wife would visit them when his schedule allowed.[49]

Riggs Bank president Timothy Coughlin sent Pinochet a letter thanking him for receiving the delegation and for the copy of the book *The Crucial Day,* which Pinochet gave him. The book is an extended interview with Pinochet conducted by an unidentified interrogator, and Pinochet is listed as the book's author. In the book Pinochet, who had become army commander only three weeks before the military takeover, describes his version of events leading up to the 1973 coup, considerably embellishing his own role. "The factual objectivity with which you tell the story of Chile in the early 1970s is both fascinating and instructive," Coughlin wrote. "History provides for fair and proper judgement only when the true facts are known." The bank president also sent Pinochet a note wishing him a happy birthday, from all his "friends and supporters at Riggs Bank."[50]

SIX Politics and Free Speech

I

Valparaíso is a port city on Chile's central coast with steep hills, few skyscrapers, and an eclectic bohemian architecture that earned it a designation as a UNESCO World Heritage Site in 2003.[1] It is also the location of the country's new congress and senate complex, a project the Pinochet regime considered one of its proudest public works. Constructed at a cost of $40 million, its brutalist, geometric design makes it an imposing landmark. From its rooftop patio, lawmakers and their staff can enjoy a panoramic vista of the city and the coast, although the complex blocks the view of the Pacific Ocean for residents of the hillside neighborhood to the east.

Prior to the 1973 military coup, the Chilean congress had been considered the most effective legislature in Latin America and was based in Santiago, along with the rest of the central government's institutions. The regime used the original congress building, a neoclassical structure with Corinthian columns, to house its justice ministry. Pinochet and his advisors grudgingly acknowledged that Chile would again someday have a legislature and no doubt believed that locating it eighty-five miles outside the capital would weaken its influence and preserve the executive branch's political power. Construction began slowly, was still underway when Chile's new senators and deputies took their seats in March of 1990, and was not complete until more than another year had passed.

The new congress and senate complex provided lawmakers with more than three times the space of the old congress, with fourteen floors of offices plus a longer, lower building containing meeting rooms and an extensive library. Valparaíso city officials hoped that the presence of the new congress might provide a much-needed economic stimulus to a port whose fortunes had slowly declined since the opening of the Panama Canal. There was speculation that a new high-speed rail link might eventually connect Valparaíso with Santiago, but for now, the only way to travel between the two cities is a ninety-minute journey along a highway that passes through two mountain tunnels.

The regime's constitution also sought to curb the congress's power by providing for nine nonelected senate seats, with one of these to go to Pinochet when he left the army. Any reform of the constitution itself would require a three-fifths majority in both the senate and chamber of deputies, and there was a clever provision for preventing this from happening: a binominal system for electing members of congress that ensured that the political Right would almost always receive more than its share of seats and that smaller political parties, such as the Communists, would almost never gain any seats.

The binominal system worked by diluting voter support for any political coalition. Each congressional district elected two representatives to each house, although each voter may cast only one vote for one congressional and one senatorial candidate. Political coalitions such as the Concertación or the rightist Alianza por Chile would present two candidates for each office in every voting district. The candidate receiving the highest number of votes would win one of the two seats in a given district. But the second congressional seat would not go automatically to the candidate receiving the second-highest number of votes. If this candidate belonged to the same political coalition as top vote-getting candidate, their combined votes would have to total more than two-thirds of the ballots cast in their district for both candidates to win both seats. If this did not happen, the second seat would go to the most successful candidate run by the other political coalition.

The unfairness of this system was evident from the start: during the 1989 elections Christian Democrat Andrés Zaldívar won 29.8 percent of the votes in one Santiago senate race, followed by Ricardo Lagos, a moderate Socialist who won 29.2 percent. But since the two Concertación candidates' combined votes fell short of the two-thirds-plus-one requirement stipulated in the Pinochet regime's constitution, the district's second senate seat went not to Lagos but to the candidate of the right-wing UDI and former Pinochet regime ideologue Jaime Guzmán, who had won the next largest number of votes, 16.4 percent.[2]

The electoral system bequeathed by the regime ensured that the Right would participate in the democratic process, giving it a stake in the country's new political order.[3] Most of the conservative political leadership appeared to relish being out from under Pinochet's shadow and seemed keenly aware of the political benefit to be gained from working toward political consensus rather than adopting a spoiler role. And no one wanted to return to the bitter divisions and political stalemates of the past, including the very few older legislators who had served in Chile's pre-1973 congress. But how would such a congress function, with so little institutional experience?

David Aronofsky, a legal scholar and U.S. State Department consultant, said that despite the seventeen-year closure of Chile's congress, the country's new senators and congressional deputies made up the best assembly of lawmakers he had ever seen. "They were a remarkable group of people," he said. "What hit me immediately was how little learning needed to be done." Aronofsky was in Chile giving an eight-week seminar on legislative procedures, such as how bills are drafted, how committees are organized, and how meetings are conducted, but Chile's new lawmakers showed a full understanding of the material after barely one week had elapsed. Aronofsky had worked with congresses in Mexico, Colombia, Peru, and Bolivia as well as various U.S. state legislatures and said, bluntly, "The Chileans put everyone else to shame." One congressional staffer who had been employed by the Venezuelan congress while an exile during the Pinochet regime told Aronofsky that the difference between the two legislative bodies "was like night and day."[4]

Aronofsky said that in contrast to the unruly atmosphere in so many other countries, a typical parliamentary committee meeting in the Chilean congress would take place in a tidy room, with no onlookers talking among themselves and all discussion taking place in respectful, serious tones. There was pride in the legislative process, he observed, and even the appointed senators were treated with deference, for they seemed to work just as hard as their elected colleagues. And when events in Chile took a more dramatic turn, such as the discovery of bodies buried in unmarked graves in Pisagua, "there was no showboating, but sensitivity toward the families of the victims."[5]

Other scholars concurred with Aronofsky's positive assessment, and the promise shown in the new Chilean congress's early period carried on into the next electoral term. By 1998 John M. Carey, a political scientist at Washington University, wrote, "According to the standard criteria by which legislatures are compared, Chile's Congress is re-establishing itself as an unusually professionalized and technically competent legislature."[6]

The Chilean congress and senate may have been the best in Latin America, but they lacked the staff and resources enjoyed by more-established democracies. The executive branch continued to dominate legislation, with almost all bills proposed by the president and either passed, vetoed, or modified by congress. At the same time, relations between the two branches seemed surprisingly good, considering the Right's strong presence in both the senate and chamber of deputies. U.S. ambassador Charles Gillespie observed that the Aylwin government had devoted considerable resources to its congressional liaison to further its legislative agenda. "The organization and staffing of the office is impressive, with the government's best and brightest diligently drafting and tracking government legislation at every stage of the process," he wrote in a cable. "The watchword is negotiation, not confrontation, and nothing characterizes the legislative process more. Even the opposition has rallied around the banner of 'gobierno de acuerdos' (government of accords)."[7] One survey of Chile's congress showed that 90 percent of all deputies and 83.4 percent of conservative opposition deputies agreed that relations with the Aylwin government had been "fluid and cooperative." When questioned about the quality of legislation proposed by the executive branch, 86.7 percent of deputies and 75 percent of opposition deputies rated the measures as "good or average."[8]

The issue persisted of whether to remain in Valparaíso or move the congress back to Santiago, for few senators or deputies liked making the ninety-minute drive from the capital. But a strong grassroots campaign to keep the congress and senate in Valparaíso sprang up among community groups from around the country, suggesting greater support for decentralization—or perhaps resentment toward Santiago— throughout Chile. In the end, the more spacious and modern facilities in the new complex and the difficulty and expense of relocating back to the capital combined with the decentralization campaign to convince Chile's new lawmakers to keep the congress in Valparaíso—just as Pinochet had wished.

The World Bank helped to finance an extensive modernization plan for the congressional library, adding Internet and intranet capabilities and providing senators and deputies with streamlined research services. The result was a "one-stop information shop," according to librarian Marialyse Delano, although the new facility had to be promoted to parliamentarians unfamiliar with such resources.[9] The new informational facilities contrasted sharply with a more archaic holdover from the Pinochet regime: a collection of over one hundred laws drafted in secret and never published. These would remain secret until lawmakers finally declassified them. Like researchers examining items from a library's rare book collection, members of congress had to seek permission to view these legal texts, which were stored at a secret location in Valparaíso, and read them under the supervision of an officer at the senate's general secretariat. It was permissible to take notes but not to make copies or reveal their contents—though some information did leak to the public.

Many of the secret laws dealt with the armed forces and included information regarding salaries, weapons purchases, and troop movements, while other laws established Pinochet's secret police organ, the DINA, and its successor, the CNI. Some laws referred to military finances, including million-dollar grants sent to secret accounts and one authorizing sizeable funds transfers from the Chilean Central Bank to the military for unspecified purposes. Declassifying these legal texts might have helped the judicial inquiry into Pinochet's million-dollar bank accounts abroad, but although the congress passed such a bill in 2003, the legislation became stuck in a Senate committee for several years. "No one has ever really addressed the situation," said Pilar Silva, a senate secretariat officer. "It's not easy to break away from this past. This is something that was just left pending . . . the laws put away in a safebox and forgotten."[10]

Some legal provisions from the past have simply been ignored. The Pinochet regime's 1980 constitution contained clear provisions requiring members of congress to have resided for at least two years in the district they represent.[11] This may have been an attempt to undermine the influence of Chilean political parties, whose organization in rural areas was often weak, rather than to encourage local leadership. The regime's constitutional drafters might also have recalled the early political career of socialist president Salvador Allende, who began as a congressional deputy representing Valparaíso and went on to serve four terms in the senate from four different electoral districts around the country. But the residency requirement was very loosely enforced, and, as had been the case prior to the 1973 military coup, many senators and deputies were not from the regions they represented (though some rented second homes in their electoral districts).

According to Chilean political scientist Patricio Navia, the practice of candidates seeking office in regions where they did not and never had resided has become so entrenched as to not even be an issue among voters. "It's called clientelism," he said, referring to the paternalistic relationship political elites in developing countries often have with the general public. "Do you want someone who represents you in the sense that they dress and speak like you, or someone who can advocate for you?" he said. "In this way the elections are like job interviews." Navia noted that Chilean political leaders, including socialists, all tended to reside in the same affluent suburbs of eastern Santiago—and that this included even the mayors of poor municipalities.[12]

II

Francisco Javier Cuadra had been one of the youngest members of Pinochet's cabinet, an ultraconservative lawyer acting as *secretario general de gobierno,* the regime's official spokesman, and later as its ambassador to the Vatican. He was now a political analyst and a member of the Center-Right Renovación Nacional but had declined an invitation to stand as one of the party's candidates for congress, opting instead to take a job at a conservative think tank.[13]

Many regime opponents had vivid memories of Pinochet's former minister as a manipulator of news who disseminated the security forces' often dubious versions of events. This did not preclude them from maintaining professional contact with Cuadra or from participating in the occasional social meeting to discuss the current state of the country. And during the Aylwin administration, Cuadra had sometimes acted as a back-channel emissary between Pinochet and the new government. Shortly before the former dictator had ordered troops to the streets of Santiago in 1993, Cuadra had been summoned to the home of the director of the Chilean War Academy and asked to warn government officials that tension levels were rising in the army and that the situation was becoming very serious. "I had very fluid relations with the leadership of the Christian Democrats, the Socialists, the UDI [Union Democrática Independiente], and Renovación Nacional," he said.[14] But Cuadra was about to be caught up in a Kafkaesque legal battle with the political establishment that would be studied by future generations of Chilean law students. In October 1994 Cuadra was invited to dinner at the home of a Frei administration interior ministry official who was a member of the Socialist Party. Also present was a public works ministry official and a member of the Chilean senate, also a Socialist. According to Cuadra, the senator discussed drug use among certain members of congress, mentioning some parliamentarians by name.[15]

A few weeks later Cuadra gave an extended interview to *Qué Pasa* magazine, a Center-Right newsweekly, in which he discussed political developments over the past year and, almost as an afterthought, expressed concern over illegal drug consumption in Chile. Until now, he said, most of the media attention had gone to drug use among the poor, but there were worrying signs of increasing use among the country's elite. "There are some parliamentarians and other public functionaries who consume drugs," Cuadra told the interviewer. "The most serious thing is that they are potentially significant politicians. By using drugs these people are converted into indirect protectors of the narcotics network and are vulnerable to being pressured." He went on to note that Chile was in a stage of democratic consolidation and said he would be very concerned if this process were jeopardized, "because part of the political class is incapable of assuming its responsibilities in due manner." When his interviewer pressed for details, Cuadra declined to give any names and almost seemed to backtrack, adding by way of clarification that "fortunately the problem is one of individuals, and of a few individuals, it has nothing to do with the congress as an institution, nor with the political parties as such, nor with any other public institution in particular."[16]

The former regime official's statements brought on a chorus of disapproval from Chilean senators and congressional deputies across the political spectrum, all demanding that Cuadra substantiate the allegations. His refusal to do so seemed to spark even greater outrage, prompting accusations that he was deliberately casting aspersions upon the integrity of Chile's legislative branch. The events that followed were not the congress's finest hour.

On January 30, 1995, the senate president, Christian Democrat Gabriel Valdes, the president of the chamber of deputies, filed charges against Cuadra before a court in Santiago. The president of the chamber of deputies, Vicente Sota Barros, also filed suit. The legal basis for this suit was the State Security law contained in the Pinochet's 1980 constitution, which the regime had frequently used to prosecute and censor its political opponents. The return to democratic rule had not prompted Chilean officials to get rid of the State Security law, and lawmakers would not amend it for several more years.

Variations of this law had been in force in Chile since 1958 and have a long tradition in many Latin American countries. The purpose of such laws is to ensure the smooth running of government by obliging people to show respect for public functionaries because of their rank. Allowing criticism might have a destabilizing effect on the government, since it might reflect not only on the individual in question but also on the office held and the administration he or she serves. Such contempt-of-authority provisions reflect a view of the public not as citizens but as subjects.

Article 6 (b) of the State Security law made it "an offense against the public order" for anyone to publicly slander, libel, or offend the president or any other high-ranking government, military, or police official, and the definitions of these offenses were vague enough to give the Pinochet regime an effective tool for controlling the media and restricting free speech.[17] Valdes himself had been briefly arrested under the State Security law during the regime, as had several others now serving in congress. However, although the congressmen had experienced persecution under a dictatorship, this did not mean they would always respect a political opponent's right to freedom of expression or to engage in a debate on such a politically charged issue.

Some members of congress defended Cuadra, particularly Evelyn Matthei, who recalled the ugly feud she had endured with Renovación Nacional leadership two years earlier. "I have no doubt that there are congressional deputies who use drugs," she told the press. Her comments led some Renovación Nacional leaders to suspect she was referring to them, though the only parliamentarian Matthei later named was a Socialist Party member who adamantly denied any drug use.[18] One congressman from the right-wing UDI even proposed that the chamber of deputies conduct an investigation into possible drug use by its members. The motion was rejected.

A peculiar multipartisan viewpoint seemed to be emerging: it was perfectly acceptable for the congress to stifle criticism to uphold its own prestige. Accompanying this view was the unspoken fear that in this new, more open political climate, activity that previously had been private and well hidden from public inspection might now be exposed. Chilean society had strict, conservative norms for such matters as family life and personal behavior, but there was an inevitable gap—some would say hypocrisy—between these standards and their actual observance.

And it was not only members of the ruling Center-Left coalition who were calling for sanctions against Cuadra. Renovación Nacional expelled him from the party and filed its own suit against the former Pinochet cabinet minister. The Santiago court combined this suit with the charges filed earlier by the senate and chamber of deputies presidents into a single case. As the case invoked Chile's State Security law, the investigation proceeded quickly—much more quickly, in fact, than many judicial investigations into far more serious crimes.

After four months, the court judge indicted Cuadra under both the Security law and the criminal code for "defaming the honor of congress." That Cuadra had no intention of causing offense or that his statements might be true were not considered a defense. He was arrested five days later and taken to Santiago's Anexo Capuchinos, a jail for nonviolent criminals, where he spent nineteen days before being released on bail. Recalling the experience years later, Cuadra said he felt a great rebellion against "the world of law and the courts of justice."[19]

It was not over yet. The court judge continued to process the case while Cuadra's lawyer attempted to gather witnesses and additional information for his defense. The Socialist senator with whom Cuadra had dined prior to his magazine interview insisted he had not mentioned the names of any drug-using parliamentarians. He also suggested that former secret police agents spying on Chilean politicians were behind Cuadra's statements. A discotheque owner who earlier had claimed to have witnessed three of the congress's most prominent members using cocaine (two conservatives, one Center-Leftist) denied making such comments.[20] On December 19 the judge convicted Cuadra, sentencing him to a 540-day suspended prison term, a ban on holding public office for the duration of this sentence, a fine, and an order to pay court costs.

Cuadra appealed, and a month later the verdict was reversed, with a ruling by a respected jurist who would later investigate Pinochet for tax evasion and fraud. Judge Carlos Cerda ruled that the former regime official's statements had been no threat to public security. On the contrary, the judge said that Cuadra had made a constructive use of his right to free speech by criticizing actions that could have brought the Chilean congress into disrepute—which thus might have undermined the country's fledgling democracy. In Cerda's interpretation, Cuadra's statements were an attempt to sound an alarm over a possible threat to public order.[21]

Undeterred, the senate and chamber of deputies filed a writ of complaint in the Supreme Court against Cerda and the other court judges who overturned Cuadra's sentencing. The Supreme Court upheld the original State Security law conviction and reinstated the prison sentence, a ruling that allowed no further legal appeal. The justices ruled that Cerda and his colleagues had given Cuadra's actions "a different gloss from that which flows clearly and naturally from the legal text" and that his statements "sow doubt about who are the people who may be enslaved by drugs, consequently diminishing their loyalty to the law and national interests."[22] The two court rulings showed diametrically opposed views of public order—one based on human rights, the other based upon the more authoritarian concept of protecting the honor of state institutions.

Cuadra noted that if the Supreme Court had been following the letter of the law, it would have sanctioned Cerda and the two other court judges for making such a decision in his favor—but this did not happen. A court official told Cuadra's father, also a lawyer, that the Supreme Court was afraid of offending the congress by not ruling against the former cabinet minister but was considering imposing a very short, token prison sentence and no fine.[23]

Cuadra's case, however, was drawing international attention, and many observers were troubled by the spectacle of democratically elected parliamentarians—including some who had been persecuted under the Pinochet regime—using the State Security law to silence a critic. In October 1996 Human Rights Watch and the Center for Justice and International Law brought the case to the Inter-American Commission on Human Rights, accusing Chile of violating guarantees on freedom of expression.[24] Meanwhile, in a separate investigation, a criminal court in Valparaíso had begun an investigation into possible drug trafficking within the congress and senate complex. Three security guards, a former secretary, and a congressional aide were among those indicted.[25]

III

The official vendetta against Cuadra continued on other fronts. In December 1996 Fernando Paulsen, an anchorman for a public affairs program on Chile's state Television Nacional (TVN), wanted to invite the former regime official to take part in a panel discussion on Cuban leader Fidel Castro's visit to the Vatican. Paulsen, whose reporting during the Pinochet regime had earned him multiple threats and lawsuits from military prosecutors, had no journalistic interest in Cuadra's legal case. Instead, the journalist had wanted Cuadra to take part in the program because he had served as the Pinochet regime's ambassador to the Vatican. The station's director vetoed the suggestion.

Government control over TVN and *La Nación* newspaper had loosened since Patricio Aylwin took office, and the new administration wanted to distance itself from the Pinochet regime's censorship and intimidation of the media. Under Pinochet, TVN had been an aggressive propaganda machine, sometimes airing "news footage" produced by the security forces, and had become notorious for mismanagement and corruption during the regime's final year in power. The channel was now restructured as an autonomous entity with more editorial independence. The actual change took place during Aylwin's inauguration, when two respected Chilean journalists began hosting the event. Aylwin also appointed two more journalists to be the director and associate director of the station, rejecting the nonjournalist candidates backed by some in his cabinet.[26] But if TVN and *La Nación* were no longer government mouthpieces, they were still constricted in what they reported, along with much of Chile's independent media.

Cabinet ministers and other officials often called to complain about press coverage. "They thought they had the right to ask us to publish what they wanted, and not to publish what they did not want," former *La Nación* deputy editor Alberto Luengo told Human Rights Watch. In one incident, the minister of agriculture complained about a story on a group of Mapuche Indians with a grievance against his department. When the paper published photographs of their protest, the minister demanded that the journalists covering the story be fired. The paper's editors refused, and the journalists kept their jobs, but there were many more instances of official pressure on *La Nación*'s journalists.[27]

Chilean print media was also becoming less diverse, an unexpected development in a new democracy. During much of the Pinochet regime, only one publication, the weekly newsmagazine *Hoy,* presented any editorial independence, and part of the periodical's financial backing came from Christian Democratic Parties outside the country. By the mid-1980s a handful of other independent publications were allowed to circulate, a point Pinochet regime supporters often made when arguing that press freedom was respected in the country. Their editorial staffs were largely young, energetic, and willing to work for little pay, buoyed by the feeling they were performing a much-needed public service. None of these publications received enough advertising revenue to cover their costs, and they depended upon the generosity of foreign supporters to stay afloat.

This support began to dry up after Pinochet left the presidency, and, one by one, periodicals that had enjoyed wide readership during the 1980s—*APSI, Cauce, Análisis,* and *Hoy*—began dying off, followed by two newspapers, *La Época* and *Fortín Mapocho.* Within a few years the Chilean news media was dominated by two conglomerates: the *El Mercurio* chain, which owned the conservative daily of the same name plus nineteen regional newspapers and several radio stations; and the rival COPESA media group, which owned three tabloids and the country's most widely circulated newsmagazine, *Qué Pasa.* These two conglomerates broadened their editorial line considerably and eventually hired many journalists from the now-defunct publications. But as journalist and media analyst Ken Leon-Dermota observed, the Chilean media seemed far less interesting in the absence of these independent media. "The Pinochet-era journalism that used wit, sarcasm and humor has given way to dull, bland pack-journalism that sticks to the official story in times of democracy," he wrote.[28]

The most serious threats to freedom of expression continued to come from the State Security law, which allowed officials to bring charges of contempt against their critics. Repealing or amending the law was not high on the congress's list of priorities, although it was the subject of periodic debate. Not until April 2001 did congress vote to remove article 6 (b), which allowed military chiefs, judges, and members of congress to bring charges of contempt against their critics, and article 16, allowing authorities to seize publications deemed insulting to public officials. But congress rejected a proposal to reform Chile's criminal code, which also contained provisions for libel and defamation similar to those in the State Security law. "In Chile, freedom of expression has a limit," José Joaquín Brunner, the Frei government's spokesman, told the *New York Times*. "I know of very few governments in the world that do not allow their citizens to protect themselves from slander by filing lawsuits. The same is true in Chile."[29]

IV

Gladys Marin, secretary general of Chile's Communist Party and former deputy in the country's pre-1973 congress, stood before a crowd at the General Cemetery in Santiago on the twenty-third anniversary of the military coup. The gathering was a memorial for those killed during the Pinochet regime, an annual event since the return to elected civilian rule, but Marin had tough words for those in office. "The main person responsible for state terrorism, for the crimes against humanity, Pinochet, is still in politics and giving orders," she said. "And he does so because the government allows him to." Six weeks later she was driving in the Chilean capital's afternoon traffic when her car was stopped and surrounded by twenty police officers who ordered her out of the vehicle, arrested her, and took her to jail. For Marin, who had spent years as an exile during the Pinochet regime and whose own husband was among the *desaparecidos,* it was a fearsome sign that political repression was still alive and well even under a democratically elected government.

Marin's arrest was one of several resulting from lawsuits Pinochet had filed against critics in his capacity as Chile's army commander since leaving the presidency. Two years earlier a Socialist youth leader was arrested, held for six days, and given a five hundred forty-one–day suspended prison sentence for shouting that Pinochet and his former security chief Manuel Conteras were murderers. In such cases Pinochet's accusations were treated with utmost seriousness by judicial authorities, who then examined the offending words and summoned witnesses, sending a clear signal that the former dictator was still powerful enough to punish his critics. Marin, who had not dared return to Chile until Pinochet left the presidency, spent three days in the women's prison while her lawyer filed a writ of protection with the Supreme Court. The court confirmed her indictment and made no allowance for the fact that Marin was a political leader expressing an opinion. Only one Supreme Court judge dissented, arguing that it was up to Chilean citizens and not the courts to make judgments about political opinions. Marin's case drew protests from abroad, and defense minister Edmundo Pérez Yoma managed to persuade Pinochet to drop the charges on "humanitarian grounds."[30]

The feisty Marin did not retract her statements and continued to challenge the Frei government to stand up to Pinochet. She later ran for senate in the 1997 congressional elections, winning 15.69 percent of the votes cast in a Santiago district covering much of her original congressional constituency (though like many Chilean parliamentarians she did not live in her district).[31] The Chilean Communist Party won no seats in congress, but its slate of candidates did win the student elections held that year at the University of Chile. Marin secured more than her share of votes from younger Chileans, who were attracted by her message of economic justice but who, as a group, were becoming increasingly apathetic. Unemployment was 6.7 percent nationwide—but three times that level among Chileans under twenty-four years old. There seemed little difference in economic policy between the ruling Concertación and its conservative opposition, and young Chileans had only a vague memory of the Pinochet regime. Many were not even bothering to register to vote.

Pinochet and the aftermath of his regime may have been a boring subject for Chilean youth, but the Frei administration was troubled by the former dictator's high profile that year, his last as army commander. To commemorate his twenty-fourth anniversary as commander, the military academy had staged a massive parade of two thousand troops, attended by the heads of the navy and air force. Pinochet was presented with a ceremonial staff representing "the unity of the armed forces under his leadership."[32] A few weeks later he appeared at the traditional military parade held during Chile's independence holiday, where he and Frei were photographed shaking hands. Pinochet told an interviewer that when he retired from the army, he fully intended to take his place as a senator for life, a terrifying prospect for those in the government coalition already worried about the impending congressional elections. Some even imagined that Pinochet might become president of the senate.

On September 30, 1997, Chilevisión, a privately owned television station, recorded a debate on the forthcoming elections. The guests included congressional deputy José Antonio Viera Gallo, who was running for senate, and the Pinochet regime's former justice minister, Monica Madariaga. There was aggressive questioning about possible corruption in the Frei government, and Viera Gallo was moved to remark, "The one who put his hands in the cash register was General Pinochet, and he is now commander in chief of the army and may get to be president of the senate."[33] When the taping finished, Madariaga notified the army's vice commander, who tried to pressure Chilevisión not to broadcast Viera Gallo's comments. The station refused, and the program was aired.

Pinochet was traveling in China at the time, having made a brief stop in London en route. He ordered a special meeting of army generals, who announced the decision to sue Viera Gallo under the State Security law. If the lawsuit proceeded, the politician could see his senate campaign derailed as well face a prison sentence. A torrent of escalating accusations and counteraccusations over Pinochet's suspicious fortune and the Frei administration's financial management might hurt other Concertación candidates as well. Viera Gallo met with Defense Minister Pérez Yoma, who worked out a scheme in which the socialist deputy would make a public, conciliatory gesture. There was a brief delay while the army vice commander contacted Pinochet in China, and then the three men met at the Defense Ministry. The Chilean press was invited to observe, and photographers prompted the deputy to shake hands with the army vice commander. The photograph that appeared in newspapers the next day showed Viera Gallo leaning toward the vice commander, reaching out his hand, while the officer stood with his arms at his side. Viera Gallo read a text saying he had not intended to cause offense but stopped short of offering an apology. The army vice commander then made his reply. "In the name of the commander in chief of the army I accept this apology and the reparation of the honor of General Pinochet and of the institution."[34] The image of a Socialist congressman seeming to kowtow to Pinochet's representative outraged many in the Concertación, and some Socialists blamed Defense Minister Pérez Yoma. Viera Gallo, however, put the blame on Chile's repressive legal apparatus. "With a law of state security like we have now in Chile that protects practically all the authorities, freedom is very restricted," he told *El Mercurio*. "If tomorrow a minister or a senator or a member of a high court or a military officer commits robbery, no one can say anything; they immediately apply the law of state security. It's not enough for the person to prove the accusation is true, for what is being punished is the imputation of a crime."[35]

Viera Gallo won his senate seat in the 1997 elections, but the overall returns were disappointing for the Frei administration, which had expected its political coalition to benefit from the thriving economy. Although Chile would be hard hit by the Asian financial crisis the following year, for the moment the indicators were encouraging: overall growth was 7.1 percent that year; inflation and unemployment were at 6 percent each.[36]

The election results were, in the words of Chilean pollster and political scientist Carlos Huneeus, "a bucket of cold water" poured on those who presumed that economic gains would automatically translate into electoral victory.[37] The Concertación lost one of its senate seats, leaving it with twenty out of the thirty-eight elected senate seats (not counting the nine appointed senators). The coalition maintained its control of the chamber of deputies, with seventy out of one hundred twenty seats. Its overall share of the vote was 50.5 percent, five points lower than in the 1993 election.

The right-wing UDI obtained 14.5 percent of the overall vote, and though it had less electoral support than the Center-Right Renovación Nacional, it seemed to be consolidating itself as the leader of the opposition. It had become the second-biggest party in the Chilean senate, and its candidate had beaten a popular Renovación Nacional politician in a key senate race. "Our closeness to Pinochet is no handicap," UDI secretary Juan Coloma told *The Economist.* "He is history. The voters aren't interested in the past. They want solutions to their everyday problems."[38]

It was the first time that parliamentary elections had been held separately from presidential elections since the return to democracy, and the low voter turnout suggested that many Chileans viewed their legislative bodies with indifference. An opinion poll by the Centro de Estudios de la Realidad Contemporanea revealed an abrupt decline in the way Chileans perceived government. Those polled were asked, "In general, would you say the country is run by a few interest groups seeking their own benefit, or is it run for the benefit of the public?" In June 1990, a few months after the Aylwin government took office, 39 percent chose the first option while 48 percent chose the second. Seven years later, 80 percent of respondents said Chile was being run by interest groups for their own benefit, and only 14 percent said it was run for the benefit of the public.[39]

Out of those Chileans eligible to vote, one in six did not bother to register for the congressional elections of December 11, 1997, and out of that number, only 86 percent actually voted—despite the fact that the country's electoral laws provided fines for registered voters who did not vote. An astonishing 18 percent of the ballots were either deliberately spoiled or left blank.[40]

SEVEN Justice Delayed

I

The most feared man in Chile, retired army general Manuel Contreras, was beginning to have fears of his own. Since organizing and directing the Pinochet regime's secret police agency, the DINA, he had amassed a vast network of contacts throughout the country and was used to calling in favors or resorting to blackmail to achieve his goals. After leaving the regime and retiring from the army in 1978, he had formed his own private security agency, Alfa Omega, and had served as a board member of several businesses, including a private telephone company with an exclusive contract to provide service in an eastern Santiago neighborhood.[1]

The Frei government's future defense minister, Edmundo Pérez Yoma, who was running a construction firm during this period, happened to meet the former DINA chief when Contreras contacted his office to offer Alfa Omega's security services. Many Chileans suspected that Contreras continued to freelance for the regime, but it seemed to Pérez Yoma that the former DINA chief's security company was a legitimate business. "Contreras came across as an intelligent, affable man," he recalled. "But even Pinochet was afraid of him."[2]

The case against Contreras and his former operations chief, Pedro Espinoza, for the 1976 Letelier-Moffitt car bomb assassinations had been slowly moving through the Chilean judicial system since 1991. That year the Aylwin government renewed charges against the two officers after managing to push through a law giving civilian courts jurisdiction in cases involving the military if Chile's relations with another country were involved. Of the nineteen judges on the Chilean Supreme Court, only one—Adolfo Bañados—had been appointed by Aylwin; the rest were holdovers from the Pinochet regime. Bañados painstakingly put together an indictment, using evidence collected by the FBI, while Contreras employed a formidable team of lawyers who argued that the regime's amnesty law for crimes committed prior to 1978 should be applied and left no legal stone unturned. But on January 25, 1995, the Supreme Court indicted Contreras and Espinoza, much to the surprise of many observers. Several military officers, including the commander of the Santiago garrison, attended the proceedings in a show of support for the two former regime officials and were not pleased to find television cameras inside the courtroom as the ruling was announced.[3] And now the court would now decide a sentence.

Earlier that month Chile's congress approved the construction of a $2.7 million special detention facility for human rights offenders. The prison, the first of its kind in Latin America, was located twenty-five miles north of Santiago in the farming town of Punta de Peuco. The prison had nine-foot-high walls, television surveillance, plus state-of-the-art metal and bomb detectors. A staff of sixty, including two dozen noncommissioned army officers guarding the interior, would oversee the incarceration of one hundred inmates. This last provision came at Pinochet's insistence, according to Pérez Yoma. "Once Pinochet realized that Contreras's imprisonment was absolutely inevitable he began to negotiate the way in which he would be kept—where to put him?" he said. "An army general could not be held by *gendarmes,* whom Pinochet regarded as socialists, but had to be in a military installation. In a way it was a delaying tactic, but it was also a completely unfamiliar situation: there had never before been an intelligence chief jailed in his own country."[4]

Getting the Punta de Peuco prison project through the Chilean congress had not been easy. Some left-wing politicians objected to what seemed like a luxury facility for torturers and murderers; human rights campaigners said that the prison would at the very least incarcerate these offenders, who otherwise would be held at military installations, which would allow them more freedoms. The Frei government bargained hard with its right-wing opponents, securing their support for the prison in exchange for promising that there would be no be no more modifications to the military justice code, which gave military courts jurisdiction over judicial cases involving military officials.

The court finally issued sentences of six years' imprisonment for Espinoza and seven for Contreras on May 30, 1995. The penalties may have seemed like a slap on the wrist for a double murder, but neither man was going to prison just yet. From his farm in southern Chile, Contreras told a television interviewer that he would not go to jail, an assertion he repeated the next day to a group of journalists arriving from Santiago. His constitutional rights were not respected, and he did not receive due process, he asserted, because "the judges were scared by Marxists." He also implied he would resist any attempt to arrest him. "I will decide what is necessary at that moment," he said. "As a general I am not going to run away because I am going to face the battle. I am a winner and do not want to lose."[5]

The army issued no comment on the prison sentences for Contreras and Espinoza, though one retired general close to Pinochet said the institution was "deeply wounded by this ruling. We are returning to confrontational situations, which could be extremely delicate for the country's fate."[6] Pinochet met with twenty-seven army generals to discuss the sentences. Some officers thought that Frei might issue presidential pardons for the two former DINA officials or be persuaded to do so.

That evening Pérez Yoma and another defense ministry official went to the Club Militar in eastern Santiago to meet with Pinochet and two of his legal advisors, who suggested alternatives to imprisoning Contreras. The former security chief was elderly, ailing, and had suffered financial reversals in recent years. Would it not be possible to let him stay at his farm in southern Chile, under house arrest? When Pérez Yoma turned down this suggestion, Pinochet thumped his hand on the table and declared the meeting adjourned.[7]

Pérez Yoma had at least two other meetings with Pinochet prior to Contreras's eventual imprisonment and craftily pushed a wedge between the former dictator and the man who had once been his closest collaborator. Poker-faced, he said that perhaps Pinochet had not been fully aware of the extent of Contreras's crimes and that the former DINA chief had been deliberately undermining him with his actions. "Pinochet was afraid Contreras might launch a coup against him. He would say, look it's not convenient to imprison him," Pérez Yoma said. "I would respond by detailing the crimes Contreras had committed during his government, phrasing it in such as way that by the time the meeting ended, Pinochet would feel very angry with Contreras. I would say, 'This man tried to undercut you. How can you defend a man who has committed these barbarities against you?'" The defense minister acknowledged that this was a completely cynical maneuver but one that proved effective, because it allowed Pinochet to save face.[8]

Meanwhile, Contreras's former operations chief had taken refuge in a Santiago army barrack. After a three-week standoff, the military finally allowed civilian police to arrest Espinoza on June 20, after first stripping him of his army rank. As he was led away, he told Chilean journalists he never expected the army, which he had served for forty-six years, to surrender him. The traditional military history of Chile had been demolished, he said.[9]

Espinoza became the first—and for a time the only—inmate held at Punta de Peuco, at an estimated cost of $21,000 per month, as opposed to the $800 per month for prisoners at Chile's other prisons. According to family and friends, he spent his time writing his memoirs, reading, or watching television in his ten-foot by ten-foot cell. Espinoza was allowed visitors three times a week, and one young right-wing politician told the Associated Press news agency that the former DINA official's accommodations were fairly comfortable. "It may sound odd, but it's a rather pleasant place. It's nice to be inside," Rodrigo Eitel said. "The windows were made in such a way that you don't see any bars."[10]

The Frei government, which was then in the midst of negotiations with the United States over a free trade agreement, may have breathed a sigh of relief that at least one of the two officers indicted in the Letelier case was now in prison. Much of the Chilean army, however, was outraged. On July 22 a caravan of about three hundred cars carrying army officials and their families left Santiago to show of support for Espinoza. Chile's television news programs had been alerted beforehand and recorded what was to be known as *el picnic de Punta de Peuco,* in which officers wearing civilian clothing and their wives and children rallied outside the prison. The approximately one thousand demonstrators waved Chilean flags and sang the national anthem, including the verse about brave soldiers added by the Pinochet regime (but removed by the Aylwin government). Among those present was the head of the Santiago army garrison.[11] Small groups of officers were allowed inside to visit Espinoza, and the demonstration broke up about four p.m.

Back in Santiago, the Defense Ministry was already monitoring the situation. A few days earlier, a retired general had alerted War Secretary Jorge Burgos that part of the army's officer corps was planning this show of support for Espinoza, giving officials just enough time to partially defuse the situation.[12] Not all the Chilean army had backed this demonstration—no one from the War Academy or other military institutes had taken part, and, aside from the commander of the Santiago garrison, most of the officers at the Punta de Peuco rally held the rank of colonel or lower. But the entire episode was sufficiently alarming to cause Pérez Yoma to cancel a planned trip to a conference of defense ministers held in Washington, D.C., and to summon Pinochet for a meeting.

At this meeting, Pinochet once again argued that Contreras, who had yet to be taken into custody, should not go to prison. A communiqué issued by the Defense Ministry after this meeting said that Pinochet was ordering an investigation into the Punta de Peuco gathering, which violated a long-standing prohibition on the military taking part in political demonstrations. "We knew that an army general had organized this demonstration," Pérez Yoma said. "And that general was retired by the end of the year."[13] Others believed that Pinochet had orchestrated the entire episode, which marked the third incident of army defiance since the country's return to civilian government.

II

Getting Espinoza behind bars had been difficult enough, and it would take a few more months before Contreras was finally brought to the Punta de Peuco prison facility. The Chilean army continued to insist that Contreras, still at his farm in southern Chile, was gravely ill and was recovering from surgery to remove a malignant growth from his abdomen. He might even die if moved, it was argued. Pérez Yoma noted that Contreras had certainly seemed well enough during his recent television interviews, and even Pinochet was somewhat uncomfortable with the former DINA chief's public statements that his conviction and sentencing constituted a "judgement against the army."[14]

Contreras's friends and associates were keeping him informed of any police or government officials arriving in the region, and upon hearing reports that a group of civilian detective police were heading his way, he moved from his farm to a neighbor's, taking three bodyguards with him. His son Manuel remained behind with two more bodyguards and a machine gun, which he used to fire several rounds in the direction of suspicious noises heard on the family property. The civilian detective police never appeared, and Contreras then traveled along back roads to the nearest army regiment, which designated him as its guest.[15]

The Frei government was dreading a confrontation with the army and wanted to avoid an armed standoff or any action that might make Contreras look like a martyr at all costs. Technically the former DINA chief was not a fugitive from justice—he had been tried and sentenced but not yet officially notified and taken into custody. A senior general from Santiago visited the army regiment where Contreras was staying and, after a series of tense phone conversations with the Defense Ministry, Contreras was assured that the coast was clear, that there were no detectives or other officials in the vicinity. The army then escorted him back to his farm.

While the Frei government was trying to devise a way to get Contreras to begin his seven-year sentence for murder, an Italian court issued a twenty-year prison sentence against him for attempted murder—the 1975 attack against an exiled Christian Democratic politician and his wife. Bernardo Leighton, who had been a member of Frei's father's cabinet, was living in Rome with his wife, Anita Fresno, trying to build a network between his party and other Chilean exile groups. One evening, when the couple was returning to their apartment, a gunman belonging to an Italian fascist fringe group with ties to the DINA shot Leighton in the back of the head and Fresno in the side. Miraculously, both survived. Two decades later, an Italian judge who had tirelessly investigated the links between the DINA and the right-wing extremists in his own country sentenced Contreras in absentia to twenty years in prison. Judge Giovanni Salvi had traveled to Chile and Argentina and secured an agreement with U.S. authorities to get American-born DINA agent Michael Townley to testify. The Italian court also sentenced another DINA official, Raul Iturriaga, to eighteen years in prison.[16] The Frei government refused Italy's extradition request, as the Pinochet regime had done with the U.S. extradition request for Contreras, Espinoza, and a third DINA agent involved in the Letelier assassination.

Meanwhile, Contreras continued his secluded existence at his farm in southern Chile. Another army general persuaded him that he was putting his health in jeopardy by remaining there and that the Chilean naval hospital in Talcahuano, a port located roughly halfway between the farm and Santiago, was ready to admit him. An elaborate plan was hatched to move Contreras under cover of night, with the help of the army and a group of his local friends: two former mayors, a businessman, and a farmer. Three military jeeps were seen entering the former DINA chief's property and then leaving in different directions. Contreras was taken to another army regiment and then transferred by helicopter to Talcahuano's Hospital Naval. The Chilean army said

Contreras had suffered a medical emergency during the journey to Santiago.[17]

According to his lawyers, Contreras was suffering from diabetes and high blood pressure, two conditions he was not known to have had prior to his hospital admission. While Contreras's physicians appeared to extend his medical treatment for as long as possible, his lawyers filed appeal after appeal, eventually getting the authorities to agree that he could begin serving his sentence at the hospital. Contreras underwent a hernia operation, and there was further discussion among doctors, lawyers, and the government about whether he could be safely moved to Punta de Peuco. Finally, on October 21, 1995, after being declared fit and well, Contreras left the hospital and joined Espinoza at the Punta de Peuco prison. Personnel and patients at the Hospital Naval were relieved by his departure, having grown tired of the constant presence of attorneys, government officials, and journalists at the facility. By then enough time had elapsed for the proud Chilean army to adjust to the idea of one of their emblematic generals going to prison, though reporters and cameras were blocked from recording Contreras's arrival. "He thought he was untouchable," Pérez Yoma said. "But with a lot of patience and time, we advanced to the point where he was finally jailed."[18]

Pinochet was out of the country when his former security chief went to prison. He was traveling abroad, making what was becoming an annual trip to the United Kingdom, and then he went on to Malaysia, where the Chilean army was said to have joint ventures with authorities in those countries. But he had followed with keen interest Contreras's actions, for the former DINA chief's pattern of stonewalling and claiming illness would provide Pinochet with useful strategies in the future.

III

Some conservative members of congress, along with a handful of Concertación politicians, wanted prosecutions for human rights abuses to end, regardless of whether justice had been served. In July 1995 opposition senators presented a bill for a full stop law that imposed a deadline for court investigations of human rights cases. The Pinochet regime's amnesty law gave human rights violators immunity for crimes committed before 1978 but left open the possibility for courts to investigate them. Sometimes the courts pursued such cases, for disappearances could be considered unsolved until the fate of the victim was resolved. But that August the Supreme Court declared the case of a missing Socialist Party leader closed, ruling that the victim be considered legally dead from the time of his disappearance in 1976. It made similar rulings on seven other cases, a worrying trend for Chile's human rights campaigners.[19]

A few weeks later Frei appeared on national television and addressed the nation. The Letelier case had forced Chile to confront the limitations of its democracy, and the country had to face the truth about human rights abuses of the past, he said. "We should be capable of arriving at a great understanding to ensure our future development," he stated. "We have to face reality: the country is not fully reconciled; our democracy is imperfect; the military and a great part of the civilian world have not established points of communication."[20]

Frei announced he was sending three bills to congress. The first would simplify judicial investigations into human rights abuses. This bill provided for specially appointed Supreme Court judges who would work exclusively on disappearance cases. They would be given access to classified government documents and military and police installations—investigative powers not enjoyed by the rest of the judiciary. They would take over all the cases on file in military courts, and human rights violators would be guaranteed immunity if they cooperated in the investigation by providing information on the fate of the disappeared. The cases would only be closed if the victims' remains could located or the fact of their death established.[21] The second bill Frei proposed modified the armed forces law to restore the president's power to remove military officials. The third provided changes to the country's constitutional tribunal and the state security council and eliminated government appointees from the senate.

It may have seemed like a moderate, even cautious package of legislation, but getting it through congress would be difficult. The president of the association of families of the disappeared, the Agrupación de

Familiares de Detenidos-Desaparecidos, criticized the first proposed law for not punishing human rights violators. In the five years since democratic rule returned, the Agrupación de Familiares de Detenidos-Desaparecidos had become a visible presence in Chilean public life, and even right-wing politicians who had supported the Pinochet regime felt obliged to meet with its representatives. Most of the Concertación deputies and senators backed Frei's bills, although the rightist UDI offered support for the human rights bill but rejected any curtailment of the military's power or other changes to the Pinochet regime's authoritarian legacy. The most moderate members of the Center-Right Renovación Nacional party indicated they would support the human rights law and the constitutional reforms, pending their own consultations with the military. This last proviso showed how much influence the armed forces still enjoyed among conservative politicians.[22]

A compromise seemed unavoidable, and two months later Frei announced some concessions to his government's conservative opponents. Human rights cases would only be opened at the express wish of the families, those cases currently in the military courts would not be transferred to civilian judges, and the requirements for declaring cases closed were relaxed.[23] This watered-down package of reforms still proved impossible to get through the congress. The debate dragged on for six more months while the legislation died a slow death.

IV

At least some of the abuses of the past would be recognized in the form of memorials to the victims. One of the most notorious of the DINA's detention centers, Villa Grimaldi, became a peace park and open-air museum.

Villa Grimaldi had once been a country estate for a series of wealthy Chilean families. Its last private owner converted the main house into a restaurant and cultural venue, and it became a popular gathering place for Chilean intellectuals in the 1960s and early 1970s. Shortly after the 1973 coup, its owner was forced to turn over the property, which is located a short distance from the army's telecommunication center in south Santiago, to the military. The regime's security forces found the spacious property an ideal place to keep prisoners, and during the DINA's four years at Villa Grimaldi, an estimated 4,500 people were imprisoned and tortured there, including future president Michelle Bachelet and her mother, Angela Jeria. Of those prisoners, 226 were never seen again.[24]

The regime later sold Villa Grimaldi to a private real estate company, which tore down the remaining wooden jails and other DINA constructions and was subdividing the property into lots for future condominiums when the Aylwin government took office. The new government's housing ministry found various irregularities in the property's transfer and took control of Villa Grimaldi. In late 1995 work began on turning the site into a public memorial.

On March 22, 1997, Villa Grimaldi was reopened as a peace park. A group of former prisoners, their families, and relatives of the disappeared walked through the double metal gate where detainees had entered years before, and then the gate entrance was locked securely behind them. The keys were then presented to an elderly Jesuit priest who had helped organize demonstrations against torture during the Pinochet regime. He would be the guardian of the keys, and never again would that entrance be used. "These walls which hid death and torture today will have signs of life," Father Jose Aldunate said. He had been a priest in one of Santiago's poorest neighborhoods, where the police and army had been especially brutal.[25] Eventually the park would have a museum, a documentation center, and facilities for concerts and live performances.

It would also become a meeting place for many Chileans struggling to come to terms with a painful past. The departing secret police officials had burned down the buildings where prisoners were kept, but the park's directors put up replicas of the cell blocks, including a notorious tower where detainees were confined who were not ever expected to be released. Former prisoners were able to provide accurate descriptions for the memorial's builders to use for the reconstructions.

One day after Villa Grimaldi's inauguration as a peace park, a small group of men who had known each other since early childhood gathered at the site. As young adults they had all joined the Movement of the Revolutionary Left (MIR) and were politically active during the Allende government. After the coup, one had been arrested, tortured, and forced to reveal the others' names. All were arrested and tortured; at least one did not survive. When they were eventually released, most went into exile, bearing a burden of bitterness and guilt along with the trauma they had suffered at Villa Grimaldi. "We sat right over there," Rodrigo del Vilar, president of the Villa Grimaldi board of directors, said, pointing to a spot near the fountain. "And we talked and talked and very slowly we began to understand. It was tremendously healing." Del Vilar walked over to the fountain and recalled how one night during his detention, a guard had opened the door of the cramped cell he shared with several other prisoners and beckoned to them. Did they want to bathe? In the fountain? They had not washed for weeks, and it was, he said, "the best bath of my life." But guards who seemed too easy on the prisoners risked horrifying consequences. A massive ombu tree, a species native to the Southern Cone, stands in the middle of the park, dating from a time when Villa Grimaldi was a villa or even earlier. A young guard accused of treating detainees with too much kindness was suspended from the tree by his superiors and later beaten to death with chains. Del Vilar has made certain his case is remembered, along with those of other victims.[26]

V

He was now eighty-two years old, a full a generation older than all of his fellow generals, and Pinochet's time as army commander was finally coming to an end. In his last months on the job, he made a point of visiting every army regiment up and down Chile's narrow territory. His eventual choice of a successor, General Ricardo Izurieta, secretly pleased the Frei government, for he was an officer whose previous posts had not brought him close to Pinochet's corrupt inner circle. He had recently spent two years as military attaché at the country's mission in Washington, D.C., where he had left a favorable impression on the Chilean ambassador.[27]

On March 6, 1998, the army held a special ceremony in which Pinochet was declared Meritorious Commander-in-Chief and pledged its absolute, permanent loyalty. Four days later Pinochet formally turned command of the army over to Izurieta in an emotional ceremony at the Escuela Militar in Santiago.

Pinochet was not a man to express doubt, yet there were signs he had some misgivings about becoming a senator, unsure about how to respond to political attacks. He told journalists covering his farewell visit to an army base in southern Chile that he had background information on two prominent left-wing senators and would not hesitate to reveal it if provoked.[28] He told Pérez Yoma he would feel unprotected in the senate; the defense minister assured him he would enjoy all the personal security he needed.

Many of his future colleagues were casting about for ways to prevent Pinochet from joining them. A Christian Democratic senator, Jorge Lavandero, was seeking an official investigation into the origins of Pinochet's evident wealth, pointing out that he now owned at least seven properties in different parts of the country, worth more than US$2 million. The properties included a luxury apartment in the most affluent area of Viña del Mar, a coastal resort town south of Valparaíso, and there were questions about the ownership of a summer residence on the Chilean coast that was supposed to belong to the army but seemed to have been awarded to Pinochet. Lavandero noted that Pinochet had made a public declaration of his financial assets in 1973—would he do likewise now?[29]

Pinochet, whose annual salary as president had never been more than about $40,000, did not respond to Lavandero's challenge. It was not the first time the Christian Democrat had raised questions about Pinochet's holdings. In 1984 Lavandero had tried to get the courts to conduct an inquiry into the suspiciously low price Pinochet had paid for the government-owned land where one of his properties was built. After this unsuccessful legal bid, Lavandero was set upon by thugs, who nearly beat him to death. He spent six months in the hospital, suffered permanent deafness in one ear, and was left unable to walk without a cane.[30]

The chamber of deputies passed a resolution at the beginning of the year expressing "its rejection and repudiation of General Augusto Pinochet taking up a lifelong seat in the Senate because his presence will not help the reconciliation among Chileans." Were Pinochet to enter the senate it would "imply a grave deterioration of the image of our country abroad." The declaration was passed by a majority of fifty-six deputies, with twenty-six right-wing parliamentarians voting against the measure.

The resolution carried little weight, and Frei urged the public to accept that the former dictator was now a senator. "We oppose the existence of non-elected senators," he said. "But let's be clear: the constitution establishes the existence of appointed Senators and senators for life and everybody knows that our repeated attempts to amend the constitution have been frustrated."[31] On March 11, 1998, Pinochet, wearing a dark suit and red tie, took his seat in the Chilean senate. But before the session officially opened, legislators from the Concertación's Center-Left parties walked onto the senate floor carrying poster-sized photographs of some of the 1,100 *desaparecidos.* Several right-wing senators positioned themselves near Pinochet in a show of support while the president of the senate sought to dispel the tension and restore order. Ushers tried to clear the senate floor as a Socialist Party politician began a heated exchange with a colleague from the right-wing UDI. The argument boiled over into a fistfight, which was quickly broken up. The president of the senate delayed the start of the day's official proceedings until the protesting parliamentarians agreed to remove the photos, some bearing the caption "Where are they?" from their desks. The scene outside was even more confrontational. Thousands of people protested against Pinochet in the streets of Valparaíso. There were 573 arrested and 34 injured that day, including 12 policemen. "Today is a gray and bitter day for Chilean democracy, because the person who closed down congress today tries to shield himself with it," said Isabel Allende, a Socialist congresswoman and daughter of the late president Salvador Allende.[32]

Just two weeks after taking his senate seat, Pinochet once again received a visit from Riggs Bank president Timothy Coughlin and vice president Maria Carol Thompson. The banking executives held several meetings with Chilean military officials in addition to their lunch with Pinochet. Pinochet later received a letter from Coughlin, thanking him for the two sets of Chilean army cuff links, which he said he and Riggs Bank president Joseph Allbritton would wear proudly. Coughlin also said that he and Thompson hoped to see Pinochet's son on his next trip to Washington.[33]

During his few months as a senator, Pinochet kept a low profile. To the astonishment of many, he developed a civil working relationship with senate president Andrés Zaldivar, a Christian Democrat he had forced into exile in 1981. Zaldivar had presidential ambitions and hoped to cultivate some support from the political Right, while Pinochet viewed the Christian Democrat as preferable to the Concertación's other likely presidential contender, Socialist Ricardo Lagos. Pinochet was also visibly displeased with the Chilean Right's frontrunner in the 2000 presidential election, Joaquín Lavín, mayor of an affluent municipality in eastern Santiago and member of the UDI. As Zaldivar looked for support from conservative voters, Lavín made overtures to the Chilean Left and had infuriated Pinochet by meeting with families of the disappeared. Pinochet appears to have believed he could wield more clout under a government led by Zaldivar rather than Lavín.

Zaldivar met with Pinochet to discuss legislation to abolish the September 11 coup anniversary's status as a national holiday, suggesting that it might be substituted for a "day of national unity" on an alternative date. Previous attempts by the Aylwin and Frei governments to abolish the holiday had been unsuccessful, but Zaldivar was able to sway Pinochet, and the former dictator told fellow senate right-wingers to support the measure. But after the vote, he strolled over to the senate president's raised platform, violating protocol. Pinochet embraced Zaldivar, a man of small stature who seemed overpowered by the former dictator. It was a surreal moment, with Pinochet stealing the show and presenting himself as a conciliatory figure.[34]

VI

Judge Juan Guzmán Tapia is a soft-spoken, deliberative man with no left-wing political sympathies. He was born into a Chilean diplomatic family and has lived in El Salvador, the United States, and Argentina. He attended an elite private English school in Santiago, studied law at the University of Chile, and did postgraduate studies in Paris. He began his career in 1970, just as Allende's Popular Unity government was coming to power, and at first was a supporter of the military regime. But in early 1998 Guzmán's life and career would undergo an abrupt change.

Gladys Marin, the Chilean Communist Party's general secretary, presented a criminal complaint of genocide against Pinochet to the Santiago court. The case involved the 1976 arrest and disappearance of five party leaders, including Marin's husband, and sought the prosecution of "all the masterminds and accomplices" involved. Only Pinochet was mentioned by name. Some of Guzmán's colleagues asked him whether he planned to reject the case or turn it over to the military tribunals. Guzmán kept his thoughts to himself and carefully studied the documents, which described a DINA operation to trap the four men and one woman. It was an elaborate action, but one that had produced many witnesses.

In the early morning of April 30, 1976, plainclothes agents arrived at the home of Juan Becerra and told him that his sister-in-law had been killed in an accident and that he must come with them to identify the body. When he got into the car with the men, he was handcuffed, blindfolded, and taken to Villa Grimaldi, where his sister-in-law had been taken after being arrested the day before. Both were arrested, tortured, and forced to reveal the whereabouts of Mario Zamorano, a member of the Chilean Communist Party's central leadership who would be coming to a meeting at Becerra's house in a few days. The DINA agents brought them back home, where they found that the owner's wife and her cousin had also been arrested and released. The family was kept under guard and ordered to "maintain the appearance of going about their everyday business." Another group of DINA agents occupied the home of Becerra's mother, and when the auxiliary bishop of Santiago, Enrique Alvear, stopped by for a visit, he was also detained for a few hours. The agents showed Alvear their identification cards before allowing him to leave.

On the evening of May 4, 1976, Mario Zamorano arrived at the family's home and was shot in the leg and arrested. Gladys Marin's husband, Jorge Muñoz, also arrived and was arrested and taken away. The next day two more party activists were arrested, and on May 6 a fifth Communist was arrested upon arriving at the Becerra home. None were ever seen again, though the Pinochet regime's Interior Ministry reported that two of the men had gone to Argentina—a claim Argentine officials denied.[35]

The case was one of thousands already documented in the Truth and Reconciliation report, which concluded that the five Communist leaders had suffered "forced disappearance at the hand of government agents in violation of their human rights."[36] Guzmán considered the 1978 amnesty law, which had jettisoned so many human rights cases presented to the courts, and thought of different approach. "If you take a person away in this fashion it is, in legal terms, a kidnapping," he said. "Such a case can be considered to be a continuing violation and thus be prosecuted."[37] Since no bodies had ever been found, it could be argued that the victims were still kidnapped (*secuestro permanente*), which meant that the crime was still being committed and that the 1978 amnesty law did not apply.

And so Guzmán accepted Marin's petition on January 20, 1998, setting off a legal and political storm. No one had ever dared attempt to prosecute Pinochet, and Guzmán faced a torrent of criticism, with rebukes from his fellow judges, editorial attacks in Chile's conservative news media, and the awkwardness of being photographed wherever he went. Chilean authorities assigned Guzmán two bodyguards, who accompanied him whenever he left the confines of his home, along with a police guard posted outside his house and another patrolling the neighborhood.

But Marin's lawsuit had opened the floodgates and more would follow: two days later another suit was filed on behalf of fourteen people killed by the military in the northern city of Antofagasta; a few months later relatives of a group of twenty-six Chileans killed under similar circumstances in the mining town of Calama, to the east of Antofagasta, also filed suit.

These killings/disappearances formed part of an infamous series of mass executions in the weeks immediately after the 1973 coup that became known as the Caravan of Death. Some seventy-five Chilean political prisoners in five cities, many already serving sentences imposed by local military courts, were summarily executed on orders of a special army envoy dispatched from Santiago by Pinochet. One of the victims was the director of a children's orchestra; another was a broadcaster who had disobeyed the military's order to cease transmissions and shut down his radio station after the coup. Some of the executed prisoners had not even been arrested but had voluntarily reported to police or military authorities after their names appeared in official lists of those wanted for questioning.

The executions occurred in provincial areas, where political tensions during the Allende government had been lower than in Santiago, and the men's deaths sent shock waves across their communities. Regime authorities offered only the most terse and ludicrous explanations, if any. A short news article in the October 21, 1973, edition of *El Mercurio* bore the headline "Mass Murder Plot Uncovered in Antofagasta" and said that the executions had been ordered "to accelerate the process of Marxist purification and to focus efforts on national recovery."[38]

A lawyer and widow of one of the executed prisoners filed a criminal lawsuit against the army general leading the caravan, General Sergio Arellano, and two of his accompanying officers. She knew that more officials were involved, but theirs were the only names that had been identified at the time. Arellano, who had been one of the army's principal coup organizers—and a sometime rival of Pinochet's—responded to the lawsuit by refusing to invoke the amnesty law, saying he wanted the full truth of these events to be made known. The civilian judge declared the case to be out of her jurisdiction and turned it over to a military court, which immediately applied the amnesty law.

If Chilean judges were not yet ready to deal with the case, a number of Chilean journalists were. One was Patricia Verdugo, a courageous reporter and daughter of a *desaparecido* who tackled the subject head-on, interviewing every witness willing to talk. Her book on the executions, *Los zarpazos del puma (The Puma's Claws),* was published in 1989, its readership expanded by the freer public debate during Pinochet's last year in power. It received additional publicity when General Arellano sued her for libel and lost. Verdugo's book presented a detailed and horrifying chronicle of the killings. In one of the passages, a witness recalls "that during the night, the General's entourage took 14 detainees, whose cases were in process, from the place where they were being held to a ravine called the Quebrada del Way and killed all of them with submachine gunfire and repeater rifles. After that, they took the bodies to the Antofagasta Hospital morgue, and since it was very small and all the bodies didn't fit, most were left outside. All of the bodies were mutilated, with approximately 40 bullet wounds each. At that time, they were lying out in the sun so that everyone passing by could see them."[39]

Judge Guzmán had known little about the case before it reached his court in 1998, and he belatedly read Verdugo's book. He was shocked by the information it contained, for the actions of the officers were not those of the Chilean army he had always esteemed. He reread the book and began doing his own research, starting with a search for the bodies of the victims. Traveling north, he retraced the route General Arellano and his lethal committee had taken, aided by forensic scientists and civilian detectives. In each city they found more evidence. Clandestine gravesites were visited, human remains uncovered but not decomposed in the dry Atacama Desert.

He began interviewing retired military officers who had been on duty when the killings took place. Some denied everything, others claimed to have no memory of the events, but a number of officials provided "testimonies and sometimes confessions which chilled [his] blood." Many of the prisoners had been tortured and mutilated before being shot.[40]

There were nineteen victims of the Caravan of Death whose bodies had not been found. In June 1999 Guzmán ordered the arrest of General Arellano and three other officers for the crime of "permanent kidnapping." He also indicted former DINA operations chief Pedro Espinoza, who was already serving a prison sentence for the Letelier assassination. Guzmán continued investigating the chain of command in these crimes, and all signs pointed upward, to Pinochet.

EIGHT London and Santiago

I

It had become his custom to travel abroad in late September after Chile's two-day independence celebrations, the *fiestas patrias,* with its annual military parade. This year the army had given him special honors as the institution's longest-serving commander, and now he was looking forward to a trip to the United Kingdom. Many of his past travels to that country had been very brief, stopovers on the way to China or other Asian countries. But this forthcoming trip would be a real visit, with plenty of sightseeing and time for relaxation and a medical checkup. The trip would also provide what he expected to be a respite from the growing number of human rights lawsuits filed against him in Chilean courts—at least nine separate legal accusations.

He was hoping to have tea with Margaret Thatcher, whom he deeply admired. They had first met in 1994 when she was on a speaking tour in Santiago. At a formal reception at the British embassy, the two had posed side by side for a photograph: the Iron Lady clad in a shiny formal dress and jacket with stiff shoulder pads, her facial expression serious; Pinochet in full dress uniform and smiling broadly.[1] On a later trip to London, she had invited him to tea, and he always sent her flowers and chocolates when he came through Britain.

Thatcher was not Pinochet's only foreign friend. The Russian general Alexander Lebed, who left the army in 1995 to become a hard-line nationalist politician, credited Pinochet with "saving the state [of Chile] from total collapse."[2] Chinese authorities also seemed fond of him, for the fierce anti-Communist had maintained diplomatic relations with Beijing during his rule, and Pinochet had been given VIP treatment during his earlier visits to China.

Before Pinochet left on this fateful 1998 trip to London, he granted a rare interview to Jon Lee Anderson, a staff writer for the *New Yorker* magazine. "The people around Pinochet don't like him to talk to journalists, but his daughter Lucía had encouraged him to see me, because she thinks that if people understand her father better he will be maligned less," Anderson wrote. "She had warned me that he is brusque, and asked me not to upset him by bringing up the topic of human rights." As an army colonel and another aide sat at the table with Anderson and Pinochet, taping the conversation and taking notes, Pinochet said that England was his favorite country, an ideal place to live, with its civility and moderation, where rules were respected and motorists displayed impeccable driving habits.[3]

As had happened with Pinochet's previous visits to the United Kingdom, the Chilean embassy in London was not advised of his arrival beforehand, and it is not even clear how much attention the Frei government was paying to this trip—or, for that matter, who was paying for it. Certainly, having Pinochet out of the country provided the Frei government with a certain amount of political breathing space. Ambassador Mario Artaza later recounted that he had only been informed of Pinochet's visit after his plane left Santiago, and that neither Pinochet nor the

Chilean army had asked for any embassy assistance before or after his arrival on September 28, 1998.[4]

Pinochet had been invited to the country by Royal Ordnance, the British arms manufacturer that in 1989 had signed a deal with the Chilean army's munitions company FAMAE for a joint project to manufacture a rocket.[5] But a spokeswoman for Royal Ordnance said the company had never received a reply to its invitation and had had no contact with Pinochet since his arrival. The British embassy in Santiago had been informed of his trip and presumably notified the Foreign Office, but Foreign Office officials later said Pinochet's visit had not been approved and that he was given no special treatment. Nevertheless the former dictator, accompanied by four or five other army officers, received VIP status when he landed at Heathrow Airport and was quickly transported to the five-star Intercontinental Hotel in London's Park Lane.[6]

So just what did Pinochet do during his first few days in London? Jon Lee Anderson met with him again at his hotel, after his daughter Lucía had joined her father, having arrived on a later flight. She warned Anderson that her father was not feeling well, that he was cutting back his activities, would not be having tea with Margaret Thatcher after all, and was scheduled to see a doctor in a few days about a possible hernia operation. Anderson's observations, however, suggest that Pinochet was feeling quite well. "Pinochet was in a good mood, and after we talked for a while he set off to visit Madame Tussaud's, for the umpteenth time; the British National Army Museum; and then to lunch at Fortnum and Mason," he wrote. "He bought some books on Napoleon, and was delighted when, during a stop at Burberry's, the head salesman recognized him and was courteous."[7] Anderson had the impression Pinochet was traveling incognito—his army entourage was dressed in civilian clothes, and he seemed to be shielded from casual onlookers. On October 2 he had lunch with Peter Schaad, a Swiss businessman who had lived in Chile from 1976 to 1978 before moving to London. That evening the two had visited Thatcher and her husband, Denis, at their home. "Lady Thatcher offered us a drink. We were there for 45 minutes, and as the general does not speak English, I had to interpret," Schaad said.[8] During this visit, Pinochet informed them that he was going to have the surgery, and that the doctors had assured him he would be able to return to Chile in a week. The four posed for a photograph, which Schaad later displayed during an interview on Chilean television.

Some have suggested Pinochet may have been traveling with a false passport, perhaps one of the ones he used to open foreign bank accounts, but this was not the case: he was refused a visa to travel to France to visit Napoleon's tomb. Had Pinochet been traveling as a simple tourist, he might have entered and left France undetected, but he was using a kind of diplomatic passport that required a visa. France's refusal to grant him one hit the Chilean press October 3 and was confirmed by French government spokespeople, and thus the wider world learned that Chile's notorious former dictator was in London.

On October 9 Pinochet underwent a hernia operation at the London Clinic, a private hospital "internationally renowned for medical and surgical expertise" with a "longstanding reputation for excellence in individual care spanning more than 75 years," according to the institution's Web site.[9] The hernia was a condition he had suffered for some time, but for undisclosed reasons he had decided not to seek treatment in Chile. His daughter Lucía told Jon Lee Anderson there were concerns about the effects of using a general anesthetic on a man of his years. "No one wants to take responsibility when the patient is someone important," she said. But the surgery was apparently successful, and Pinochet was expected to make a full recovery.

II

For more than three years, Baltasar Garzón, a judge on Spain's Audiencia Nacional, the national court, had been investigating the deaths and disappearances of Spanish citizens in Chile following the 1973 coup. Garzón was especially interested in the case of Spanish national Carmelo Soria, the U.N. official found dead in his car in 1976, and the report by Chile's Truth and Reconciliation Commission contained information about this case. There would be additional information in U.S. government documents on Chile, and Garzón wanted to interview American DINA agent

Michael Townley, now living in the United States under the federal witness protection program.

Garzón also wanted to interview Pinochet about these cases and knew he would have little chance to do so in Chile. The news of Pinochet's visit to London presented a rare opportunity, but he would have to move fast. He contacted the Spanish offices of Interpol, who in turn informed their British counterparts, and the order was issued that Pinochet be located, informed of Garzón intent to question him, and prevented from leaving the country until then.

On the evening of October 16, officers of the London Metropolitan Police arrived at the London Clinic to serve Pinochet with the detention order. At that moment, a member of the former dictator's entourage notified the Chilean embassy in London of the order. Ambassador Mario Artaza was charged with explaining the situation to the heavily sedated Pinochet, who spoke little English. But Artaza, a Socialist whom Pinochet had exiled, found his access blocked by a dozen or so police officials, who delayed his entry pending authorization from the Foreign Office. Hospital medical personnel and Pinochet's wife, Lucía, were also denied access.

It was the beginning of one of the world's most complex judicial cases, a watershed in international law that some legal scholars considered one of the most important legal events since the Nuremberg trials of Nazi war criminals. Garzón based his case on the principle of universal jurisdiction, which holds that some crimes are so reprehensible they constitute crimes against humanity and can therefore be prosecuted in any court anywhere in the world. Universal jurisdiction allows the prosecution of such crimes, even if the crimes took place outside the country and neither perpetrator nor victim are nationals of that country.

Pinochet's lawyers filed two on his behalf. The first was to the Home Office, the British government department responsible for security and internal affairs, requesting that extradition proceedings not begin. The second was a habeas corpus petition to the British courts, asking that the arrest warrant be denied. The lawyers cited British extradition law, which requires that the crimes be committed in the country seeking extradition or that the accused be a citizen of that country (Spanish law, on the other hand, allowed such proceedings).[10]

The court agreed with this argument, but Pinochet was still not released. By now other groups, including Amnesty International and Human Rights Watch, had joined forces to bring Pinochet to justice. The case was presented before Britain's highest court, the House of Lords Judicial Committee. On November 25 the law lords ruled that sovereign immunity did not extend to crimes against humanity.

Pinochet's lawyers then challenged this ruling, arguing that one of the lords was a director of Amnesty International's charity division and might therefore be biased. A second panel of law lords overturned the November 25 decision on these grounds, and then a third panel pronounced Pinochet's arrest to be in keeping with Britain's obligations under the United Nations' Convention against Torture. This last ruling meant that Pinochet could not claim immunity, but then the law lords held that he could only be extradited for "acts of torture or conspiracy to torture" committed after December 8, 1988, the date the United Kingdom ratified the convention. As a result, Pinochet was required to remain in the country and await the Home Office's decision on whether extradition could proceed.

The London Clinic had given Pinochet a clean bill of health two weeks after his surgery and was unhappy with the disruption his detention had caused, but more than another week passed before he finally vacated the hospital. Under heavy police guard, he was moved by ambulance to Grovelands Priory, a leading psychiatric hospital in north London. His family and aides maintained that he was still in very poor health and unable to understand all that was taking place around him. Pinochet's nephew told the *Daily Mirror* that his uncle "would rather kill himself or be killed by his guards than face the humiliation and indignity of being sent to face trial in Spain." Pinochet's wife said her husband was "very weak and depressed about his position."[11] Grovelands Priory officials suspected the general was malingering to avoid having to appear in court and stated publicly that it had to remind Pinochet's entourage of the need to go elsewhere. On the evening of December 1, another ambulance under police escort whisked Pinochet away to a private estate south of London, where he would stay for the remaining fifteen months of his detention. Grovelands Priory, relieved, issued a statement expressing its gratitude "to the police and General Pinochet's representatives for expediting his move after it requested he find alternative accommodation following his period of rehabilitation."[12]

The village of Virginia Water in the English county of Surrey lies near Runnymede, where King John was forced to sign the Magna Carta in 1215. Many of its 4,800 residents commute to jobs in London, taking the train from the station located in the middle of the village. Heathrow Airport is just eight miles away. It is one of the wealthiest communities in the country, and many of the largest residences can be found on the Wentworth Estate, next to the Wentworth Club, home of the PGA European Tour. A number of well-known celebrities have had homes on the Wentworth Estate, including Elton John, Elizabeth Hurley, and Sarah Ferguson. And now the former dictator of Chile would be joining them, spending the remaining period of his detention in a house that was comfortable but far less spacious than any of his residences back in his own country. Two of the residence's four bedrooms would be used by Scotland Yard officers, who filled another small room near the kitchen with surveillance equipment. Pinochet had the use of a small office and a computer, but his every move would be tracked by cameras and motion sensor detectors.

III

In Santiago the news of Pinochet's detention caused an uproar. Few Chileans of any political persuasion had imagined that an arrest warrant would come out of Spain, whose prime minister, José María Aznar, was a conservative who had belonged to a pro-Franco group as a student. Aznar felt compelled to state that the case was "a legal issue and must not in any way become a political issue," but Chile's political Right was galvanized. Some right-wing members of the Chilean senate announced they would boycott future legislative sessions until Pinochet was released. Santiago's archbishop, Francisco Javier Errazurriz, ventured to remark that the whole situation might have been averted had Chilean courts been able to do their job. His comments drew such vitriol that a few days later the cleric seemed to retreat, saying that he, too, was indignant over the treatment Pinochet was receiving.[13]

Pinochet supporters staged angry demonstrations in front of the British and Spanish embassies in Santiago, burning the flags of both nations. (The latter activity did not endear them to Spanish conservatives, who might otherwise have been sympathetic to their view.) The Chilean Communist Party held a counterdemonstration, with some protestors waving the Union Jack along with their own party's sickle and hammer flag. The right-wing mayor of the municipality of Providencia, where the embassies are located, announced he was suspending garbage collections at both missions. Senator Evelyn Matthei led a women's demonstration in front of the British ambassador's residence (who was also female) and called on Chileans to boycott all British and Spanish products.[14]

A British trade boycott would have caused greater financial loss to Chile than to the United Kingdom, which imported $1 billion in Chilean goods and sold just under $400,000 worth of goods to Chile the previous year. Copper exports alone totaled $400 million, and Britain had become the third biggest market in the world for Chilean wine.[15]

Conversely, Chile enjoyed a trade surplus with Spain, importing $621 million in 1997 and exporting $345 million. But Spanish investors had considerable holdings in the country, $2.7 billion, $2 billion of which had arrived in Chile over the past year. These investments included a 43.6 percent share in the Compañia de Teléfonos de Chile and an important stake in a major hydroelectric plant. British investments had reached $1.3 billion, with another $3.6 billion authorized for future projects.[16]

On December 11 the Frei government announced it was suspending all official meetings with Britain and Spain and would be reviewing arms purchase agreements with the two countries, saying that Pinochet's arrest showed there were no legal guarantees for Chilean contracts with either nation. In addition to the rocket project between the Chilean army and Royal Ordnance, Chile had an agreement with a Spanish and French group for the purchase of two submarines. Neither of these contracts was ever suspended (though the Chilean navy made a point of taking possession of the submarines in France rather than Spain), and the announcement seemed aimed more at calming nationalistic outrage rather than reconsidering the country's trade and weapons procurement with Spain. There were other announced measures, which in retrospect appear more cosmetic than substantive: the Chilean army reduced the rank of its attaché in London from general to colonel, and the navy did likewise with its attaché in Madrid. Chile also announced it was encouraging Chilean airlines not to fly to the Falkland Islands.

There seemed to be little genuine danger of right-wing Chilean nationalists hounding British and Spanish investors out of the country, but the Frei government did not want political tension adding to the economic downturn already underway. The Asian financial crisis that began in mid-1997 had washed onto Chile's shores, depressing world prices for copper, still the country's single biggest export. The worst drought in forty years had reduced crop yields and also hydroelectric power, forcing a series of power cuts between November 1998 and April 1999. After several years of impressive growth, the economy grew by only 3.4 percent in 1998 and contracted by 1.1 percent the following year. Unemployment rose to 8.2 percent.[17]

At the same time, a sizeable majority of Chileans did not view Pinochet's detention as something that threatened their well-being. A survey published December 2, 1998, by the Mori polling group revealed that 71 percent of respondents said they were not unduly affected by the arrest, and 66 percent said Chile's democracy was not in danger. On the subject of the arrest itself, 44 percent said it was a good thing; 45 percent thought it bad. Nearly two-thirds thought Pinochet was guilty of crimes, 57 percent thought it would be best for the country if he were tried, and only 29 percent thought he should not be tried. Another poll published two weeks later by the Center-Right newsmagazine *Qué Pasa* revealed a similar climate of opinion: 41 percent backed Pinochet's arrest, 56 percent thought he bore most of the responsibility for human rights abuses during his regime, and 59 percent wanted him tried by Chilean courts. In a sign of changing times, respondents placed Pinochet's arrest fourth in a list of important issues facing the country, but almost half of those surveyed considered it unimportant.[18]

Pinochet's arrest may have presented Frei with a difficult political dilemma, but his government had no doubt about Pinochet's guilt. In addition to the suspicious circumstances of Frei's own father's death in 1982, at least three members of Frei's cabinet had firsthand experience with the Pinochet regime's repression. Foreign Minister Jose Miguel Insulza had been exiled in Mexico, and Secretary General Jorge Arrate had been exiled in the Netherlands. Public Works Minister Jaime Tohá had been arrested and tortured after the coup, and his brother Jose, one of Salvador Allende's cabinet ministers, had died in detention.[19] Frei had been in Portugal attending the Ibero-American summit, an annual conference of Latin American, Spanish, and Portuguese heads of state, when he learned of Pinochet's arrest. His government's initial response was to claim that Chile's former dictator enjoyed diplomatic immunity and had gone to Britain on official business. This not-very-credible version of events soon collapsed, and Chilean authorities then challenged Spain's jurisdiction in the case. The government's position was to argue on behalf of the Chilean state—not Pinochet himself—asserting that Chilean courts were competent to judge the former dictator. Foreign Minister Insulza was dispatched to London to lobby for Pinochet's return, answering critics by saying he was seeking to defend "principles and not persons."[20]

Although most of the Concertación political parties felt obliged to tow the official line, that Pinochet should be returned to Chile, a sector of the Socialist Party welcomed his arrest and even sent its own delegation to London to say so. The delegation, which included Congresswoman Isabel Allende, daughter of the late president, presented a letter to British home secretary Jack Straw urging Pinochet's extradition to Spain and stating that it was unrealistic to expect that a trial would take place in Chile. Foreign Minister Insulza, also a Socialist, criticized the delegation, saying it undermined the government.

Most of the Chileans arriving in London were vociferously backing Pinochet's release. A delegation of Renovación Nacional and Union Democrática Independiente politicians visited Pinochet in the London Clinic a few days after his detention was announced, presenting their trip as a humanitarian gesture on behalf of an elderly, ailing colleague. "He did not want to eat breakfast. He had barely half a cup of tea and a biscuit," Senator Ignacio Pérez Walker said after visiting Pinochet in the hospital before his transfer to the house in Surrey. "He has lost around 15 kilos. I saw him in his bathrobe and unmistakably he is a person who has lost a lot of weight."[21] Many right-wing and conservative politicians made more than one trip to London during this period; Cristián Labbé, the municipal mayor who had cut off trash collection at the British embassy, visited Pinochet fourteen times during his detention. Pinochet's appointed successor as army commander, General Ricardo Izurieta, also traveled to London for a visit and to meet with British military officials and politicians. He had not consulted Frei about the trip beforehand and declared that Pinochet was not guilty of any human rights crimes—a public position at odds with the Chilean government's position. At the same time, Izurieta made a point of wearing civilian dress and faced criticism from some sectors of the army for waiting nearly six months after Pinochet's arrest before making the trip.

There would be no official figure on the total cost of Pinochet's detention in London, but unofficial estimates put it at several thousand pounds per day. Rent on the four-bedroom house where Pinochet and his aides were staying cost around £10,000 per month, while police security was estimated at £50,000 per week. Pinochet's six-member British legal team cost about £12,000 for every day in court, and one can only speculate about the fees and expenses of the numerous Chilean lawyers jetting back and forth between Santiago and London.[22]

Pinochet and his family do not appear to have suffered any detectable economic hardship during his detention, despite a Spanish court order to international financial institutions to freeze his accounts. The U.S. Senate report on the former dictator's American bank accounts indicate that in January 29, 1999, "Ramón Pinochet," one of the false identities used for Pinochet's foreign bank accounts, wire transferred $499,985 from a Banco Atlántico account in Gibraltar. In March a Riggs Bank delegation, including chairman Joseph Allbritton, traveled to Chile for three days of meetings with military officials.[23] Later that month the law lords authorized a hearing to decide whether Pinochet should be extradited to Spain. Two days after this decision, Riggs allowed Pinochet to cash in a £1 million CD at its branch in London and transfer the funds to a new

CD in the United States without filing any report that would have alerted officials to the existence of these funds.

A joint account held by "A. P. Ugarte and M. Lucía Hiriart" at the Espiritu Santo Bank in Miami was closed two days before Christmas that same year. To further facilitate the family's financial transactions, on May 7, 1999, Pinochet and his wife formally divided their property and holdings in a *separación de bienes,* a legal move that allows married Chilean women to buy and sell property and undertake banking transactions without their husbands' consent.

Some of Pinochet's bills were being paid by the Pinochet Foundation, which had opened an account at the Banco de Chile's New York branch in January 1999. The U.S. Senate report noted the account held over $2.2 million from multiple sources, arriving in large and small amounts, and the bank had little information about the deposits' origins. There was a $200,000 deposit made by a source called American Engineering, and another for $250,000 from an account in Germany. "Questions remain about who these entities are, the source of their funds and the reasons for their substantial transfers to the Foundation," the report said.[24]

IV

If his arrest came as a shock to Pinochet, he and his associates quickly devised ways to present his case from the most compelling angle. On December 11, 1998, Pinochet made his first appearance in court, gripping a cane and seated in a wheelchair pushed by his son Marco Antonio. His voice was rasping, but his tone was defiant. "My name is Augusto Pinochet Ugarte. I was commander-in-chief of the army in Chile, captain general of Chile, president of the republic and at present I am a senator of the republic," he said through a translator. "I do not recognize the jurisdiction of any court other than in my own country to try me on all the lies that the men from Spain have said."[25]

The court session was relatively brief, just to set the conditions for a hearing the following month. Pinochet's lawyers asked that he be allowed outside to take walks in the garden of his rented house, and the judge quickly agreed, noting that it would be "inhumane" not to allow this. Senator Pérez Walker, who had accompanied Pinochet to court, praised the general's composure during the proceeding. "He was the same courageous man as ever," he told reporters. "He is prepared for everything. He is a soldier and a statesman." Pinochet, meanwhile, issued a letter to the Chilean public, calling it his "political testament." He wrote that he had been the object of "an artful and cowardly politico-judicial machination," and that his detention had been "the hardest and most unjust experience of my life." He said he was being prosecuted for having defeated Communism. "The country knows I never sought power," the statement said. "That is why when I exercised it I never clung to it and when the moment came to hand it over I loyally did so." He said he was "absolutely innocent" of the crimes attributed to him, but said he felt a "sincere grief" for those who lost their lives during these years.[26] It was as close as he would ever come to acknowledging that at least some Chileans had suffered during his regime.

The public relations campaign to improve Pinochet's image continued after Christmas, with an invitation to select British newspapers to photograph him at his rented house in Surrey. He sat slumped in a wheelchair during the photo session, saying he was resigned to his fate. A former aide to Margaret Thatcher published a pamphlet, *The Tale of Two Chileans: Pinochet and Allende,* that defended Pinochet's regime as a victory for Latin America in the cold war. While admitting that there had been some abuses, "the brutal truth is that such casualties are the inevitable price paid when order in a society is broken by civil war." He presented the pamphlet at a rally in London, where he called Pinochet "the closest thing Britain has to a political prisoner."[27]

For three more months Pinochet did not appear in public, until Margaret Thatcher paid him a very public visit that was shown live on television. The former prime minister, accompanied by an aide, was met at the doorway by Pinochet and his wife, who thanked her for visiting "this simple house." A young Chilean man sat on the sofa beside Pinochet, translating their conversation. Thatcher praised Pinochet as the man "who brought democracy to Chile" and said Britain owed him a great deal for his regime's assistance during the 1982 Falklands War: "The information you gave us, communications and also the refuge you gave to any of our armed forces who were able, if they were shipwrecked, to make their way to Chile," she said.[28]

Thatcher's visit came shortly after Britain's law lords voted six to one that Pinochet could be extradited to Spain. The new ruling reduced the charges against Pinochet, stipulating that he could be charged for the crimes of torture and conspiracy to torture for actions taken after December 8, 1988, when the International Torture Convention went into effect in Spain, Britain, and Chile.

V

If the Frei government and a majority of Chileans held that Pinochet should be tried in Chile, it seemed a good time to examine the state of the country's courts. A law establishing a judicial academy was passed in 1994, in an effort to improve standards in a field where education levels and professionalism varied enormously. The new academy, the Academia Judicial, offered both training and internships for young lawyers seeking careers as judges and continuing education programs for serving justices.[29] In December 1997 the government passed constitutional reforms that set age limits for Supreme Court justices, gave the Chilean senate the power to approve judges nominated by the president, and increased the number of Supreme Court justices from seventeen to twenty-one. Pinochet appointees had gradually retired over the years, and by the time of his arrest, only three of his designated judges remained.

Unfortunately, a significant portion of the Chilean judiciary did not take kindly to critical scrutiny. Alejandra Matus, a young investigative journalist, had been researching the Chilean court system for six years. In April 1999 she published *El libro negro de la justicia Chilena,* an exposé of corruption and cronyism in the judicial system during and after the Pinochet regime. Although the Aylwin and Frei governments had passed some reforms, "It is obvious that a lot of things are still swept under the carpet," she wrote.[30] The book described how the judiciary had resisted attempts to make its record keeping more efficient with computers, which only came into use during the Aylwin government. It also described the habits of some of the more notorious judges, including one discovered photographing underaged girls in various stages of undress in his office. The book's cover showed three monkeys in the "see no evil, hear no evil, speak no evil" pose sitting in the chairs of Chile's highest court.

A former Supreme Court justice mentioned in Matus's book read an advance copy and lodged a complaint with the Santiago court under Chile's State Security law. Within twenty-four hours of the book's launch, the court judge ordered police to confiscate all copies of the book on sale and in the publisher's warehouse and issued an arrest warrant for the author. Matus fled to Argentina and later traveled to the United States, where she quickly received political asylum.

The court judge then opened a case against the book's publisher and editor, who were arrested and held for two days. The case was later dropped, but not before a photocopied version of the book had become a bestseller on the black market. The Chilean daily newspaper *La Tercera* posted excerpts of the book on a U.S.-based Web site, attracting thousands of additional readers.

The author, editor, and publisher appealed to the Inter-American Commission on Human Rights, which called on the Chilean government to protect their security and personal liberty. The charges against the editor and publisher were dismissed, but the attempts to prosecute Matus continued, bringing Chile into considerable disrepute in international legal circles. Not until 2001, when the Chilean congress finally amended the country's State Security law and similar legal statutes, was the case dropped and Matus able to return to her country.[31]

The Pinochet regime, its beginnings and its aftermath, were about to come under still more scrutiny. On June 30, 1999, a truck pulled up to the Chilean embassy in Washington, D.C., and began unloading dozens of cartons. The boxes contained 3,300 documents totaling over 20,000 pages of recently declassified material from the State Department, the CIA, the FBI, the Department of Justice, the Department of Defense, and the National Security Council, all dealing with U.S.-Chile relations over a thirty-year period. "They [the State Department] asked us if there was anything we wanted redacted," recalled Genaro Arriagada, Chile's ambassador to Washington at the time. "But really, there wasn't."[32] The embassy set aside a separate room just to deal with the documents and began a daily routine in which several staffers would gather at 3 p.m. to read the avalanche of reports, memoranda, and cables.

Some of the newly declassified documents made bizarre, darkly comic reading. One cable from the U.S. embassy seventeen days after the coup reports that two Chilean Defense Ministry officials asked whether the U.S. could send them "a person qualified in establishing a detention center for detainees which they anticipate will be retained over a relatively long period of time." The Chilean defense minister officials making the request said there was no Chilean official with the necessary background, "and they want to ensure that detainees are given humane treatment." They also requested the loan of tents and portable housing equipment. The cable's author, then U.S. ambassador Nathaniel Davis, cites a UN High Commission for Refugees official who tells him the Chilean authorities need blankets for detainees. "While sending of an advisor to aid in establishment of detention camps provides obvious political problems, [the State Department] may wish to consider feasibility of material assistance in form of tents, blankets, etc which need not be publicly and specifically earmarked for prisoners."[33]

Other cables were chilling. A few days later, a State Department briefing memorandum reports a junta announcement that "summary, on-the-spot executions would no longer be carried out" and that military courts would process prisoners before executing them. It cites an "internal, confidential report" prepared for the junta that puts the number of executions, both summary and post-trial, at 320 for the period of September 11 to 30. "The Chilean leaders justify those executions as entirely legal to the application of martial law," the memorandum continues. "Their code of military justice permits death by firing squad for a range of offenses, including treason, armed resistance, illegal possession of arms and *auto theft*" (emphasis added).[34]

Other documents show that U.S. officials hardly remained blasé over human rights abuses. A July 1, 1975, National Security Council (NSC) memorandum tells of several officials at the U.S. embassy in Santiago who urged "cutting off all economic and military assistance to Chile until the human rights situation improved." Weapons sales to Chile had been delayed as a result, the document said, and "Pinochet called in our Ambassador on Monday to protest the run-around being given to his representative in Washington in terms of arms sales. He expressed his continuing preoccupation with the threat from Peru now that the installations for the Soviet tanks and other military equipment [are] 150 miles from the Chilean border."[35]

A few weeks later another NSC memo discusses a possible visit to the United States by Pinochet and his request for a meeting with then-president Gerald Ford. "We asked Ambassador Popper to discourage it by saying the President's schedule was already full for this period," the document said. "For Pinochet to be the first Latin American chief of state to be received by President Ford at the White House (not counting Williams of Trinidad and Tobago) would stimulate criticism domestically in the U.S. and from Latin America. On the other hand, if someone wanted to make an issue out of it, refusal by President Ford to see him could be equally embarrassing at this stage."[36]

There were documents that revealed U.S. officials' declining opinion of Pinochet over the years, beginning with a CIA biography handbook on Chile describing him as "an intelligent, competent and disciplined infantry officer and military geographer."[37] By the end of his regime, Pinochet had come to be viewed as a man who "does not really know anything about politics, either internal or especially, external. His views on the rest of the world, about which he knows little, are extraordinarily naive and simplistic." General John Galvin of the U.S. Southern Command visited Santiago, met with Pinochet, and afterward told embassy officials that he found it difficult to understand how the Chilean leader could have been an instructor at the military academy. "He reads extensively, how could someone be a professor and reader of serious books and not have a better mind?"[38]

These and other documents provided fascinating additional details but did not expose any previously unknown activities by the CIA or other U.S. agencies—the gist of which had been already revealed in the mid-1970s by a U.S. Senate investigation and report and in additional documents declassified and released in subsequent years. But these earlier revelations had occurred when Pinochet was still in power, and little of their content had filtered through the regime's wall of censorship. This time, a much freer Chilean press would access these documents, and their subsequent reports would weaken Pinochet's image even more.

Pinochet's detention in London had prompted the Clinton administration to review all classified documents "that shed light on human rights abuses, terrorism and other acts of political violence in Chile." According to State Department spokesman James Rubin, the Clinton administration had already been privately providing information to Spanish officials over the past year but was "not prepared yet to state [its] views about the legal merits" of the case for Pinochet's extradition.[39]

There seemed to be no clear consensus within the Clinton administration over Pinochet's detention. A Department of Justice official had said the department was considering its own extradition request for Pinochet to stand trial in the United States for the 1976 Letelier assassination and the killing of two Americans, Charles Horman and Frank Teruggi, in the aftermath of the 1973 coup. "There have been discussions here at a very high level, and we are discussing extradition to the United States as a backup if Pinochet gets immunity in London," department spokesman John Russell told the *Los Angeles Times*.[40]

The Clinton administration was ambivalent about international human rights prosecutions and their possible effect on U.S. interests. Earlier that year, the Clinton administration had voted against the establishment of the International Criminal Court to prosecute crimes against humanity, war crimes, and genocide.[41] But there were other requests for Pinochet's extradition. In addition to the case Italy had filed for the 1975 assassination attempt on Christian Democratic exile Bernardo Leighton and his wife, France filed three separate cases in behalf of French citizens who had disappeared or been killed during the regime. Switzerland filed an extradition request for the disappearance of a Swiss-Chilean citizen. Belgium also filed an extradition request on behalf of Chilean exiles living in that country.

VI

While the international cases against Pinochet mounted, the Frei government tried to bolster its authority at home. In May, as Frei prepared to give the annual state of the union address before congress, pro-Pinochet parliamentarians asked the British and Spanish ambassadors to leave. Their protest ended in a scuffle, with punches thrown as ushers tried to restore order, all caught on camera.

Frei reshuffled his cabinet, bringing Edmundo Pérez Yoma back to the Defense Ministry after a stint as Chile's ambassador to Argentina. He also announced a series of new public works packages—housing subsidies for the poor and new loan programs for farmers and small businesses—the kind of initiatives governments tend not to undertake with less than a year left in office. He met several times during Pinochet's detention with the National Security Council, the military advisory body Pinochet had set up as a kind of parallel executive branch. These meetings gave senior officers an opportunity to air their views and to keep informed of Chile's negotiations with Britain and Spain.[42]

Judge Juan Guzmán's prosecution of five military officers for the killing and disappearance of political prisoners after the coup heightened tensions further. But Chile's new navy commander, Admiral Jorge Arancibia, responded with a proposal for a commission to discuss past human rights abuses by both the military and armed political groups. Human rights campaigners expressed skepticism, but the proposal demonstrated that the Chilean military leadership was at least beginning to address the issue. Military officials took part in a series of discussions with academics, religious leaders, and human rights lawyers. Although the Mesa de Diálogo never produced any accord, it seemed at least a small step forward in improved civil-military relations.

Pinochet, however, was still maintaining that no human rights abuses had taken place on his watch. As Pinochet faced the increased possibility of extradition, his lawyers and aides reported that his health was deteriorating and that a Catholic priest had been summoned to his residence in Surrey to administer the last rites. In May he went to the Princess Margaret Hospital in nearby Windsor for tests after complaining of abdominal pain. Two months later Pinochet, who had always disliked journalists—especially foreign ones—gave an interview to the *Sunday Telegraph*. Despite the British newspaper's conservative editorial stance, the interview had only been granted after lengthy negotiations and a last-minute intervention by General Izurieta, who knew that Pinochet's rare press interviews almost never did his image any good. The two journalists waited for Pinochet on the patio of his Surrey residence with several military aides, who shuffled nervously. General Izurieta had been on the phone the previous day, trying to stop an interview that he knew would hurt Pinochet's image.

When Pinochet appeared, he seemed perfectly lucid and spoke in hoarse whispers that reminded the journalists of Marlon Brando's performance in the film *The Godfather.* He told his visitors that he did not normally authorize meetings with members of the press and gave them "a smile which did not reach his pale blue eyes and was not at all reassuring." Pinochet said that he had been kidnapped by British authorities, who had been "playing with the life of someone who is very old." Beating his fist on the patio table, with a copy of his regime's 1980 constitution placed before him, he called himself the only political prisoner in England and denied any direct responsibility for human rights abuses. "I didn't have time to control what others were doing," Pinochet said. "To say that is gross slander."[43]

In July he had an electrocardiogram. The following month Chile's and Spain's foreign ministers met in Madrid but adamantly denied there were any secret deals in the making. A Spanish foreign ministry spokesman said the government would not intervene in the judicial investigation but was "prepared to consider all the reasons that our Chilean friends may have to defend their arguments given the importance we attach to our bilateral relations."[44]

Pinochet's son Marco Antonio told reporters that his father was suffering psychological problems and had become so ill he might die during his detention. "He's taking 10 pills a day to keep his body in a correct chemical way. He's in a position to understand what has happened, but I don't know for how long," he said. Some of his supporters suggested moving Pinochet out of the Surrey residence to one in Spain, where he would at least be able to understand the language. But his Spanish lawyers counseled against it, saying that going to Madrid voluntarily would be legal suicide.[45]

In Santiago Judge Guzmán was contacted by an old friend and a retired army general who presented him with an unusual legal proposal. He should formally seek Pinochet's extradition to Chile, on the assumption that Britain would be more likely to accede to this request than those of Spain and other countries. Once Pinochet was back in Santiago, all the charges would be dropped, of course. Guzmán rejected the proposal.[46]

That September Pinochet had a brain scan and a series of neurological tests. He was said to have suffered two minor strokes and was excused from appearing at an extradition ruling on October 6. Meanwhile, Margaret Thatcher delivered an impassioned speech at the Conservative Party Conference in Pinochet's defense. She called him Britain's "staunch, true friend" during the Falklands War and said that "an international lynch-law" was threatening to subvert British justice and the rights of sovereign nations.[47]

The British court upheld the charges filed against Pinochet on October 8, 1999, and it was now up to Home Secretary Jack Straw to make the final decision whether to extradite him. The Frei government formally asked Britain to free Pinochet in view of his poor health. Spain said it would not appeal if Pinochet were released on these grounds, and the Home Office asked that Pinochet undergo additional medical examinations to determine his fitness for extradition.

On January 5, 2000, Pinochet had six to seven hours of tests at Northwick Park Hospital in north London. Two specialists in geriatric medicine and two neurologists, both fluent Spanish speakers, conducted the examinations after a groaning Pinochet had to be helped out of bed and held upright. His aides informed the doctors that Pinochet was unable to shave or dress himself and predicted he would suffer further physical and mental deterioration.[48] Their examination found Pinochet to be suffering a variety of ailments: a viral infection, diabetes, heart disease, and the effects of two mild strokes. Home Secretary Jack Straw then informed the British parliament that the physicians had deemed Pinochet unfit to stand trial—a position the medical specialists refuted.

Sir John Grimley Evans, one of the doctors and a professor of clinical gerontology at Oxford University, told the *Observer* newspaper that Pinochet could have recovered from the ailments they diagnosed and that the decision about the former dictator's fate was "outside our field of competence and outside our responsibilities."[49]

A Chilean air force jet was placed on standby, ready to fly to London to bring Pinochet back as soon as a decision had been made. Several more weeks of legal challenges ensued: at first Straw refused to release the medical report on Pinochet, while the British Medical Association publicly criticized this move, saying patient confidentiality was not an issue, as the doctors examining Pinochet were acting in a forensic capacity.[50] Judge Garzón requested that Spain ask British prosecutors to challenge any move to send Pinochet home, but Spanish authorities ruled out any further.

On March 2, 2000, Straw informed Britain's House of Commons that officials were dropping the extradition proceedings against Pinochet. In letters to the ambassadors of four countries seeking the former dictator's extradition, Straw said that Pinochet was suffering a "memory deficit" that impaired his ability to understand a trial procedure and work with his defense lawyers.[51] The Chilean air force plane, having landed several days earlier at the Royal Air Force Base in northern England, picked up Pinochet and his entourage at Heathrow. He had been detained in the United Kingdom for seventeen months.

Pinochet may have eluded extradition and prosecution for his regime's crimes, but the world had become a smaller and riskier place for dictators and their associates. The "Pinochet precedent" encouraged victims of human rights abuses in other countries to take their cases to international courts. Many of those brought to trial in the wake of Pinochet's detention were midlevel officials, but Human Rights Watch observed that fallout from the case caused more than one dictator to think twice about traveling abroad. "Pinochet's greatest legacy may be the cautionary lesson he provides for dictators everywhere," said José Miguel Vivanco, the organization's Americas director. "His case showed the world that even the most powerful human rights abusers can be made to face justice."[52]

PART THREE Consolidating Democracy

NINE The Dictator's Last Bow

I

Augusto Pinochet Ugarte arrived home in Chile to find that a man he had once imprisoned was about to become president. Ricardo Lagos, a Socialist, had defeated Christian Democrat Andrés Zaldivar to become the Concertación's candidate in the December 1999 presidential election. His opponent was Joaquín Lavín of the Union Democrática Independiente (UDI).

Both men had graduate degrees from American universities. Lavín had a master's degree in economics from the University of Chicago and once held a midlevel administrative post on the Pinochet regime's economic team. He was a popular mayor of Las Condes, an upper-income municipality in eastern Santiago, but presented himself as a technocrat with vaguely populist leanings. If elected, he promised that he would spend at least three months of the year governing from regions outside Santiago and proposed ending military conscription, making the Chilean army an all-volunteer institution. He said he would set up a free, direct telephone line for citizens to leave messages for the president. He also said he favored ending the designated senator seats in congress and indicated he was open to more constitutional reforms.[1] Lavín was also a conservative Catholic traditionalist, a father of seven, and a member of Opus Dei.

Lagos held a PhD from Duke University and had been a professor at the University of North Carolina before working for the United Nations in Chile and Argentina. In the mid-1980s he joined political groups opposing Pinochet and was arrested and held prisoner for several days in wake of the 1986 assassination attempt on Pinochet. "I recall when I was prisoner I was interrogated by a military prosecutor, who had a thick dossier on me," he said. "I noticed that the top page bore an old address of mine, one I hadn't used for fifteen years. I also recall some death threats used to arrive at this old address—pictures of gravestones, that sort of thing."[2] Whatever their errors in intelligence gathering, Pinochet regime officials viewed Lagos as a threat. His name was on a list compiled by the Central Nacional de Informaciones (CNI) of people to be eliminated as a reprisal for the attack on Pinochet, and the fact that he was arrested and taken into custody beforehand by Chile's civilian detective police that night may have saved his life.[3]

Two years later, during the "no" campaign against Pinochet's reelection, Lagos once again made headlines when he appeared on a panel discussion on Chile's Universidad Católica television channel. Looking straight into the camera, he accused Pinochet of deliberately misleading the country. "I will remind you, General Pinochet, that on the day of the 1980 plebiscite you said that President Pinochet would not be a candidate in 1989," he said, holding up a copy of *El Mercurio* with the relevant headline and jabbing the air with his index finger. "And now, you promise the country another eight years of tortures, murders and human rights violations . . . you intend to stay in power for 25 years."[4] No one had ever so openly challenged Pinochet in public, and many Chileans wondered whether Lagos would live to see the plebiscite vote. He and other opposition leaders felt it necessary to take precautions with their own and their families' safety during this period. Lagos stayed at his son's house the day of the vote and recalled that when he left that morning, he wondered whether he would be returning that night. But he said it was important to project a sense of confidence.

Lagos joined Aylwin's cabinet and found that even then he had to deal with the former dictator. During Chile's 1992 independence celebrations, Aylwin asked those members who had not yet attended the annual military parade to accompany him, which would mean greeting Pinochet in his role as army commander. The encounter was mercifully brief; Lagos and other the other cabinet officials were presented to Pinochet "as some of the ministers."[5]

The 1999 election marked the second time the Concertación candidate was chosen in a primary rather than a caucus of party leaders. Lavín was chosen by leaders of his own UDI and Renovación Nacional, who formed the Center-Right Alliance for Chile coalition. There were other candidates running for president as well: Gladys Marin of the Communist Party; Tomás Hirsch, a former Chilean ambassador to New Zealand who ran on the Humanist Party ticket; environmental activist Sara Larraín, who ran as an independent; and Arturo Frei Bolívar, a cousin of the former president, who represented a populist conservative party, the Progressive Center-Center Union. All the candidates received a share of free television time during the thirty-day period leading up to the December 11 vote, with the two largest Chilean newspapers, *El Mercurio* and *La Tercera,* backing Lavín. Much of the Chilean business community also supported Lavín, but a number of otherwise conservative business leaders backed Lagos, who had promised there would be no radical change in economic policy. Lavín enjoyed a larger campaign budget than Lagos, approximately $35 million, but the latter's supporters charged that Lagos's reported $5 million was really three times as high and did not include the free publicity he received while attending the Frei government's public works inaugurations.[6]

Pinochet and his detention did not figure as major issues during the presidential campaign. Indeed, both candidates seemed to have found it rather convenient to have Pinochet out of the country. "There were more important issues to be discussed in Chile. But our position was that Pinochet had to be returned, and in this sense we were both in agreement," he said. "Lavín saw it would do him no good to be close to Pinochet. He went to London, saying it was a humanitarian journey."[7]

A poll published in November showed a slightly higher percentage of Chileans had a favorable opinion of Lavín than Lagos—57 percent versus 55 percent, respectively. But when asked whom they would vote for if the election were held in a few days' time, 36.2 percent said they would cast ballots for Lagos, against 34.3 percent for Lavín.[8]

Both men seemed to espouse the same general social and economic policies, with promises to create hundreds of thousands of new jobs and reforms in the areas of housing, social security, and health care. Both refrained from personal attacks, though some of Lavín's supporters made much of the fact that Lagos was an agnostic and married to his second wife (though they had been married some thirty years). Although Lagos's personal life was hardly the stuff of scandal, there was still no divorce law in Chile, and his first marriage had been annulled. He made a point of meeting with the Catholic Bishops' Conference to assure them he would not introduce legislation to legalize abortion—as some Lavín supporters insinuated he would.

Lavín's candidacy was somewhat hurt by his association with the Pinochet regime, but his public discourse emphasized the future. The fact that congressional elections were not being held that year made it easier for Lavín to present himself as an independent-minded leader. The results of the December 11 voting were agonizingly close: with 7.2 million ballots cast, Lagos received 47.96 percent and Lavín, 47.52 percent. Gladys Marin received 3.19 percent; Tomás Hirsch received 0.51; Sara Larraín, 0.44 percent; and Arturo Frei Bolívar, 0.38 percent. As no candidate received a majority, Lagos and Lavín would face each other in a runoff, competing for a share of the minority candidates' votes.

The runoff election, the first in Chilean history, took place on January 16, 2000, and was also close. Lagos won, with 51.31 percent to Lavín's 48.69 percent. The two candidates were photographed with their wives as Lavín graciously conceded and then promised Lagos his cooperation on issues of shared concern. It was a promising finale to a close but civil electoral process and seemed to bode well for the future of Chile's democracy.

II

Judge Juan Guzmán watched the television coverage of Pinochet's arrival, taking careful note of the general's movements and demeanor. As the aircraft door opened, Chilean officials could be seen preparing a folding wheelchair for Pinochet's exit. A covered platform was used to lower Pinochet to the ground, but once his wheelchair touched the tarmac, he stood up quickly, embraced army commander Ricardo Izurieta, and walked toward the waiting crowd. He made little use of the cane he was carrying.[9]

Against the Frei government's express wishes, the army had prepared a brief welcoming ceremony for Pinochet at the airport. A military band played as the general embraced and greeted family members, army officers, and other well-wishers for several minutes. A few right-wing politicians—but not former presidential candidate Joaquín Lavín—were in the crowd but emphasized to reporters that they were there as individuals rather than representatives of their political parties. After greeting his supporters, Pinochet was ushered back to his wheelchair and transported in a helicopter to the military hospital. On the rooftop landing pad, a group of soldiers dressed in camouflage and carrying machine guns surrounded Pinochet's wheelchair as he was moved inside. The streets below were filled with pro-Pinochet demonstrators. A hospital spokesman said Pinochet would undergo further tests and examinations but might be able to go home that afternoon or the following day. "He boarded the airplane a destroyed man, and with the passing of hours began to recover," Pinochet's daughter Jacqueline later told Chilean reporters. "Even I was surprised, but I don't want to say he is healthy. Bit by bit he recovered while he flew." A drunken bystander told the Reuters news service that his country was "miraculous." "They arrive in wheelchairs and [then they] walk, they arrive beaten down and sad and [then] they smile," he said. "God is with Chile."[10]

The following day some four thousand protestors marched through the streets of downtown Santiago, shouting, "Put Pinochet on trial!" and "Punish the guilty!" When the demonstrators reached the La Moneda presidential palace, police tried to disperse the crowds with water cannons and arrested ten people.

Guzmán had read the report by the four independent medical specialists who had examined Pinochet and scoffed at the notion that Pinochet was unfit to stand trial. Pinochet's agility, even after a twenty-four-hour flight, was further evidence that he might well have duped his British hosts. And on the same day Pinochet returned to Santiago, lawyers in the Caravan of Death case asked the court to revoke his parliamentary immunity. "Pinochet left Chile as the king of the world, and he returns a criminal condemned morally by the world," said Viviana Diaz, president of the Relatives of the Disappeared. A few weeks earlier, Diaz and the group's secretary general had received a Christmas card with a death threat. "Let's hope that Father Christmas will give us the opportunity to meet face to face in the year 2000 so that we can blow your brains out," the inscription said. "Enjoy your last Christmas." The card was signed by the Nationalist Front for Fatherland and Freedom, an organization almost certainly made up of fanatical Pinochet supporters and former military officials that had issued similar threats during the general's detention in London. But the threats ceased once Pinochet returned to Santiago.[11]

The court agreed to revoke Pinochet's immunity, ruling that there were "well-founded suspicions" of his culpability in the Caravan of Death case. Pinochet's lawyers challenged this ruling, but on August 8, 2000, Chile's Supreme Court voted fourteen to six to uphold the lower court's decision. The decisions reflected the judiciary's growing autonomy as Pinochet-appointed judges retired and army influence waned in wake of Pinochet's retirement. The Frei government had been insisting that the Chilean legal system was capable of dealing with Pinochet, and for many judges, it was now a matter of professional pride to show they were up to the challenge.[12]

Some members of the Chilean congress, however, were not pleased with the ruling. In wake of the Supreme Court ruling, a group of right-wing parliamentarians visited Pinochet to express their support, while Guzmán began to receive discreet visits from Concertación's own leaders. The contacts typically began with an insistent request for just a few minutes of the judge's time. The politician would begin by complimenting Guzmán on his work, saying the judge's efforts constituted an important step on the road to justice. And then would come the real reason for the visit: a request that Guzmán back away from prosecuting Pinochet in the interest of national reconciliation and the preservation of social peace. In other words, Chilean judges were supposed to understand that there were certain boundaries that could not be breached.[13]

On December 1, 2000, Guzmán formally indicted Pinochet as the *autor intelectual* of fifty-seven killings and eighteen kidnappings during the Caravan of Death. The higher court ruled that Guzmán could not prosecute Pinochet without interviewing him and that the general should undergo a series of psychiatric exams. The judge arranged for a team of specialists to exam Pinochet at the military hospital on January 2, 2001. Guzmán arrived at the facility at the appointed time, but the supposedly ill and infirm Pinochet never showed. The Chilean press found the former dictator with his family at one of his residences near the Pacific coast. Several days later Pinochet's lawyers announced that their client had agreed to the medical exams, which showed the former dictator to be suffering from "mild to moderate" dementia. "This might mean he would have trouble remembering very recent events, such as where he left his keys, but he should certainly have no trouble recalling past events," Guzmán said.[14]

He negotiated the terms of his interview with Pinochet, insisting that none of the general's five children be present. On the appointed day, Guzmán found another army general and two members of Pinochet's legal team waiting at the former dictator's home. Guzmán, his notary, and a court secretary were shown into a room where they found Pinochet seated in an armchair. After asking the lawyers to leave the room, Guzmán began his questions and found Pinochet to be "very alert, with his intellectual capabilities intact."[15] The interview lasted barely thirty minutes. Guzmán was almost finished when one of the lawyers entered the room and whispered that the general was very tired and that the session should stop. Guzmán and his two aides moved into another room to transcribe the interview, leaving Pinochet still seated. But through a half-opened door, the judge noticed Pinochet stand up unaided and walk quickly to the other side of the room.

On July 9, 2001, the Santiago court ruled two to one to suspend criminal proceedings against Pinochet on humanitarian grounds, citing his "moderate vascular dementia."[16] Pinochet then announced his retirement from the Chilean senate and from public life. The Supreme Court upheld the court decision one year later, but there would be more judicial inquiries to come, and Pinochet would remain very much in public view.

III

The dressmaker's killers assumed her body would never be found. Marta Ugarte was last seen in the backseat of an unmarked car driven by plainclothes policemen on August 10, 1976. But a month later her corpse washed up on a beach northwest of Santiago. The damage to her skeleton suggested the body had been dropped from a considerable height. Her legs were almost detached from her hips, her skin showed signs of recent burns and punctures, and her fingernails and toenails were missing, as was part of her tongue. Her arms and neck had been tied with wire.[17]

For years Chilean human rights groups had received reports of prisoners' cadavers being dumped into the ocean, including some testimonies from former regime officials.[18] But few had ever washed ashore. A Santiago court had rejected a habeas corpus petition filed shortly after Ugarte's disappearance, accepting regime authorities' denials that she had ever been arrested. The discovery of her corpse was reported in the Chilean press, which speculated that Ugarte had been the victim of a crime of passion. In reality, Ugarte had been taken to Villa Grimaldi, where she was interrogated and killed. Then her body was moved to a military airbase and loaded into a helicopter along with other dead prisoners. The military tied the cadavers to iron railings to ensure they would sink to the ocean floor, but Ugarte's body had broken free and provided a clue to the fate of hundreds of other Chileans.

On January 7, 2001, President Lagos went on television to present a report from the military-civilian discussion panel begun during his predecessor's government. The talks had yielded information on the fate of at least some of Chile's *desaparecidos,* including 130 whose remains had been dropped into the Pacific Ocean or other bodies of water. The Chilean military's high command, he said, had acknowledged that country could not "look toward the future without clearing up the debts of the past." The families of those victims recently identified would be contacted personally, he said, and the information would be turned over to the Chilean judiciary for further action.[19]

Guzmán moved his investigation to the stretch of coastline where Ugarte's body was found, taking a boat with divers to the area where former regime officials reported that bodies had been dumped. The Chilean army's Puma helicopters had made approximately forty such excursions between 1974 and 1978. Some of the victims had been killed and dropped into the water immediately after, whereas others were killed and buried in unmarked graves but had their remains later exhumed, fastened to iron railings, and dropped into the sea. Much of the information on these "flights of death" came not from senior officers but from mechanics working at the military air base where the helicopter flights originated. One of the mechanics told Guzmán that his commander had warned him and others at the air base that these operations were "secret missions" not to be discussed with anyone. Although Guzmán tried to protect the identity of his witnesses, some still received threats. The son of one of the mechanics was briefly kidnapped by two men who forced him into a car, tied him up, placed a hood over his head, and warned him to tell his father to "shut his mouth."[20]

The helicopters had not taken their grisly cargo very far out to sea. Guzmán's divers, searching less than a mile from the shoreline, managed to locate several railings and bring them to the surface. The railings, rusting and cracked after nearly two decades under water, did not by themselves constitute proof of the crimes. But one of the railings held a shirt button that had become stuck between the metal fragments.[21]

Eventually Guzmán was able to identify a colonel and four former pilots who had been part of an army aviation unit that had dumped bodies into the sea between 1974 and 1977, charging them with complicity in the death of Marta Ugarte. Between four hundred and five hundred bodies of political detainees had been disposed of in this fashion, but the dressmaker's corpse was the only one discovered.

IV

It was not unheard of for former political prisoners to cross paths with their former torturers and jailers. Angela Jeria de Bachelet was in the elevator of her apartment building when she came face to face with a man who had interrogated her. "At some point I am going to have to talk with you, because we met at Villa Grimaldi," she said. The retired official froze and then walked away quickly. The two neighbors, former prisoner and former jailer, managed to avoid each other for a while, but another encounter was inevitable. "I told him I didn't hate him for what he did," Jeria de Bachelet said. "His eyes filled with tears and he thanked me. At that moment, I felt liberated."[22] Other encounters were far less benign. Felipe Aguero, a political scientist with a PhD from Duke University, had left Chile in 1982 and was making his first trip back to Santiago to attend an academic conference six years later. He found himself seated at the same table with a man who had stripped, beaten, and tortured him in the National Stadium shortly after the coup. He was too shaken to react, but at later academic conferences he continued to notice the former naval officer, Emilio Meneses, who had a PhD from Oxford University and had become a respected professor at the Universidad Católica's Institute of Political Studies.

Aguero finally mustered up enough courage to try to talk to Meneses during another visit to Santiago, going to his university office but not finding him. He found himself avoiding academic conferences where Meneses was likely to appear, when he finally realized he was not the one who should be suffering such anxiety. In 2001 he sent a carefully worded letter to the head of Meneses's department, saying he felt it his ethical duty to inform his academic colleagues of Meneses's past activities and that his earlier silence had effectively made him an accomplice to deceit. "Mr. Emilio Meneses took part in the team which personally tortured me on repeated occasions in the national stadium in 1973," he wrote. "About his participation I have no doubt whatsoever."[23] The letter, which contained no request for Meneses's dismissal, was leaked to the Chilean press. Meneses responded with a libel suit against Aguero. He admitted he had been in the National Stadium, but said that his role had been limited to processing arriving prisoners. Aguero received the backing of fellow academics around the world, including two hundred scholars in the United States, Europe, Latin America, and Japan who signed a letter promising to boycott any academic conference in which Meneses was a participant. Other academics, including critics of the Pinochet regime, maintained that Meneses should not be condemned until proven guilty.[24]

Within the Chilean military there was a small but growing number of active and retired officers who were willing to admit that human rights abuses had occurred. The army had a new commander, General Juan Emilio Cheyre, a man who somehow managed to earn the respect of both Pinochet and President Lagos. Cheyre and Lagos had met several years earlier at a conference on Spain's democratic transition. Lagos recalled that by the time he took office, the Chilean army had already become a more outward-looking institution. When he visited Chilean troops taking part in peacekeeping missions in Haiti and Timor, there was no Pinochet memorabilia in view.[25]

There was also a new defense minister, the first woman in Latin America to hold such a post. Michelle Bachelet, daughter of an air force general who died in detention following the coup, encouraged conciliatory gestures from military officials. General Cheyre published an article early in 2003 saying that the coup of thirty years ago had not been a triumphant "military pronouncement" but a time of "acute civic enmity," and that human rights violations could have no justification.[26] Six months later Cheyre made a speech that the Chilean press described as historic. It contained a sharp critique of those civilian groups that had urged the military to overthrow the Allende government. "Never again, the sectors that incited us and officially backed our intervention in the crisis which they provoked. Never again, excesses, crimes, violence and terrorism," he said. "We are building an army for the 21st century. At the same time we have given proof that our process has committed itself to never again repeat human rights violations." It was time, he said, to move away from cold war–era thinking.[27] Cheyre consulted Lagos on both his article and the speech beforehand, showing his institution's deference to civilian rule.

Cheyre's "never again" speech irritated some sectors of the military, and he later reported receiving death threats. But there would be more expressions of mea culpa. A few weeks later, eight retired generals who had served in high-ranking posts during the Pinochet regime issued a statement condemning the clandestine exhumation and disposal of human rights victims' cadavers as illegal and deploring "the pain of the victims and their families."[28]

Human rights organizations praised these incidents but still found much to criticize in the slow pace of justice. In an open letter to Lagos, Human Rights Watch urged that Chilean courts investigate the secret removal of bodies from clandestine graves and hold accountable those responsible for covering up evidence of such crimes. The letter went on to suggest that the government coroner's office, the Servicio Médico Legal, should receive additional resources to carry out its forensic work and that military courts' jurisdiction should be limited to strictly military offenses.[29]

The Aylwin government's Truth and Reconciliation Commission had reported on deaths and disappearances under the Pinochet regime, but there had been no official reckoning for the thousands of Chileans who had survived torture during detention. On August 12, 2003, President Lagos announced on television an initiative to deal with the country's unresolved human rights legacy. One proposal provided for any human rights cases still under the jurisdiction of military courts to be transferred to civilian courts within a month. In addition, civilian courts would be given authority to subpoena documents from the armed forces. The government would offer the Servicio Médico Legal an external specialist to advise on ways to improve its procedures for identifying victims' remains. He rejected a proposal from conservative political leaders to place a time limit on court investigations into human rights cases. And a special commission would be formed to draw up a list of victims of torture, with some form of compensation given to those who had suffered.

The eight-member National Commission on Political Imprisonment and Torture, led by Bishop Sergio Valech, spent six months interviewing 35,868 people, of which 27,235 were judged to have valid cases. An additional 8,000 cases were investigated over the next six months. The commission's work was publicized throughout the country, though not every victim opted to testify, and some observers criticized the lack of psychological support offered to those reliving horrific experiences.

The period in which the most human rights violations were committed was the time immediately following the 1973 coup, when more than 18,000 people were tortured. Arrests were indiscriminate, and most victims were innocent civilians. Of the 3,400 women who testified, nearly all reported some form of sexual abuse or rape, and many told the commission they had never reported their experiences to anyone until then.

Another 5,266 people were tortured by the DINA or another specialized military group, the Comando Conjunto, in the period from January 1974 until August 1977, when the regime reorganized its security forces. The commission identified over one thousand sites, including schools and hospitals as well as police and military installations, where prisoners were tortured.

In a televised presidential address November 28, 2004, Lagos said the victims identified by the commission would receive monthly pensions of about $190 as well as health, education, and social welfare subsidies. The victims' identities and personal details were to be kept secret, though the commission published some extracts of their testimonies.

Human Rights Watch noted that the report, which concentrated on the suffering of the victims rather than investigating the perpetrators, was unlikely to have much impact in any judicial prosecutions. But it did at least give official, public recognition to experiences that tens of thousands of Chileans had endured. The physical trauma had taken a heavy psychological toll on many torture victims, leaving them humiliated, depressed, and often unable to keep a job or sustain close relationships.

Each person who testified was given a copy of the commission's report. Lagos said that on a number of occasions on his travels within Chile he was confronted by a former prisoner holding the report. "Even in some of the most remote parts of the country, someone would approach to say, 'I am case number such and such' and ask me to sign his copy of the report," he said. "As if to verify that yes, I was a prisoner but for political reasons. I am a part of Chilean history."[30]

V

More than a decade had passed since the Sociedad Benefactora y Educacional Dignidad, better known as Colonia Dignidad, had lost its status as a charity. The Aylwin government had tried various legal maneuvers against the secretive German colony, as had officials during the Frei government. But Colonia Dignidad continued to flourish as lawyers for the sect fought what one Chilean senator described as "a guerrilla war in the courts," while enjoying the support of an extensive network of right-wing political contacts—including former junta member and conservative senator General Rodolfo Stange. It had transformed itself from a charity to a diversified business group, with holdings in mining, real estate, and agriculture worth an estimated $100 million.[31] Villa Baviera, as the community was now called, still remained impenetrable to outsiders, its premises accessible only by a long dirt road and protected by high walls and elaborate security systems.

Its leader, former Luftwaffe medic Paul Schafer, had fled the country when the parents of several Chilean children attending the colony's boarding school filed charges of sexual abuse. The families had believed their offspring would receive an excellent private education, comparable to what was offered at the German bilingual schools in other parts of the country. When Chilean police raided the farm property and two other sites owned by the sect, Villa Baviera's attorneys filed no less than seventy different lawsuits, accusing the authorities of "state terrorism."[32] Schafer, who was living under an assumed name in Argentina, had turned the administration over to a trusted associate, and for a while it appeared that nothing would ever change.

There were some fears that an aggressive police action might result in an armed confrontation with colony residents and their local supporters or perhaps a mass suicide similar to the 1978 events at the Jonestown compound in Guyana. The judicial investigation proceeded slowly in the face of Villa Baviera's legal stonewalling, and it seemed extraordinary that the sect had continued to operate with such impunity under three democratically elected governments.

Finally, on March 10, 2005, Schafer was discovered in a Buenos Aires suburb and, after two days of negotiations, was extradited to Chile. At a court hearing he was charged with the sexual abuse of twenty-five children and was also under investigation for the disappearance of political prisoners during the Pinochet regime. Some twenty-two other leaders of the sect were also charged with child abuse.

Another raid on the colony by Chilean police turned up the largest privately owned weapons arsenal ever discovered in the country. The cache included three containers filled with machine guns and other automatic weapons, hand grenades, rocket launchers, and large quantities of ammunition, along with an armored tank. Some of the arsenal was of WWII vintage with German inscriptions whereas other weapons were newer. Officials also discovered an old electroshock machine, similar to what was once used on psychiatric patients, and parts of automobiles later traced to missing political prisoners.

A policeman taking part in the raid recounted how they discovered a trapdoor covered by a rug under Schafer's bed. The door led to a chamber containing high-tech gadgetry such as pencils that could shoot bullets, a dart-shooting camera, and several walking canes fitted to shoot projectiles.[33] Investigators found a second weapons cache with more rocket launchers and grenades on the grounds of a restaurant run by the colony in a nearby town.

On August 25, 2005, Chilean authorities entered Villa Baviera to officially take control of the property and its assets and assigned a government-appointed lawyer to administer the colony. The few hundred remaining residents told of living under a totalitarian cult leader who never allowed them to leave the property and backed up his rule with beatings and torture. The sexes were segregated, and some residents were forced to take drugs to curb physical desire or as a form of sedation.

In April of the following year, two representatives of the community delivered a three-and-a-half-page letter to La Moneda apologizing for the sexual and human rights abuses committed at Villa Baviera. They had been brainwashed by Schafer, their charismatic leader, they said, and offered more details of life at the settlement. "Among the children, our own children, Schafer was the ultimate authority," the letter said. Children born into the colony were separated from their parents, and Schafer selected his victims in such a way that adults would not have been aware of sexual abuse. "Some of us came to be his slaves, robots who just obeyed his order and worked without a schedule or any breaks." Failure to carry out Schafer's instructions could result in "electric shock, tranquilizers and isolation treatment, sometimes for long periods of time." The letter also said Colonia Dignidad's inhabitants now understood the gravity of their crimes and were willing to cooperate with judicial investigations. "We want to make the effort to say how sorry we are and to reintegrate into society."[34]

VI

There was yet another investigation underway that would expose the sordid financial practices of Pinochet and those close to him. A report by the U.S. Senate showed that for twenty-five years, Pinochet and his associates had amassed a personal fortune and concealed it in a complex network of foreign bank accounts and offshore shell corporations.

The investigation originated as an in-depth study of money laundering activities in the U.S. financial sector. This research provided the basis for many of the bank secrecy sections of the USA Patriot Act passed shortly after the 9/11 attacks (a date that also happens to be the anniversary of Chile's 1973 coup). The Patriot Act required American financial institutions to exercise due diligence when dealing with foreign political figures. Enabling corrupt foreign officials to hide funds of dubious provenance would result in prosecution for money laundering.

In February 2003 a Senate subcommittee began investigating just how well the Patriot Act's bank secrecy provisions were working. In the case of the Riggs Bank, the subcommittee investigators found two foreign clients for whom the money laundering regulations seemed never to have applied: the tiny African country of Equatorial Guinea and the former dictator of Chile, a country often praised for its modern, free market economic policies.

Riggs had twenty-eight Pinochet-related accounts and certificates of deposit, which it had concealed from U.S. banking regulators at the Office of the Comptroller of the Currency (OCC) for two years. In addition to the $1.6 million it helped Pinochet move from London to the United States during his detention, the bank had delivered over $1.9 million in four batches of cashiers checks to Pinochet in Chile, allowing him to withdraw substantial amounts of cash. The bank had also "resisted OCC requests for information, failed to identify or report suspicious account activity, and closed the Pinochet accounts only after a detailed OCC examination."[35]

The Allbrittons initially tried to downplay their relationship to Pinochet, telling the *Washington Post* through a family spokesman that Joseph Allbritton had "met Pinochet twice and the two men were not friends."[36] But as the U.S. investigation continued, Riggs Bank officials pleaded guilty to felony charges, paid more than $41 million in civil and criminal fines, and agreed to a takeover by the PNC Financial Services Group of Pittsburgh. The bank and the Allbrittons also agreed to pay $9 million to victims of the Pinochet regime after a human rights lawyer successfully petitioned a Spanish court to begin criminal proceedings.[37]

The Riggs Bank was the largest but not the only recipient of Pinochet funds. Other financial institutions included Citigroup, the U.S. branch of the Banco de Chile, the Espiritu Santo Bank in Florida, the Ocean Bank and Pine Bank in Miami, the Bank of America, the Banco Atlántico, and Coutts and Co., a finance company that later became part of Banco Santander. The Senate report *Money Laundering and Foreign Corruption: Enforcement of the Patriot Act, Supplemental Staff Report on U.S. Accounts Used by Augusto Pinochet* was 406 pages long, but its authors said there was evidence of still more Pinochet accounts in the United States, of which "limited Subcommittee resources prevent an exhaustive analysis."[38]

Among the more damning items in the report's appendix was a photocopy of three different passports Pinochet had used to open his accounts. The U.S. Senate report found Pinochet had used ten different identities, along with his own name, to open his bank accounts: Augusto P. Ugarte, A. Ugarte, A.P. Ugarte, José Pinochet, José P. Ugarte, José Ugarte, José Ramón Ugarte, J. Ramón Ugarte, José R. Ugarte, and Daniel Lopez. His wife and children had also used multiple identities to open either joint or separate accounts, and there were also at least ten offshore companies controlled by Pinochet and his associates.

The U.S. Senate report sparked a political storm in Santiago. The Chilean congress formed a commission to determine whether Pinochet's accounts contained stolen government funds while the judiciary and tax authorities began their own investigations. Court-appointed physicians determined that Pinochet, who was suffering from heart, circulatory, and neurological problems, was still fit to stand trial. The press coverage ranged from critical to scathing, even in conservative news media. The *Clinic,* a satirical magazine founded during Pinochet's detention in London, featured a cover designed as a wanted poster with a well-known 1973 photograph of the former dictator in dark glasses, offering an $8 million reward for his capture.[39]

Pinochet and his wife, two sons, and three daughters gave statements to a judge during a preliminary inquiry in August 2005, and all claimed ignorance of any financial wrongdoing. Pinochet's wife, Maria Lucía Hiriart, testified that her husband had always been "very savings-minded, very orderly."[40] She couldn't recall having opened any bank accounts abroad except for one joint account with her husband. Augusto Jr. attributed any unexplained funds as having come from Cuban-American donors to his father's defense fund during his arrest in London. Lucía, the eldest of the Pinochet offspring, said she had heard something about a Riggs account in London and some donations but claimed not to know much more than that. Her sister Veronica said she had no knowledge of her parents' finances, and that, in her judgment, their lifestyle was fairly modest. Marco Antonio Pinochet said he knew his father had a foreign bank account but didn't know whether it was in Switzerland or Luxembourg. The youngest Pinochet daughter, Jacqueline, said her parents had always encouraged them to save, and that a Riggs Bank official had once offered to open an account for her but that she did not have the money to do so. It is unclear whether any of the family had read the U.S. Senate report, which documented bank accounts in all their names.[41]

A revealing moment came when the judge questioned Pinochet, who was supposed to be suffering from memory loss, about the millions of dollars held in U.S. bank accounts. When the judge misspoke, giving a figure in pesos rather than dollars, Pinochet reacted abruptly. "Whaaaat?" The judge quickly corrected himself, repeating the amount in dollars, and Pinochet agreed.[42]

Carlos Cerda, one of Chile's most respected and independent jurists, headed the subsequent inquiry into Pinochet's foreign bank accounts. At his first meeting with Pinochet at his home, the former dictator was evasive and meandering in his answers, blaming others for any irregularities in his accounts. "I have a very bad memory, I never evaded taxes. When it was time to prepare the tax return, others prepared the papers for me. I didn't intervene, I signed," he told Cerda. When asked about the false passports, Pinochet claimed not to recall either the number of documents or any of the aliases used. "They told me that for my own security they were going to give me some passports, for my security, but I didn't use these passports, I don't remember what happened with them," he said.[43]

Later in the interrogation Pinochet seemed to admit to having opened bank accounts under false names. Cerda showed him documents with his signature, which Pinochet acknowledged as his own, and asked why he had opened an account under the name of Augusto Ugarte. "I don't know what it could be, it was because of the permanent threat, because Garzón [the Spanish judge seeking his extradition] did not stop looking for accounts," he said. But as Cerda's questioning became more specific, asking about offshore investments and monetary transfers, Pinochet became vague in his answers, claiming not to remember. He admitted he had an account in his real name at the Riggs branch in London, to which people in Chile had sent funds during his arrest, when he was "without a cent." Cerda then asked him if Riggs Bank had allowed Pinochet's associates to deliver funds in cash to him when he was under arrest.

Pinochet answered that Scotland Yard detectives had stolen the money from him. "I was guarding the money in a very safe place but I noticed that these gentlemen [Scotland Yard] had surveillance throughout the house," he said.[44]

A second interrogation took place two days later, and once again Pinochet expressed ignorance or no memory of the various shell companies or the circumstances of his real estate transactions. There was a third interrogation the following week, when Cerda handed Pinochet a passport bearing his photo and the name José Ramon Ugarte. But even when confronted with concrete evidence against him, Pinochet seemed agitated but remained defiant. He insisted it was not his and that he was not the man in the photo. He maintained he used whatever passport his officials provided and that his accounts were administered by "those who managed my finances." Who were they? Pinochet said he could not remember, but there were numerous individuals. Cerda showed him another passport with the name Augusto P. Ugarte, and once again Pinochet refused to say whether he had ever used that alias or whether the signature and fingerprint were his.[45]

During a fourth interview, Cerda produced documents showing travel expenses and "service commissions" charged during some of his trips abroad. Among the funds listed was $2.5 million for a 1997 trip to China and Britain. Pinochet answered that he didn't know who was in charge of his finances. He admitted he had used the name Daniel Lopez at some point in his U.S. banking transactions, "But in the United States that is not a sin." Cerda tried to elicit information about holdings he might have in other countries, and Pinochet indicated that he might have accounts or property in Britain, Gibraltar, and Switzerland as well as in the United States. But he could offer no specific information.[46]

On November 23, 2005, Cerda issued four indictments against Pinochet: tax evasion, falsifying official documents, use of false passports, and failing to report his financial and real estate holdings on his tax statements. He was placed under house arrest but released on bail in view of his age and the fact that, having just celebrated his ninetieth birthday, Pinochet did not represent a threat to the public. His family and associates maintained that he was too sickly to undergo any further judicial investigation, but Pinochet's legal troubles were far from finished.

Another judge was investigating Operation Colombo, a notorious human rights case from 1975 in which one hundred nineteen Chilean leftists disappeared and were alleged to have died in shootouts in neighboring Argentina. The missing Chileans were in fact being held in Chilean detention centers or dead, but the regime's security agency, the DINA, planted bogus stories in the Argentine press, with photographs of dead bodies and a list of one hundred nineteen names. The Chilean press had picked up the story, with one paper using the headline, "Chileans Exterminated Like Rats." It was later discovered that the bodies in the photographs were Argentines killed by a death squad, and that the list of Chilean names was the same one the Catholic Church's human rights department had used when filing a habeas corpus petition in their behalf. The fact that the names bore the same misspellings in both in the habeas corpus writ and the DINA-inspired "news" stories was a giveaway.[47]

The investigating judge brought Pinochet and former DINA chief Manuel Contreras face-to-face for a joint interrogation on November 14, 2005. The two men, once the closest of collaborators, had not seen other for years but had already begun blaming each other. Contreras had told judicial investigators that Pinochet was the one responsible for the DINA's actions, whereas Pinochet claimed that the former DINA chief had wanted to take over the country and had attempted to bribe him. "I remember why I fired him. He offered me some funds deposited abroad and I fired him for this. I rejected the offer he made me." Pinochet acknowledged that Contreras did not operate independently but denied that the two of them maintained frequent, almost daily contact. "I don't remember, but it's not true. It's not true and if it were true, I don't remember," he said.[48]

VII

Judge Cerda was still trying to estimate the value of Pinochet's fortune, even as the former dictator feigned memory loss. In early 2006 he sent a research team to each of Pinochet's residences as well as to the army's war and military academies to take an inventory of the former dictator's massive private library. The investigators discovered at least fifty-five thousand volumes and would spend over two hundred hours cataloging Pinochet's books and another two hundred hours trying to establish their value.

They did not find a well-tended collection, cataloged and carefully stored on shelves; instead the former dictator's massive collection was less a library than a jumbled hoard of books. At Los Boldos, Pinochet's coastal estate, investigators were amazed at the sheer number of volumes crammed into boxes or stacked, unshelved, in the library, which had become a kind of forgotten storage room for clothing, toiletries, and various household goods. The library had not been cleaned for some time, and many of the books were covered with dust, which suggested that among the former dictator's family, friends, and extensive staff, no one had thought to look after the collection or was even aware of its worth. It was not clear whether the books were read or even handled very often after their acquisition, for none of the Pinochet family members were known to have intellectual or academic interests.

The investigative team found many rare volumes and first editions "of an extremely high patrimonial value." Cerda's investigators located some book dealers in Santiago who had counted Pinochet among their clients; one recalled him as a compulsive customer who wanted to have everything ever published about Napoleon Bonaparte. Cerda also discovered that Pinochet had ordered military attachés at Chilean embassies abroad to acquire certain titles for him. His investigators estimated Pinochet's collection to be worth at least $2.8 million, mostly acquired with public funds.

While the researchers took their inventory, Pinochet made an appearance, dressed in a Lacoste T-shirt and Bermuda shorts and accompanied by a doctor, an attendant, and two armed bodyguards. Pinochet was walking by himself with his cane and sat at the desk to watch what was taking place. At one point he asked one of the researchers about a small magnifying glass she was wearing as a pendant. He said he had some magnifying glasses as well and began rummaging in the desk drawer but failed to locate any. Pinochet then left a short time later and did not reappear during any of the team's subsequent visits. One of the researchers remarked afterward that it must have been painful for him to see them sorting through some of his most prized possessions. Pinochet's grandson reported that he was so disturbed by the investigators' visit that he took to his bed for a few days after this incident.[49]

Pinochet's family and associates continued to maintain that he was too frail to withstand the multiple judicial cases descending upon him. They were also under investigation: a few days after the visit to Los Boldos, Pinochet's wife, Lucía, and their five grown children were ordered to appear before the Santiago court on charges of tax evasion and falsifying passports. Also ordered to appear were Pinochet's private secretary, a daughter-in-law, and his personal financial advisor. All but one obeyed the order and duly appeared at the court, where they were released on bail. The missing Pinochet family member was about to make headlines in Washington and Santiago.

Inés Lucía, the eldest of the Pinochet siblings, drove across the Andes to Argentina and took a plane from Buenos Aires to Washington, D.C., with an eccentric plan to request political asylum. Why she would seek refuge in the United States, the very country where her father had been afraid to travel and where the investigation into her family's fortune had originated, is something of an enigma, but her actions probably reflected the extreme stress she was experiencing. Chilean officials immediately issued an international warrant for her arrest, as the country's tax authority claimed she owned approximately $850,000 in back taxes. That evening Argentine Interpol officials notified the Chilean government that the sixty-year-old Inés Lucía Pinochet—now officially a fugitive from justice—had in fact entered the country and was headed to the United States.

She later issued a statement claiming that she had asked for a meeting with Judge Cerda to inform him of her travel plans and to respond to a story in the *El Mercurio* newspaper concerning her unpaid taxes but had not been given an appointment.[50] This version of events is undermined by the fact that she opted to take a longer overland route across the Argentine border rather than simply catching a flight from Santiago, and that family members claimed she told them she'd taken a plane to

Washington rather than her intended destination, Miami, because there were no available flights to Miami.

Upon arrival at Washington's Dulles Airport, Inés Lucía Pinochet was pulled over for special screening, informed that her multiple entry visa had been canceled, and placed under guard by U.S. customs and border protection agents. A spokesman for the Department of Homeland Security said she was in custody at the Arlington County detention facility "pending resolution of her immigration status."[51]

Her son Rodrigo García Pinochet flew to Washington to help his mother. As a schoolboy, García Pinochet had been riding in the same automobile with his grandfather in 1986 when leftist gunmen ambushed the motorcade, killing five bodyguards, and he was steadfastly loyal to the former dictator. He was irked by the presence of reporters and television cameras outside the detention center and even more annoyed when he was refused access to his mother for security reasons. "It had taken me over a day to arrive there and now a stupid gringo was not going to stop me from seeing my mother," he later wrote. Immigration officials said he might be able to speak with her by telephone, and then they informed him his mother had been moved to a different detention center and asked him to leave. García Pinochet was shepherded out of the building through a back exit "for [his] own safety" and to a nearby taxi stand. He felt "beaten down, exhausted, just wanting it to be over," but also worried that this could be the beginning of a prolonged London-style detention for his mother.[52]

In Santiago, Chilean authorities seemed somewhat embarrassed by the whole affair, as if the Pinochet family tax fraud case was the kind of dirty laundry best not washed under the glare of international publicity. President Lagos told reporters that negotiations were underway to arrange for Inés Lucía Pinochet's return. "All of this has an effect on the country—it's sad," he said.[53] Two days after she arrived, U.S. immigration officials managed to persuade Lucía to fly back to Chile voluntarily. On her return, she found Judge Cerda waiting for her at the Santiago airport. "Ms. Lucía, how nice that you've arrived," he said. "Please come with me so that I can arraign you."[54]

TEN Unfinished Business

I

"I am trying to trust Judge Guzmán, but it is so slow down there. I understand that he is very decent and that he has a lot of cases, but sometimes I get very upset, because I have this feeling inside that my brother may still be alive."[1] Olga Weisfeiler, sister of the Pennsylvania State mathematics professor who disappeared in southern Chile in 1985, was horrified to find information about her brother's disappearance in some of the documents the U.S. State Department had declassified in 2000. She read and reread the documents, which suggested the U.S. embassy had neglected to pursue the case. "The 'Mickey Mouseing' around we've done with this case is disgraceful and though I think forcefulness should have been applied a long time ago, it wasn't," U.S. consul Jayne Kobliska wrote in a

1987 cable to an embassy colleague in Santiago.[2] Another memo, written by the CIA several months later, quotes a Chilean official whose identity is redacted: "Source states that among the many groups that were sent out to search for Weisfeiler after his disappearance was a group of CNI agents from Chile. Source labelled these CNI people as 'delinquents and assassins.' Source said they were among the first to search the area. Source believes they were sent in to clean the area of any evidence that would indicate that Weisfeiler had been murdered. COMMENT: This group may have also been used to plant evidence such as Weisfeiler's backpack."[3]

Later documents showed embassy officials wanting to launch an investigation, only to have Washington stipulate there would be no extra funds allotted for such expenses. For its part, the Chilean justice system had effectively dismissed the case, even going so far as to sell off Weisfeiler's backpack, tent, and other possessions—which might have offered vital clues to serious investigators—as part of a judicial auction of unclaimed goods. But a lawyer for the Weisfeiler family was able to get the case reactivated, with Judge Juan Guzmán presiding.

Olga, accompanied by her two children, traveled to Chile for the first time at the end of 2000, meeting with Guzmán and U.S. embassy officials, who promised full cooperation and support for the investigation. The family was interviewed by Chilean newspapers and television, raising hopes that the publicity might prompt new witnesses to come forward. Olga met with Viviana Diaz, the head of the support group for relatives of the disappeared, and was surprised to learn that the activist was unfamiliar with the case—though she assured the Weisfeilers they would be welcomed into the group. Olga was also disappointed by the lack of support from the Chilean Mathematical Society, which had hired a private investigator with funds raised by Boris Weisfeiler's academic colleagues shortly after his disappearance. The investigator turned out to be a former police officer fired for corruption.[4]

For two years Guzmán worked on the investigation, along with a sizeable backlog of other cases of Chileans missing or killed during the military regime. Even as U.S. officials raised the issue with their Chilean counterparts and the government of President Ricardo Lagos professed its support for the investigation, the judge encountered so many obstacles that he was unable to rule out any hypothesis in the case.

U.S. officials were reluctant to identify the unnamed informants in the declassified State Department and CIA documents, while some of the army and police records requested by investigators had disappeared, were reported to have been destroyed, or were simply denied.

Meanwhile, Olga made repeated trips to Chile, meeting with government officials and holding press conferences at the U.S. embassy to appeal for information on her brother's disappearance. Mustering her courage, she toured the area where Boris Weisfeiler was last seen and even visited Villa Baviera, formerly Colonia Dignidad. The colony's new leaders, she said, proved evasive. "They are not saying he isn't there, they just say that they are too young to know what happened twenty years ago," she said. "It is very depressing. I kept looking and thinking in which corner, under which tree is my brother kept."[5]

In October 2002 the Chilean Supreme Court appointed four new judges to take over some of Guzmán's burdensome caseload, in a renewed effort to investigate the eleven hundred cases of forced disappearance during the Pinochet regime. The Weisfeiler case was transferred to Judge Alejandro Solis, who later interrogated Colonia Dignidad leader Paul Schafer following his extradition from Argentina. But Shafer, ailing and in a wheelchair, refused to say anything about the missing mathematician.[6]

Then in April 2005, Chile's judiciary reorganized the human rights caseloads once again, transferring the Weisfeiler case to another magistrate, Jorge Zepeda, who was also in charge of investigating Colonia Dignidad. Zepeda's work was praised by human rights attorneys; the judge conducted extensive interviews with former detainees and documented the torture and other abuses that occurred at the colony during the Pinochet regime.[7] Zepeda visited the area where Weisfeiler disappeared in 1985, retracing his route through the Andean foothills, and concluded that the mathematician had not drowned while crossing a river, as Chilean authorities had originally claimed.[8] U.S. ambassador Craig Kelly also visited the region, telling a local radio station that he was confident that the authorities were closer to solving the case. "The FBI is coordinating an investigation with Chilean authorities," he said. The opening of Colonia Dignidad and the arrest of Paul Schaffer had opened new possibilities, Kelly told Radio Bio Bio.[9] And Olga Weisfeiler received support from several members of the U.S. Senate and Congress, who signed letters urging the government to press the case with Chilean officials.

And yet the investigation stalled. On a 2008 trip to Chile, Olga Weisfeiler held a press conference at the U.S. embassy to decry the lack of progress in the case. Judge Zepeda had not responded to offers of help from the FBI, and many of the declassified U.S. documents dealing with the case had not been translated into Spanish. Zepeda had refused the Weisfeiler's Chilean lawyer access to documents prepared by local police detectives. "I have waited for better times, while other human rights cases have been solved," Olga Weisfeiler told reporters. "I am extremely disappointed that we have not made more progress when we have had so many opportunities to do so."[10] The case of Boris Weisfeiler, the lone American among Chile's *desaparecidos*, remained unsolved, along with over a thousand other cases.

Meanwhile, Judge Juan Guzmán had reluctantly retired from the bench in 2005 but did not abandon the cause of human rights. He joined the law faculty of the Universidad Central in Santiago and lent his legal assistance to members of Chile's largest indigenous group, the Mapuches, who were making their long-pent-up grievances felt in southern Chile.

II

> In the time of the Spaniards the Indians could not hold land; and a family, after having cleared a piece of ground, might be driven away, and the property seized by the government. The Chilian authorities are now performing an act of justice by making retribution to these poor Indians, giving to each man, according to his grade of life, a certain portion of land. The value of uncleared ground is very little.
>
> —Charles Darwin, *The Voyage of the Beagle*, November 26, 1832

Shortly after the 1960 earthquakes, volcanic eruption, and tsunamis that ravaged southern Chile, the owner of a large estate had a retaining wall built along the fence separating his property from lands occupied by the local indigenous community, the Mapuches. The dike did its job, preventing flooding on the Durán estate, whose owner was a well-known figure in conservative political circles and served as the president of Chile's national agriculture society. But it also blocked the flow of water running toward the local river and caused periodic flooding on nearly thirty acres adjacent to the estate. Over the years his Mapuche neighbors watched as Durán's cattle grazed on the green fields of his estate while their own undernourished livestock tried to survive by foraging in waterlogged, sticky clay.[11]

In May 2001 Domingo Durán, the estate's eighty-five-year old patriarch, was found unconscious outside his office in the nearby market town of Temuco. He had two severe head injuries and died in the hospital a few days later. Although a police investigation found no evidence that Durán had been attacked, his grieving son told the press that disputes with local Mapuche communities might have something to do with Durán's death. "It's a problem that goes back many years and affects not just ourselves but many people," he said.[12] And yet two years later the estate's contentious retaining wall came down, after protracted negotiations among the Mapuche community's representatives, officials from a variety of government agencies, and the Durán family. There was a 1991 law and a much older civic code prohibiting any property owner from actions liable to cause flooding on another property. More significantly, the Mapuche community leaders had the benefit of advocacy training and a working knowledge of how to negotiate Chile's legal system. In a ceremony attended by both Mapuche community members and Durán's son, indigenous leaders broke through the dike and happily predicted a brighter future for the community. The younger Durán remarked that his father had erred in building the retaining wall more than four decades earlier. "Nowadays it is necessary to work together in order to construct a country for us all," he said.[13]

The Mapuches have a fiercely proud history of resistance to outside invaders. In the fifteenth century, the Incas conquered much of what is now northern Chile, superimposing their society upon the Atacama

Desert's smaller indigenous groups. But as the Incas attempted to move into the southern forests, their expansion came to an abrupt halt.

Approximately one hundred fifty miles from Santiago, the Incas received word from defiant Mapuche leaders that their offers of "peace and friendship" were being rejected. At the Maule River, the twenty thousand Incan troops were confronted with fifteen to twenty thousand Mapuche warriors. Another diplomatic overture was proffered, with the Incans insisting they did not want to deprive the Mapuches of their lands but to "give them the means to live like men, to recognize the Sun god and his son as their king and lord." The Mapuches responded that they were determined to "waste no more time with words or vain reasoning but to fight to death or victory." Send us no more messages, they said, for we do not wish to hear them.[14] A bloody three-day battle ensued, and the larger Incan army was forced to retreat.

In the sixteenth century, the Spanish managed to gain control of lands south of the Maule River, building a series of forts in the territory they called the Araucania. Three centuries of conflict, uprisings, and Spanish military campaigns later, the colonial government had still not conquered the Mapuches. Alonso de Ercilla, a Spanish nobleman who had joined the Spanish crown's army, was so moved by the Mapuches' fearlessness that he composed an epic poem, *La Araucana*. It became one of the most important literary works of the period, a Spanish version of Homer's *Iliad* or Virgil's *Aeneid* in which the Mapuche leaders are depicted like heroes from the Trojan War. There is Caupolican, chosen to lead his people after demonstrating his superior strength by holding up a tree trunk for three days and three nights. He is later captured and executed by the Spanish forces, and *La Araucana* contains vivid scenes in which he is led in chains to a gruesome execution by slow impalement on a pointed stake. Caupolican never flinches during his ordeal and even manages to survive for a period until six archers shoot him full of arrows.[15]

His second in command, Lautaro, was captured by the Spanish and spent his childhood as the personal servant of Chile's conqueror, Pedro de Valdivia. After learning the tactics and ways of the Spanish, Lautaro escaped and rejoined his people, introducing the use of horses and building an army out of dispersed Mapuche communities for a brilliant offensive against Valdivia's forces. His story also inspired Pablo Neruda, the 1971 recipient of the Nobel Prize for Literature, to compose the poem "The Education of a Chieftain":

> He sniffed the scattered ash
> He wrapped his heart in black skins
> He deciphered the spiral thread of smoke.
> He made himself out of taciturn fibres.
> He oiled himself like the soul of the olive.
> He became glass of transparent hardness.
> He studied to be a hurricane wind
> He fought until his blood was extinguished
>
> Only then was he worthy of his people.[16]

The Mapuches continued to control a territory of almost thirty-eight thousand square miles beginning at the Bio Bio River some three hundred miles south of Santiago. Even after Chile gained independence, the Mapuches resisted domination, and southern Chile remained an autonomous region until a thirty-year military campaign finally annexed the territory in 1883.

As had happened in other countries of the Americas, the Mapuches were confined to reservations covering a fraction of the land they once owned. This destroyed their economy of agriculture and trading, even as increasing numbers of white settlers moved into the region and built large agricultural estates. Anthropologist Louis Faron observed that by 1968, so little land was available to Mapuche farmers that they were unable to let any part of their fields lie fallow for even a single season.[17]

The names of the Mapuche heroes, however, would be invoked during the country's war of independence and later passed down through generations of Chilean history and culture. Santiago's biggest entertainment venue is the Teatro Caupolican, while the figure of Lautaro has been appropriated by militant groups from the Far Right to the Far Left. One of the most notorious divisions of the DINA was the Lautaro Brigade. For more than thirty years its members maintained a pact of silence, until a tenacious judge investigating the disappearance of Chilean Communist

Party leaders finally elicited confessions from some of the group's former members. The Lautaro Brigade's brief was to kill and dispose of party members other DINA agents had arrested, with some of the victims injected with cyanide or other toxins before their bodies were dumped into the sea.[18] A small, armed leftist group, the Lautaro Popular Rebel Forces, operated for a period during the 1980s, and an anarchist youth organization also named itself after the Mapuche leader. *Lautaro* was a name selected to inspire fear and respect, but few Chileans were inclined to actually explore their own Mapuche roots.

III

The Allende government's agrarian reform program distributed two hundred seventy square miles Mapuche families between 1972 and September of 1973 and enacted legislation intended to improve social welfare in Mapuche communities. But the 1973 military coup and its aftermath hit Mapuche communities especially hard. Vengeful landowners joined the army and police in a manhunt to locate Mapuche beneficiaries of the land redistribution program. "The landowners had lists of names of the activists," said Reynaldo Mariqueo, general secretary of the Mapuche International Link. "The local police only had police cars, but the landowners had trucks and larger vehicles which they lent them to round up prisoners."[19]

The report by the National Commission on Truth and Reconciliation includes the cases of one hundred Mapuches killed or missing after being detained by the army or security forces, along with another twenty-three cases in which the commission could not reach a conclusion. According to Amnesty International, the real figure is likely to be higher, and that fear, poverty, and despair meant that only a small percentage of families affected came forward to present their cases at the time of their relatives' arrest or disappearance. Many Mapuches live in isolated rural communities, with some speaking little or no Spanish, and they may have been fearful about coming forward with their testimony, especially in situations where civilians who worked with the regime's security forces still lived nearby. One Mapuche activist told the organization in 1991 that he knew of several forced disappearances not included in the Truth Commission's report, and that in one case that was reported to the panel, a family later retracted their statement because they were still terrified of what might happen to them.[20] Four years later, members of the Pehuenche branch of the Mapuche told a visiting anthropologist that during the aftermath of the coup, twenty of their leaders had been roped together and thrown into the raging waters of the Bio Bio River. None survived.[21]

The division and loss of Mapuche lands reached a peak during the Pinochet regime, even as the former dictator was frequently photographed with Mapuches wearing traditional dress—one such picture on the Fundacion Pinochet Web site bears the caption, "Loved by the Araucana ethnic group."[22] Such images were part of the regime's propaganda machine, according to Reynaldo Mariqueo, though there were Mapuches with right-wing political sympathies who had good relations with the Chilean military. During the Pinochet years, roughly ten thousand acres of land that Salvador Allende's government had marked for redistribution was sold to private forestry companies.

At least 60 percent of all Chileans have some Mapuche ancestry, but in the face of widespread discrimination, many opt to deny this heritage. A study by a Universidad Católica sociologist revealed that between 1970 and 1990, 2,365 Chileans sought to legally change their names, and all but 19 of these applicants were Mapuche, Aymara, or Easter Islanders. The practice was still observed in 1999, when 200 Chileans of indigenous descent sought to change their names, with many citing discrimination as their motive.[23] The Chilean tennis player Marcelo Rios, asked by a reporter at an international tournament if he happened to have Indian blood, reacted by saying, "What if I called you a son of a whore?"[24]

Chilean advertising tends to employ only models and actors with lighter skin and hair coloring, though this is an observed practice even in Latin American countries with much larger indigenous populations than Chile. A giant billboard on the capital's main avenue showed a group of attractive young adults, all with light skin and European features, urging students to apply to the Universidad Central de Chile in

2007. And yet a subsequent visit to the Santiago campus where Judge Guzmán teaches reveals an ethnically diverse student body. "We are a society that is not openly racist, but there is discrimination against people with darker hair and darker skin. It is something nobody wants to talk about," said Marta Lagos, director of the Latinobarómetro polling agency. "Nobody wants to see dark-skinned models, even if they are dark-skinned themselves."[25]

Jaime Andrade Guenchocoy, a former advisor on indigenous affairs to the Lagos government, summed up the social results of centuries of discrimination: "In Chile we have a saying: there are no blond bus drivers and no dark-complected university professors." He observed that although poverty had decreased among the Chilean population as a whole, "Rural people tend to be poor, the Mapuches even poorer, and rural Mapuche women the poorest of all."[26]

Researchers have begun closer study of the effects of this impoverishment on indigenous Chileans. A study by the University of Chile School of Medicine revealed that the shorter stature of the Mapuches was not due to genetic differences—as many had previously believed—but to poverty. The authors compared Mapuche and non-Mapuche children in three separate socioeconomic categories employed by UNICEF: extreme, middle, and low poverty. They encountered some difficulty in compiling their samples, for there were "few nonindigenous children in the extreme poverty group," and in all three strata the Mapuche were always the poorest. Nevertheless, they were able to conclude that the Mapuche children's lower growth reflected their poorer living conditions and demonstrated "the need for socioeconomic development programs and effective public health measures."[27]

IV

Of the four civilian governments in office since the Pinochet regime, the Aylwin administration may have had the best relationship with Chile's indigenous groups. Aylwin took some initial steps to address long-standing grievances by passing a law making it a duty of the state to protect indigenous rights and lands. The National Corporation of Indigenous Development (CONADI) was set up to help mediate property conflicts and provide additional lands for displaced communities. Another proposal, a constitutional reform recognizing the existence of Chile's indigenous people, stalled in congress. The reforms fell far short of what the Mapuche and other Chilean indigenous groups had hoped: recognition of them as people and holders of collective rights.

CONADI and other government agencies undertook a number of programs, including the incorporation of indigenous languages in the Chilean school curriculum and the establishment of academies for teaching the languages. CONADI also launched a Mapuche television news show, to be broadcast twice a week. The Chilean foreign ministry sponsored Mapuche cultural exhibitions abroad, including a show of art and artifacts at a Beijing museum in 2008 and another in New York in 2009. The ministry's export department, ProChile, has helped some Mapuche enterprises find overseas markets. A cooperative of seventy Mapuche families produce *merken,* a traditional seasoning made from dried and smoked red chili, toasted coriander seed, and salt and sold to gourmet shops and restaurants. Another group of one hundred fifty Mapuche women produce traditional woolen textiles sold in Chile and abroad.

One Santiago municipality showcased a young opera student performing an aria from Bizet's *Carmen* in the Mapuche language, Mapudungun, which the mayor announced would be recorded on a CD and distributed at cultural venues around the country.[28] The official promotion of indigenous cultures appears to have changed the way some Chileans view their heritage, and more young Mapuches living in urban areas are proclaiming their identity.

If some progress had been made in raising awareness of Chile's indigenous heritage, events in the far south suggested a long and bitter struggle lay ahead. Since its formation, CONADI has distributed thousands of acres of land to the Mapuches and other indigenous communities, but this has not been enough to restore traditional livelihoods, and ancient territorial conflicts have reemerged in a different form. Budget constraints have limited the agency's ability to obtain land, and in some parts of southern Chile real estate prices have doubled as private companies compete to buy land. The growing Chilean economy in the 1990s expanded forestry, commercial fisheries, road construction, and hydroelectric projects near Mapuche communities, and by 2000 an estimated 3.7 million acres had been planted with pine and eucalyptus trees for commercial timber operations. The growth of the Chilean forestry and wood products industry has not produced many jobs for local Mapuches, and community leaders complain that the commercial tree plantations dry up their water, cause soil erosion, and damage the growth of native plants used in traditional medicine. "The Mapuches are not against development," said Reynaldo Mariqueo. "The problem lies in the fact that these big projects are being carried out without any consultation or participation on the part of the local communities, just imposed from above."[29]

In late 2007 the Chilean congress finally approved a forestry protection law, fifteen years after it had been presented, the longest period any law had been under negotiation. The country's powerful forestry industry, led by two of the largest business groups, had lobbied long and hard against the legislation. The new law created a fund for conservation, environmental recovery, and sustainable projects, plus an additional fund to "boost scientific and technological research related to the native forest and the protection of its biodiversity, soil, water sources, flora, fauna and associated ecosystems."[30] It also sought to protect water sources by prohibiting the felling of trees near rivers, glaciers, and other bodies of water or on land with steep slopes.

Critics of the law called it only a small step forward, with a weak system in place for enforcement. One senator compared it to "putting cops on the street with toy guns." "Roughly 97 percent of the fines which the National Forestry Service hands out are not paid," Senator Alejandro Navarro said.[31] The new law contained a special clause that allowed the harvest of dead alerce trees, an endangered species that is protected by law, but no provision to strengthen the forestry service's authority, raising concerns that loggers would continue to cut the trees and sell the wood.[32]

There have been a few success stories in which indigenous communities have been able to protect local resources. A group of the Pehuenche branch of the Mapuche people joined forces with the World Wildlife

Fund to create a twelve thousand–acre park to preserve araucaria trees and other local species and to promote low-impact tourism. The project also received support from the Chilean state development corporation and the local municipal government.[33]

And on the coast of Chiloé, the northernmost island in Chile's Patagonia archipelago, a small community of the Huilliche branch of the Mapuches complained to government authorities and NGOs that a nearby fish farm run by the Norwegian company Marine Harvest had damaged local fish and shellfish. For generations the Huilliches had used stone corrals for fishing, working with the tides to trap their catch in shallow pools. After the fish farm opened, residents noticed the mussels were darker and had a bad taste and that fresh-caught fish had a different texture and rotted more quickly. There was fish oil accumulating on the rocks where algae used to grow. Huilliche fishermen reported that the selling price of local sea urchins had been cut in half, with a corresponding drop in their income. Marine Harvest representatives visited the community, met with Huilliche leaders, and afterward announced they would remove the fish farm within five months. A community spokesman pointed out that the company's departure did not result in any job losses. "They make millions and millions and none of it stays here," said Alex Coicheo. "There are no people from our community that work for the company and no social benefit for our community. Not any kind of relationship."[34]

V

An earlier, unsuccessful struggle ensued during the Spanish utility company ENDESA's construction of the Ralco dam on the Bio Bio, which would create a one thousand–acre reservoir. The Pehuenche are forest dwellers, and they rely on access to renewable woodland resources to survive. The company offered the six hundred indigenous residents living in the area a relocation package, including new land, housing, a school, and credit. Some ninety families accepted the buyout; one young goatherd commented that the land was unproductive anyway and that she was ready to seek new opportunities. Other residents were resolute in their determination to stay, noting that the dam would flood their community burial ground and that several herbs they needed for their traditional medicines did not grow in the lands ENDESA had offered.

In Santiago, environmental groups opposed the dam, noting that it would destroy an ecosystem that was home to several species of fish found nowhere else in the world. The director of the national environmental commission was fired after the agency's board ruled against the project, and its decision was soon reversed under the commission's newly appointed management. The Frei government also removed three members of CONADI when it looked as though the indigenous affairs commission would vote against the project. A former CONADI director raised questions about those families willing to leave the area, noting that many were illiterate and may have believed they had no choice in the matter.[35]

It is unclear how well CONADI was able to deal with the needs of indigenous communities during this period; although providing legal services was part of its mission, its means to do so were severely limited. A report by the American Anthropological Association's Human Rights Committee noted that the agency "lacked the institutional capacity to defend the interests of the Pehuenche communities. Its single lawyer does not have a staff and receives a gasoline allowance of only 150 dollars for the entire fiscal year; his regional office is 300 kilometers [186 miles] from Pehuenche territory. The Pehuenche do not have travel funds to meet with him. CONADI has been ineffective in dealing with small conflicts and is already overwhelmed by the negotiations with ENDESA over the issue of land exchange in Ralco-Lepoy, which is only one part of the overall resettlement planning problem."[36]

The International Finance Corporation (IFC), a member of the World Bank group that was helping to finance ENDESA's hydroelectric projects, hired anthropologist Theodore Downing to investigate charges by environmental and indigenous organizations. The report Downing produced was highly critical of ENDESA's actions, but the Pehuenche community would not have access to the information it contained, even though Downing's contract with the IFC stipulated that the anthropologist would report his findings in a series of workshops and assemblies with the entire tribe.

The report described how the Bio Bio area was undergoing rapid transformation, with unchecked migration, land speculation, and deforestation. Nonindigenous traders paid the Pehuenche only half the going rate in the region for livestock and timber, and, in some cases, timber dealers were giving local Pehuenches small amounts of money to harvest their trees before abandoning the area, leaving the indigenous landowners to face charges of breaking Chilean forestry laws. In some cases, Pehuenches were unable to pay the fines and lost the rights to their land. Downing also noted that from 1988 to 1994, millions of dollars' worth of timber had been taken from Pehuenche community lands as a direct and indirect result of dam construction; in other words, an impoverished indigenous community was subsidizing the Chilean hydroelectric industry at an enormous cost to its own livelihood.

Downing reported that the Pehuén Foundation, an entity set up by ENDESA to help indigenous families affected by the hydroelectric project, had laudable goals but was not effective in its actions, in large part because it failed to provide for the Pehuenche families' informed participation. He also visited an area where ENDESA proposed to relocate the families, high in the Andes and covered with eleven feet of snow in the winter months.

The IFC did not release the report to the Pehuenche community, even as ENDESA was negotiating with indigenous families for their land. When IFC staff presented ENDESA officials with a summary of Downing's findings, the executives rejected it and threatened to sue both the IFC and the anthropologist if the report were released to either the Pehuenches or the public.[37]

According to the terms of Chile's 1992 indigenous rights law, land could not be sold or exchanged without the unanimous consent of the community. But Chilean officials, only too aware of the country's rising energy demands, cited another law allowing for expropriation in the interest of providing energy for the general good. They also said that hydroelectric power would cause less pollution than importing additional natural gas from Argentina.

In August 1998 a few hundred Mapuches held a demonstration outside the Chilean congress in Valparaíso to protest the government's noncompliance with the indigenous rights law. The project went ahead, but so did the protests. In March 2002 a group of Mapuche families blocking an access road to the construction site were violently broken up by carabinero police, who indiscriminately hit women, children, and old people and arrested fifty demonstrators, whose cases were handed over to a military court.[38] The Ralco dam was inaugurated later that year, providing a case study of "an authoritarian culture where dialogue is not practiced, where decisions are taken by those who have political and economic power, where those who are powerless are not heard," according to José Aylwin, director of the Observatory for Indigenous Rights. He said that both ENDESA and the government had been less than transparent in handling the project.[39]

The Pehuenche Mapuches may have failed to stop the Ralco dam, but the campaign had increased contacts among indigenous groups throughout Chile and in other countries, as well as with environmental and human rights organizations. There were more protests, ranging from nonviolent marches and sit-ins to road blockades, arson, and vandalism. The official reaction was heavy-handed, drawing the attention of human rights groups. When two digger machines were set on fire at a forestry plantation near the Mapuche community of Temucuicui, two hundred heavily armed special forces police arrived at the village.[40] "The police often fail to distinguish peaceful protest from illegal actions that present a genuine threat to public order by clamping down equally hard on both, sometimes with indiscriminate violence and racist insults," Human Rights Watch said in a 2004 report.[41]

As protests and property crimes mounted, so did demands from landowners and rightist politicians in the Chilean congress for a government crackdown. Reports in the conservative news media mentioned possible links with leftist extremist groups, who allegedly viewed the Mapuche conflict as an opportunity for a comeback. During a 2002 congressional debate, one conservative senator, representing a district with a large Mapuche population, urged that "the full rigor of the law" be applied to any violent Mapuche groups. "Their conduct has created a state of insecurity and fear that is incompatible with the full functioning of the rule of law," said Alberto Espina, who led a senate committee to study the public security aspects of the conflict but not the origins of the conflict itself. Those invited to testify included fifteen prominent landowners, who described how their properties had been attacked. Only one Mapuche representative was invited.

The draft of the hearings' report was criticized as one-sided; at the insistence of a Christian Democrat senator, the committee agreed to hear more testimony from Mapuche leaders, who offered a different view of the issue. One indigenous leader told the committee that it was difficult to analyze public security in the region, because "from a Mapuche point of view their security has been under threat for a long time." The Mapuche representatives did not justify the violence but spoke of the destruction of their lands and government indifference to their culture.[42]

VI

The Mapuches do not speak with one voice, and around thirty organizations representing different indigenous groups and communities have formed since 1990. In 2005 one Mapuche leader, Aucan Huilcaman of the Council of All Lands, attempted to run for president. He caused a stir when he entered Santiago on horseback, bearing thirty-nine thousand signatures backing his candidacy. Chile's electoral service did not recognize the petition, saying the list needed to be notarized. The fee for such a service was approximately $2 per signature, beyond the means of a small farmer. The Mapuche leader also had issues with Chile's Communist Party, complaining that indigenous members of the party had been expelled when they wanted to support his candidacy.[43]

Huilcaman also challenged the Chilean education ministry over an impending agreement with Microsoft to produce a version of Windows in Mapudungun. This had been done without the Mapuche people's consent, he said, and the version of the language Microsoft proposed to use was inaccurate. "We feel like Microsoft and the Chilean Education Ministry have overlooked us by deciding to set up a committee without our consent, our participation and without the slightest consultation," he said. "This is a form of piracy, the usurpation of our collective creation and language."[44]

But Huilcaman seemed to spend as much time traveling abroad to confer with other indigenous groups or NGOs as he did in working on local Mapuche issues. A Chilean journalist, consulting immigration records at the Santiago Airport, discovered that Huilcaman had made no less than 187 trips abroad over the past decade. When asked about his frequent travels, he admitted to having been all over the world and being as familiar with Zurich, New York, and Washington, D.C., as he was with Temuco, a city in southern Chile that lies in the heart of Mapuche territory. He dismissed criticism of his travels as "a typical campaign against our people. International organizations from New Zealand to Guatemala invite me," he said. "My friend Evo Morales has suffered these same attacks."[45]

Huilcaman's Council of All Lands is part of the Arauco Malleco Coordinating Group of Communities in Conflict (CAM). The group formed from Mapuche communities either making or defending land claims, and its leaders admit to engaging in some violent actions as a means to their end. According to Human Rights Watch, "Some of what its members consider defensive actions is in fact criminal actions that warrant prosecution."[46]

In other cases, however, authorities have chosen to apply antiterrorist statutes, and under Chilean law, anyone can file a criminal complaint charging that they have been the victim of a terrorist offense. This opened the way for landowners and companies to initiate terrorist proceedings against Mapuches, who might otherwise be charged with more mundane crimes such as arson or vandalism in the wake of a police investigation.

The governor of the southern province of Bio Bio brought terrorism charges against a Mapuche leader, Victor Ancalaf Laupe, for setting fire to four trucks and a digging machine in three separate incidents. The trucks and machinery were owned by ENDESA, and the fires occurred during protests against the Ralco dam. In 2003 Ancalaf was sentenced to ten years and one day of imprisonment after finding him responsible for all three incidents; the following year the sentence was halved when a court acquitted him of two of the attacks.[47]

Chilean officials have tried to draw a distinction between terrorist crimes and the existence of terrorist groups, believing in the former but not the latter. A 2003 U.S. survey on world terrorism said that "no incidents of explicit terrorism" occurred that year in Chile. Nevertheless, eight people were convicted of terrorism in 2003 and 2004, while others were awaiting trial on similar charges.

Developments over the next few years caused the U.S. State Department to revise its view of certain Mapuche organizations. According to the report for 2007,

> Chileans requested FBI support on two domestic terrorism cases. Coordinadora Arauco Melleca (CAM) is a violent Mapuche Indian group in southern Chile that has burnt fields and attacked police while fighting for land it claims belongs to it. CAM appeared to have begun organizing itself more like a guerrilla group, attacks late in the year demonstrated increased planning and a more professional use of weapons and tactics. Walter Wendelin, a representative of the Spain-based Basque Fatherland and Liberty (ETA) political branch travelled to Chile to meet with CAM members. Chilean police were monitoring for possible contacts between Mapuche groups and armed political movements in Latin America.[48]

Some anarchist groups have also sought association with Mapuche organizations. In early 2009 Chilean police arrested a man suspected of ninety-three bomb explosions near banks and police stations. Witnesses had placed him at the scene of several of the attacks, and police said he had frequently traveled to Mapuche communities, including Temucuicui.[49]

Many indigenous leaders are uncomfortable with such contacts. "These masked guys, dressed in black, come down and commit violent attacks, then leave our people to deal with the consequences," said Reynaldo Mariqueo of the Mapuche International Link. "They aren't even Mapuche."[50] Such tactics have been reported in a number of violent incidents in and around Tirúa, a coastal town known as a staging ground for Mapuche resistance against the Spanish four centuries ago.

Tirua also has one of the few indigenous mayors in the country, but that has not spared the town from rising levels of tension, fear, and violence.

In October 2008 approximately ten masked men opened fire on a police car that was leaving a local government prosecutor's office to deliver a legal notice. The attack occurred in broad daylight, and an elderly couple who helped the injured carabineros were later threatened. When an official from the prosecutor's office, accompanied by a police car, tried to visit the couple, they too came under attack from masked men.

A few days later carabineros confronted two people who had put up a roadblock, which they later determined was a diversionary tactic. While the police were dealing with the roadblock, masked men were setting fire to a local farmer's house and had forced their way into the storeroom of another nearby farm, also setting it on fire. A Chilean interior ministry official in Santiago said the incidents were not the work of Mapuches but of criminals.[51]

I contacted a Catholic priest in working in Tirúa, explaining that I was interested in seeing local living conditions and mentioning the name of a mutual acquaintance who had urged me to meet him. But he was too nervous to let me visit his mission, perhaps fearing a negative reaction from Chilean officials. Other Mapuche sources said the authorities, aided by an extensive network of local informants, were keeping watch on all visitors and movement in the area.

The president of Chile's congressional human rights commission denounced the "militarization" of Tirúa. In April 2008 a special carabinero police command arrived in the area with water cannons, an armored tank, and riot gear and set up camp on a forestry estate not far from a Mapuche neighborhood. The elite police unit specializes in counterterrorism operations, search and rescue, and explosives. To some observers, it was a scene more befitting a war zone than the peaceful Chilean countryside. "This is a completely unacceptable situation for a democratic country," Deputy Sergio Aguilo said. "The use of light tanks and military special forces against the Mapuches is outrageous. I've never seen such a use of force in my three terms as a representative." He believed that the carabinero special unit was there not to keep public order but to protect the property and employees of a Chilean forestry products company.[52]

More ugly incidents would follow. Citizen Watch, a human rights NGO based in Temuco, reported the case of two Mapuche teenagers injured during a raid by police who did not show a search warrant and were looking—not for weapons, explosives, or accused terrorist fugitives—for a missing horse. One of the youths suffered a broken leg from a police bullet, and his companion's jaw was fractured when he was hit in the face with the butt of a riot control shotgun. According to Citizen Watch, the police departed, leaving the teenagers behind with their injuries. The NGO's report on the incident to the Chilean interior ministry "received no substantive reply."[53]

VII

"The police actions are brutal. They periodically invade Mapuche villages with the pretext of looking for weapons. In the best of cases they manage to find, as their only proof, a sharpened knife, a machete, instruments used by campesinos to survive in the area," Judge Juan Guzmán said. "In many cases it's an excuse to make arrests and apply antiterrorist laws."[54]

Guzmán was returning from Geneva, where he had presented a letter from Mapuche leader Aucan Huilcaman to the United Nations High Commission for Human Rights. One of the cases he took on was that of a Mapuche leader accused of arson in Tirúa. One judge had absolved his client of all charges, but prosecutors had appealed, and the case was once again before the courts.[55] Another case involved the director of the more militant CAM, who was accused of arson, illegal arms possession, and receipt of stolen goods. Prosecutors had tried to show that Hector Llaitul was part of a group of six arsonists setting fire to machinery at a forestry company on Christmas Day 2006, though the Mapuche activist maintained he had been visiting a friend at the time, accompanied by two of his children. Guzmán and other defense lawyers found numerous irregularities in the prosecution's case: a forestry company caretaker who claimed to have identified Llaitul among the arsonists had been about 300 yards away in a wooded area at the time of the attack and could not give a credible eyewitness account. Another suspect in the case said he had been kidnapped by armed civilians, who brought him to the police station, where he was tortured until he incriminated Llaitul. The three court judges dropped all charges against the Mapuche activist, who had spent a year and a half in prison.[56]

In late 2008 the head of Amnesty International visited Chile for a week, meeting Mapuche community activists and representatives of other indigenous groups. Irene Khan said that while the country had made significant improvements in human rights issues, "Indigenous peoples are severely discriminated and marginalized in Chile and see themselves as the victims of an economic strategy that is destroying their lives and livelihoods."[57]

A few months later, the Mapuche School of Self Government held its first day of classes in Temuco, the capital of Chile's indigenous heartland. Its mission was to train Mapuche leaders, and it boasted a stellar faculty, including Judge Guzmán, an expert on international indigenous law, a former member of congress, and several indigenous leaders and human rights attorneys. Its first class was a teaching module on international law as it pertained to "Mapuche self-determination and self-government," according to a press release. It opened with a traditional blessing ceremony, followed by the planting of two araucaria trees.[58]

ELEVEN Michelle Bachelet

I

She had been Latin America's first female defense minister and would soon become president, one of the few female heads of state in the world whose career owed nothing to a husband. She was a Socialist and a general's daughter, a pediatrician and a specialist on defense matters who had studied at the National War College in Washington, D.C., and obtained a master's degree in military science at the Chilean army's War Academy. She spoke five languages and had lived in three foreign countries.

Michelle Bachelet's personal story was as impressive as her curriculum vitae. Part of her education included two years at a public school in Bethesda, Maryland, while her father, air force general Alberto Bachelet, served as Chile's military attaché in Washington. He was later transferred to the Allende government's food distribution department, earning him the enmity of Chile's political Right. He was arrested and tortured after the coup, dying of a heart attack while in detention in March 1974. Bachelet, then a medical student, and her mother were arrested early the following year by security agents and taken to Villa Grimaldi, where they were separated, blindfolded, and beaten. She was spared electric shock and the worst forms of torture but was told her mother would be killed if she didn't cooperate. She was kept in a cell with eight other female prisoners, including a sixteen-year-old and three pregnant women. Two of the pregnant women had been raped by their captors, and several of her other cellmates had been brutally tortured.

Bachelet and her mother were moved to another DINA detention center, Tres Alamos. After two weeks she was released without explanation, but her mother was held for another two weeks while Bachelet frantically called on every family friend and contact to try to secure her release. Bachelet's brother helped arrange political asylum in Australia, where he was living, and mother and daughter were reunited in the airport shortly before their departure.[1]

Bachelet and her mother later made their way to East Germany, where she diligently learned the language, took a job as a hospital orderly, and eventually resumed her medical studies. In 1979 she returned to Chile with her husband, a fellow former exile, and two young children. Her German medical credentials were not recognized in Chile, and so she had to get additional training to qualify as a doctor. During this difficult time, her marriage broke up. Undaunted, she got further training and managed to establish a medical practice as well as work with a medical charity to help Chilean children traumatized by political violence. With the return of democracy, she took a job as a health advisor at the Defense Ministry and later joined President Ricardo Lagos's cabinet, first as health minister and then as defense minister. "The military respected her; they knew her from her previous job at the Defense Ministry," recalled Ricardo Lagos.[2]

A new generation of officers were now leading the country's armed forces, though many Left-leaning Chileans wondered how Bachelet, a former political prisoner, could bear to do the job. "In a certain way I was re-encountering part of my roots, which had been severed during that period of Chilean history in which our society was so polarized," she said. "Most people with my background feel a profound rejection towards anything that has to do with the military, but I felt like I was recovering part of my being." Her conciliatory demeanor and academic defense credentials won over many skeptics in the military, who sent her a combat jacket with her name on it when her appointment was announced.[3] She quickly became the most visible and popular member of Lagos's cabinet, a symbol of resilience and reconciliation.

Lagos, who had won the presidency by a fraction of votes, proved to be one of Chile's most admired presidents ever, with an approval rating of 71 percent as he neared the end of his term. Per capita income had risen from $4,860 in 2000 to $5,903 in 2004, unemployment had decreased, and the number of students in higher education rose from 411,000 to 600,000.[4] Lagos had also presided over a number of public projects, such as the extension of Santiago's metro to poorer areas and an ambitious scheme to construct a footpath over five thousand miles long from the Peruvian border to Tierra del Fuego.[5] He had opened the inner courtyard of the La Moneda presidential palace to the public and oversaw the construction of a museum and cultural center in the underground warren that had once been Pinochet's bunker. He had made friends in Chile's conservative business community and moved confidently in international forums, signing additional bilateral trade deals with the European Union and China.

At the same time, the public mood toward politics and government seemed negative. A poll in August 2005 revealed that most Chileans had little faith in public institutions: only 22 percent expressed confidence in the senate, 20 percent in the judiciary, 18 percent in the chamber of deputies, and 9 percent in political parties. The two institutions with the highest approval rating were the Catholic Church (57 percent) and the carabinero police (54 percent).[6] There was a generalized sense that after three consecutive governments led by the Center-Left Concertación coalition, Chile might be ready for a change—and may even elect the candidate of the Center-Right Alianza Democratica coalition.

After sixteen years in power, the Concertación needed to present a fresh face to the electorate and appears to have deliberately picked a female candidate for this reason. Bachelet's rival for the coalition candidacy was also a woman, Soledad Alvear, a Christian Democrat who had held cabinet posts in the Aylwin, Frei, and Lagos governments. The two were due to compete in a primary, but Alvear pulled out of the race when polls showed she trailed Bachelet.

Women in Chile do not face as much ugly harassment in public places as do their counterparts in many other Latin American countries, but Chilean women's participation in the labor market was among the lowest in the region. The traditionally male preserves of mining and forestry had long dominated the Chilean economy, rather than the service sector, where women have been more likely to seek jobs. According to World Bank figures, 41 percent of Chilean women between the ages of fifteen and sixty-four were in the workforce, while in Colombia, Bolivia, and Brazil, it is 60 percent, and in Peru, Argentina, and Venezuela, 50 percent. The proportion of women in the Chilean congress was well below that of ten other Latin American countries.[7] Divorce had only been legalized the previous year.

The Aylwin administration had established a government agency for women's issues, the Servicio Nacional de Mujer (SERNAM). It was housed in the Chilean planning ministry and could present policy recommendations for other government departments as well as undertake research studies. Although it had some funds to make grants to local groups such as legal aid clinics for women, its own budget was limited, and SERNAM often worked on projects with better-funded NGOs.[8]

Domestic violence against women was a serious problem, and an issue consistently mentioned in human rights reports on Chile. According to a 2004 SERNAM study, 34 percent of married women suffered physical violence from their husbands, and another 16 percent reported psychological abuse.[9]

Bachelet promised to appoint women to half of her cabinet posts and ran on a platform of increased citizen participation in civic affairs. She faced two conservative opponents, though one was closer to the political center than any conservative candidate of the past. Sebastián Piñera of Renovación Nacional had opposed Pinochet's reelection in the 1988 plebiscite, and then went to work in the campaign of the regime's candidate, Hernán Büchi, before becoming a senator in Chile's new parliament. Despite his time as a lawmaker, Piñera seemed more businessman than politician, and in this sense he was an untraditional presidential candidate. He had a PhD in economics from Harvard University and was one of Chile's wealthiest men, owning a private television station and 27 percent of the Chilean airline LAN, as well as having business interests in numerous other countries.

Piñera financed his own campaign, often appearing with his wife and their four children, as if trying to present himself as more likely to uphold traditional social values than Bachelet, a self-described agnostic and single mother. He also sought to distance himself from Chile's traditional right-wing parties, openly criticizing Pinochet, describing his own political philosophy as Christian humanism, and at times even veering toward populism. At one point he said he favored pensions for Chile's housewives. This position was attacked by the Concertación, who pointed out that it was financially unworkable and that the current pension system, designed by the Pinochet regime, was unable to cover its existing obligations, much less extend coverage to housewives. It was an interesting exchange, with the Center-Left coalition arguing fiscal prudence while Piñera proposed more social spending.

Piñera's brother José was a former labor minister in the Pinochet regime who had designed the private pensions program. And yet Piñera had also stated that reforms were needed in the pensions system, and on this point both he and Bachelet agreed. Chile's private pensions program began in 1981, requiring salaried workers to deposit at least 10 percent of their earnings into personal retirement accounts managed by private pensions companies, who invested the funds in accordance with strict guidelines. Chileans were allowed to choose the company and switch to another if they liked. If, by retirement age, an individual pension had not reached a minimum level, the government would make up the shortfall. The military and police were not required to use the private pension companies, and the system also left out those in the informal economy, the poor, and the self-employed, who make up roughly a quarter of the Chilean workforce.[10]

On broader economic issues, Bachelet and Piñera seemed to agree, and much of the campaign seemed focused on their personalities: Piñera was confident and energetic, while Bachelet was warm and down to earth. A third presidential candidate, Joaquín Lavín of the Union Democrática Independiente, was also running in his second bid for the presidency, after having narrowly lost to Socialist Ricardo Lagos in 1999. A fourth candidate, Tomás Hirsch of the small Humanist Party, was backed by a loose coalition of small left-wing parties that had been excluded from the Concertación. Hirsch had sharp criticisms for Chile's economic model, the government's environmental record, as well as the right-wing opposition.

On a televised debate among the candidates October 19, 2005, Hirsch did very well, coming across as articulate and persuasive, while Bachelet seemed unsure of herself. A poll taken in Santiago after the debate showed that 59 percent thought Hirsch had given the best presentation, followed by 19 percent for Piñera and 18 percent for Bachelet.[11] One issue both Bachelet and Piñera seemed to avoid was Pinochet, who was ailing but still managing to fight the judicial investigations into his foreign bank accounts and his role in human rights abuses, with the support of his formidable team of lawyers. At one point Bachelet observed that Pinochet seemed to receive more attention abroad than in Chile, and many Chileans agreed with her.

Despite her impressive résumé and considerable charm, Bachelet endured some attacks that she lacked seriousness or the requisite leadership skills for the job. Her appointment as Lagos's health minister a few years earlier had been a surprise, for she was viewed as a relatively junior member of Chile's Socialist Party and not someone likely to be groomed for a political career. Although she is credited with reducing waiting times within the health service, and as defense minister helped bridge the chasm that had long existed between the country's armed forces and the political world, critics still accused her of lacking the political and administrative skills needed for the job of president. One of her opponent's campaign slogans was "Piñera, mas presidente," suggesting that he was presidential material whereas she was not. Conservative pundits also decried the fact that she had once dated a man with ties to the Far Left Manuel Rodriguez Patriotic Front, though the same critics did not mention a more recent long-term relationship with a politically conservative fellow physician, with whom she had a daughter.

Her opponents also suggested she would open the way for abortion, which remained illegal in Chile even in instances where a pregnant woman's life was in danger, and gay marriage, though she had not made either subject an issue in her campaign. But the new generation of young Chilean voters was increasingly tolerant of such matters. Bachelet also received the backing of environmental groups, and in her speeches promised more social inclusion for those Chileans left on the margins of the country's economy.

The December 2005 election put Bachelet in the lead, with 45.6 percent, followed by Piñera with 25.4 percent, Lavín with 23.2 percent, and Hirsch with 5.4 percent. Once again there was a runoff vote, and Bachelet beat Piñera with 53.5 percent of the vote.[12] She was about to make history, and her electoral victory would attract attention around the world. But her political honeymoon would be short-lived, even though the Concertación had also won a majority in both the senate and the chamber of deputies.

II

Almost all Chileans with the means to do so send their children to private schools, and Bachelet was no exception.[13] The Pinochet regime had radically overhauled Chilean education, decentralizing the entire system by moving control of state schools from the education ministry to local municipal governments. The regime subsidized both private and public schools in accordance with the number of students enrolled, but overall spending on education during the 1980s declined by 30 percent. The idea was to support parental school choice and make education improve through competition. Approximately one-fifth of the students in the state school system moved over to private schools, which today educate 50 percent of Chilean children. The figure for Organization for Economic Cooperation and Development countries is 19 percent.[14]

On their last day in power, Pinochet and the junta passed a new education law that prohibited the state from funding schools above the subsidies. The Concertación governments more than doubled spending on education over the next decade but did not tamper with the basic system left in place by the regime. "It is part of the landscape," an education ministry official under the Lagos government told *Education Week.* "We have accepted that the pressures of competition can be put to good use, and the focus of attention now is not the funding system, but the quality of our learning results." He said that during the 1980s there had been a very marked difference between the public and private schools, but that with the additional investments the new civilian governments had made, "the material differences don't exist."[15]

Chile's students and their parents and teachers were not in agreement with this last assertion. Schools reopened in March, after the southern hemisphere summer, and within weeks of Bachelet's inauguration, a million high school students were holding demonstrations throughout the country to demand an end to educational inequality in Chile. The protests erupted after officials announced that the fee to take Chile's university entrance exam would be raised to about $50 and that students would have to limit the number of free trips they could take on the country's buses. When a few hundred students began demonstrating along Santiago's main avenue, they were dispersed by carabinero police, who arrested forty-seven students.[16] More protests followed, culminating in a massive demonstration on May Day in a downtown Santiago park. Violence broke out—according to some accounts, egged on by provocateurs wearing hoods—and over a thousand students were arrested.

The rioting did not win the students much public support, but two and a half weeks later, two of Chile's top private schools joined the protest. On the night of May 19, 2006, students occupied the school campuses, demanding that Chilean schools be transferred away from municipal governments and back to the Education Ministry. They also demanded the abolition of the regime's 1990 education law and a statement acknowledging their demands during Bachelet's forthcoming address to the Chilean congress. The protests had spread to other schools, including a girls' school Bachelet had attended. At some of the schools the student takeovers became school strikes, backed by parents and teachers. On May 30 nearly eight hundred thousand students throughout the country joined the strikes and protests. The movement was soon dubbed "the march of the penguins," a reference to the students' white and dark uniforms.

On June 1 Bachelet went on television to announce a new educational package that included a reorganization of the Education Ministry, a presidential advisory panel on education, a proposal to congress to reform the regime's education law, and free lunches and transportation for the poorest students. The fee for the university admissions exam would be waived in 80 percent of cases. But she said the government could not extend free bus passes to all students.

The student protest leaders met for eight hours to discuss the proposals at the Instituto Nacional, one of Chile's most prestigious schools, then met with Bachelet's education minister Martin Zilic. The official left the meeting announcing he had not been able to reach agreement with the students, who planned to organize a national strike for June 5. One of the student leaders called Zilic "a stupid man, who went around saying that this was all just a hormonal attack on the part of the students."[17]

Bachelet called the strike "unnecessary," in view of the fact that her government was working to reform Chilean education, had granted some of the students' demands, and had kept open a channel of communication. The strike went on ahead, while a government spokesman announced that the crisis would not cause Bachelet to cancel her imminent state visit to Washington. More than a hundred other groups, including teachers, university student organizations, trade unions, and the Manuel Rodriguez Patriotic Front announced they would join the protest. Student spokespeople said the Front had a right to exercise its right to demonstrate but must take full responsibility for its actions.[18]

Not all schools joined the protest, but the extent of mobilization, which included the lone school on Chile's distant Pacific territory, Easter Island, was remarkable. The next day leaders of the student movement wrote a letter to the government saying they supported the creation of a presidential advisory panel, and Bachelet announced the group would include six seats for student representatives. The protest movement seemed to be coming to an end, but many Chileans were unimpressed by the new government's handling of the crisis. A poll taken in June and

July that year gave Bachelet a 46 percent approval rating, with 31 percent disapproving and the rest either neutral or abstaining.[19]

On June 8 Bachelet visited a public school where the band played the Chilean national anthem and she received several gifts from awe-struck students. As part of her trip to Washington, D.C., she made a stop at the Westland Middle School in Bethesda, Maryland, where she had been a student in 1963. "We are humbled and excited," the school principal said. "It's not every day we can welcome a woman who had made history." Bachelet took questions from the students, who wanted to know what it was like to be Chile's first woman president. She paused before answering. "I feel enormous responsibility," she said. "I feel a huge responsibility because there are lots of expectations by women and by men. I won't fail. I'll do my best and I'll work hard."[20]

Bachelet and her entourage drove into Washington, where she laid a wreath at the spot where Orlando Letelier and Ronni Moffit had been killed in 1976. She had a lunchtime meeting with George Bush, who described Bachelet as "a very charming person" and said he was impressed that she had visited a school before coming to the White House. That evening she was the guest of honor at a dinner hosted by Hillary Clinton and other influential women, who seemed even more star-struck than the schoolchildren Bachelet had met that morning. The *Washington Post* described a scene in which "Rep Janice Schakowsky (D-Ill) is rubbing Michelle Bachelet's arm as if she hopes her glow will somehow rub off. Rep. Carolyn Maloney (D-NY), in a straw hat, is bending her ear. Everyone wants a picture, and all of them keep gushing: 'We love you! We support you!'"[21]

Bachelet had dazzled her American hosts and would frequently encounter a similar reception in her other travels abroad. In a later visit to the United Nations, she gamely agreed to appear on the daytime television show *The View,* smiling patiently when cohosts Rosie O'Donnell confessed to not knowing where Chile was and Barbara Walters asked why she was single. She encouraged those watching to come to Chile, describing the country's extraordinary geographic range from the Atacama Desert to the Antarctic and assuring them that it was "very safe" for visitors.[22] *Time* magazine included her in its 2008 list of the world's twenty most influential leaders, while *Forbes* ranked her in the top quartile of the world's most powerful women.

Back in Santiago, she replaced education minister Martin Zilic with Yasna Provoste, a former planning minister during her predecessor's administration and one of the few cabinet-level officials of indigenous heritage. Bachelet had made a point of forming a cabinet of ten men and ten women who were relative newcomers to the political scene, but her critics said she had chosen image over competence. Provoste's appointment ended in disaster two years later, when the Education Ministry was unable to explain why $21.6 million was missing from its accounts.

There were no signs that Provoste or anyone under her had been siphoning off public money for themselves, but investigators found that fourteen hundred schools had inflated their enrollment figures to obtain additional funds. The Education Ministry, which spends nearly a fifth of the government's budget, was unable to keep an accurate record of its expenditures. A congressional hearing into the case, led by conservative parliamentarians, resulted in Provoste becoming the first cabinet minister to be impeached since Chile's return to democracy.

III

An even worse political nightmare lay ahead. Santiago's French-built metro was clean, efficient, and well run, but the Chilean capital's bus system was an antiquated mess, an unregulated fleet of aging buses that belched black fumes and duplicated many of the metro's routes. Many of the buses carried only a few riders, and the vehicles often competed with one another to reach passengers waiting at stops, driving at high speeds and swerving across traffic lanes.

A new citywide mass transit system, the Transantiago, had been in the works for at least five years, providing for new buses whose routes would be coordinated with the Santiago metro. Passengers would use a single swipe card for both buses and the metro; the improved service would be cleaner and more efficient and would encourage more Chileans to use public transport. It was one of the most ambitious mass transit programs ever undertaken by a developing country, but its debut proved to be a disorganized catastrophe.

The government might have avoided any number of obstacles had Transantiago been introduced in stages, allowing time for the public to adjust to the new system and to correct any hiccups. But Bachelet's administration opted for a "big bang" approach, inaugurating Transantiago before all its components were in place. There were not enough buses to meet demand, and long lines of frustrated passengers began gathering at stops. A GPS system to track bus movements was not working, and there were not enough kiosks selling the required "bip" card. The Santiago metro groaned under double the passenger load, and Chile's physicians' association issued a statement warning the ill and infirm not to use the service.[23] "Gabriel Garcia Marquez wrote a book called *Chronicle of an Announced Murder*," former Santiago transport coordinator German Correa later told a World Bank and World Resources Institute meeting. "Starting Transantiago the way it did, it was a Chronicle of an Announced Disaster." He said the system had serious design and implementation problems and that the government had not considered the consequences for its users if Transantiago failed.[24]

The lack of buses hit residents of poor Santiago neighborhoods especially hard, and many took to walking for hours in search of available transport, in some instances rising before dawn and walking to work. After several weeks of commuter chaos, Bachelet made a televised apology. "It is not routine that a president comes before the nation and says, 'Things have not been done properly here,'" Bachelet said in a speech televised on March 27, 2006. "But that is what I want to say tonight in the Transantiago case."[25] She also announced a cabinet reshuffle for the second time in less than a year, firing her transport minister, replacing three other cabinet officials, and bringing in a veteran political operator, former chamber of deputies president José Antonio Viera Gallo, as her chief of staff. But her government still seemed weak and indecisive, reacting to problems but not really adopting a proactive approach. Transantiago was not the self-supporting system it was claimed to be, and the government had to seek additional public funds. Many Santiago residents were choosing to drive to work rather than risk arriving late on public transport, and far from helping to improve the capital's air quality, the new public transportation system's problems had made things even worse. Bachelet turned down an offer of financial assistance from Venezuela's Hugo Chávez but was frequently faced with an intransigent congress demanding a full accounting of the disaster before it would approve any additional money.

A year later there had been some noticeable improvements, with more buses and stops and a functioning operations center to coordinate bus movements and routes. But the system still suffered a suffocating backlog of passengers during rush hour, and an estimated 30 percent of Santiago had begun using black market forms of transport such as unlicensed taxis, vans, and buses. A study by the engineering faculty of the Universidad Bernardo O'Higgins revealed that Santiago's "trans-pirate" system was being used not just by poorer Chileans in outlying areas of the capital but by high school and college students as well—including some from private institutions. Those using the illegal transport cited cheaper fares and "opportunity, consistence and better routes" than what Transantiago could offer. The study's authors said their findings demonstrated how black market economies can chip away at an official infrastructure.[26] To make matters worse, an estimated 40 percent of those using Transantiago buses were fare dodgers, causing further losses to the system's problematic finances. Chilean authorities responded by putting inspectors, sometimes accompanied by carabinero police, on some routes.[27]

IV

Bachelet's foreign policy seemed, at first glance, a continuation of her predecessors' approach, but she would be faced with a few awkward dilemmas they had not encountered. Shortly before her election, former Peruvian president Alberto Fujimori, wanted in his own country on corruption and human rights charges, surprised the governments of both countries by landing in Santiago in a private plane that had left Tokyo and had stopped for refueling in Tijuana, Mexico. In 2000, faced with a corruption scandal, he had faxed his resignation to Peru's congress and fled to Japan, where he held dual nationality. Peruvian authorities had tried and failed to extradite him from Japan. His decision to come to Chile was part of a carefully designed plan to mount a lengthy legal battle—which he imagined he could win—and relaunch his political career.

The two countries had an extradition treaty, but previously Chilean courts had refused to extradite four Peruvians who had worked with Fujimori's security forces, and it was not clear if arrest warrants issued by Interpol were legally binding in Chile. Fujimori knew Chilean judges were more demanding than their Peruvian counterparts and would insist on closely studying the evidence prosecutors had collected against him, a process that could take months.[28] He did not expect Chilean police to arrive at his hotel within hours of his arrival with an arrest warrant, issued immediately after Peru requested extradition.

Fujimori spent six months in prison, during which time the courts rejected two petitions for bail. A third bail request was finally granted, on the condition that he remain in the country, and Fujimori strolled out of prison, smiling, waving, and looking as if he were already campaigning. He seemed to enjoy the crush of reporters and television crews who followed him to a waiting car.[29]

Peruvian officials were indignant. Nearly a year and half would elapse before Chile's Supreme Court finally granted his extradition to Peru. The Fujimori episode occurred during a delicate moment in bilateral relations, for Peru's congress had passed legislation redrawing the country's sea boundary with Chile and would take its petition to the international court at The Hague. During the 1879–83 War of the Pacific, Peru lost its southernmost territory, and Bolivia, its sea outlet, to Chile. These were wounds that had never quite healed, and in both countries there was an underlying view of Chile as an aggressive, militaristic country with a suspiciously large defense budget.

Peru and Chile had been discussing a free trade agreement, but these negotiations had stalled. Nevertheless, Peruvian officials and the public seemed to warm to Bachelet when she arrived in Lima to attend the presidential inauguration of Alan García. She was seen singing along when the Peruvian national anthem was played and gave an extended interview to a television public affairs program. She mentioned that her mother had lived in Lima and Arequipa as a child, that her maternal grandmother was Argentine, and that she had a strong commitment to Latin American regional integration. Bachelet acknowledged the difficult bilateral issues but said that both countries faced similar challenges such as improving education and reducing poverty, and there were more areas of cooperation than conflict.[30] The two countries finally signed a free trade agreement early in 2009, after quadrupling their trade over the previous five years.

Chile and Bolivia had strained diplomatic relations for years, maintaining consulates but not exchanging ambassadors. Evo Morales's election, which occurred about the same time as Bachelet's, changed this. Outgoing president Ricardo Lagos was invited to Morales's inauguration, and Morales came to Santiago for Bachelet's inauguration. The two new presidents had what was described as a cordial meeting, and if no discernible progress was made on Bolivia's intractable demand for a sea outlet, the personal rapport Bachelet built with Morales would go a long way toward easing tensions. Two years later, when a constitutional crisis and civilian violence seemed to be pushing Bolivia to the verge of collapse, Bachelet quickly convened a summit of eight South American presidents to help mediate the crisis—and managed the gathering in such a way as to preclude Venezuela's Hugo Chávez from dominating the proceedings.[31]

Six months later she hosted another summit, the Progressive Governance Conference, to discuss the world financial crisis. Those attending included the presidents of Argentina, Brazil, and Uruguay; the prime ministers of Norway and the United Kingdom; and U.S. vice president Joe Biden. She told her visitors that Chile had made a point of saving part of its windfall copper revenues during the economic boom, when prices exceeded $4 per pound, and was now using them to fund a $4 billion stimulus program. Bachelet's handling of the economic downturn improved her standing among Chilean voters—after months of low ratings, polls now showed a majority of Chileans, 58.5 percent, "approved of the way Michelle Bachelet governs." But of the same respondents, only 44.6 percent approved of the way the Chilean government was performing, and only 21.2 percent approved of the Concertación political coalition.[32]

V

It was something that the Bachelet government had been anticipating for some time but in many ways dreading, an unavoidable and inflammatory event that would raise Chile's political temperature once again, no matter what her administration's response was. There were far more pressing issues at hand, but this shoved the country into the world's headlines once again. How would Chile bid farewell to its former dictator? "We all knew that there was a high probability that he would die during the Bachelet government," recalled Vivianne Blanlot, an economist who was defense minister at the time. "But he no longer had any influence on national life during this period—in that sense, it was a tranquil period."[33]

And yet Pinochet remained in the news: Judge Carlos Cerda continued his investigation into Pinochet's foreign bank accounts while the former dictator's lawyers continued to fend him off. Pinochet had had multiple health crises in the six years since his return to Chile, which tended to occur just as Cerda or another investigating judge took a further step in the judicial proceedings. That August the Supreme Court had stripped him of his immunity, opening the way for Cerda to complete his prosecution, but then a series of medical emergencies and sudden internments at the Hospital Militar had jettisoned the judge's attempts to pursue the case.

On December 3, 2006, Pinochet was taken to the military hospital after suffering an acute myocardial infarction. Small groups of Pinochet supporters gathered nearby, sometimes fighting with regime opponents and other onlookers. The next day General Emilio Cheyre, the former army commander who had vowed the Chilean military would never again be party to human rights violations, came to pay his respects to his former commander. He was booed and hissed at by Pinochet supporters.

One woman screamed that he was a traitor and threw herself against Cheyre's automobile before she was restrained by carabinero police.[34]

The pressure was mounting. Bachelet's government made no statement concerning Pinochet's hospitalization, and in answer to reporters' questions, her spokesman said it would be "tasteless" to discuss funeral arrangements.[35] But preparations for this event had been underway long before Pinochet would make his final trip to Santiago's military hospital. "The issue of the funeral was the first thing I discussed with army commander Oscar Izurieta when I became defense minister," Blanlot said. "In the armed forces, you plan everything down to the last detail as much as possible. And the army was worried about what would happen the day Pinochet died."[36]

Izurieta was acting as the intermediary between Bachelet's government and the Pinochet family, who thought that Pinochet was entitled to the full honors of a state funeral, which would have involved a long funeral cortege through the streets of Santiago, attended by all government officials and former presidents. The government adamantly refused—state funerals were for elected presidents—but it was impossible to imagine that the general who had ruled the country for seventeen years could ever have had a private funeral. The issues under discussion were the symbols of public life: how Pinochet's death was observed would affect Chile's image. "General Izurieta and I discussed what was the maximum possibility within a democratic framework. And he took charge of discussing the reality of the situation with the Pinochet family," Blanlot said. "There would be no state funeral, but a funeral for a former army commander."[37] The only government official to attend would be Blanlot, to signal that, in a democracy, the Chilean armed forces were under the command of the Defense Ministry.

After a week in the military hospital's intensive care, unit Pinochet died of heart failure and pulmonary edema. A Bachelet government spokesman gave a terse statement that Pinochet had died and that his remains would be taken to the military academy. The government had given its authorization for flags to fly at half-mast at military installations, he said, while Bachelet herself kept a low profile. But the news electrified the country.

Thousands of people began gathering in the streets, some marching toward the center of Santiago. By nightfall there were clashes as police tried to keep the demonstrators away from the smaller groups of Pinochet supporters near the military hospital. Some demonstrators erected burning barricades in the streets while carabinero police used water cannons and tear gas to disperse the crowds.[38]

That night, Pinochet's body was moved in a caravan of vehicles from the military hospital to the military academy, where it was placed in a glass-topped coffin for a wake. A Spanish television crew broadcasting live outside the military academy was harassed by Pinochet supporters, still furious with the country for attempting to extradite the former dictator. At one point a man grabbed the microphone away from correspondent María José Ramudo, shouting, "You Spaniards are sons of bitches and assholes!" The carabinero police looked on but offered no assistance.[39]

Thousands of Chileans lined up to pay their last respects, in some cases waiting for hours for a chance to file past the coffin. But one of the visitors had a very different mission in mind. When his turn came after a twelve-hour wait, he defiantly spat at Pinochet's coffin before being set upon by outraged supporters of the former dictator and then ushered outside by guards.

The spitting man was identified a few days later. Francisco Cuadrado Prats, cultural director of the eastern Santiago municipality of Las Condes, was the grandson of the late army commander Carlos Prats, who had died with his wife in a car bomb explosion in Buenos Aires in 1974. The double murder was one of the first missions the Pinochet regime's security forces had made abroad, and Cuadrado Prats had long dreamed of making some symbolic gesture to avenge his grandparents. It was, he said, "an act of contempt."[40]

The incident cost Cuadrado Prats his job. The mayor of Las Condes, a conservative Pinochet supporter, said his conduct had been unbecoming for a public official. The mayor insisted he was not politically intolerant and had often worked with people of different political views. "I don't care what people think, but I do care how they act," he said.[41]

Defense Minister Blanlot did not go to the wake but did go to the funeral, accompanied by Chile's military commanders, who formed a protective escort around her. She saw Lucía Hiriart, Pinochet's widow, and greeted her "as one would greet a woman who has lost her husband."[42] That encounter took place inside the academy and was relatively calm, but outside on the open patio, Blanlot faced approximately four thousand enraged Pinochet supporters who were glaring, shouting, and jeering as she entered. The defense minister took her place on the pavilion, but her calm demeanor seeming to infuriate the right-wing crowd even more. The late dictator's daughter Lucía spoke on behalf of the family. "The international press will not understand how hundreds of thousands of people who are informed and under no pressure could show their gratitude and affection for a man whom the press described in the worst terms and epithets one could use in describing another human being," she said to loud cheers from the crowd.[43]

One of Pinochet's grandsons, army captain Augusto Pinochet Molina, then spoke, praising his grandfather's war against the Marxists and saying that he was a fighter and a visionary who had produced a stable and prosperous country. "Goodbye my president, goodbye my general, goodbye my grandfather," he finished to loud applause.[44]

As the service was ending and Blanlot prepared to leave, a group of women rushed up and tried to punch her. The military commanders and their aides formed a tight ring around the defense minister and quickly moved her out of the premises. "What surprised me was their violence," she recalled.[45] The dictator's coffin was moved to the Pinochets' country estate on the coast, where his ashes were kept after cremation; the family recognized the fact that keeping his remains at a cemetery mausoleum would inevitably attract vandals.

Blanlot and other government officials later learned that masses had been said for Pinochet in almost all the military chapels in Chile. She and Bachelet met with army commander Oscar Izurieta, and it was agreed that Pinochet's grandson had violated military protocol for giving a politicized speech. The young officer, whom Pinochet supporters might have seen as a possible successor to the late dictator, was retired from the army, along with a general in southern Chile who had also given a fiery speech praising Pinochet.

Blanlot, who is from a military family, said she received several calls afterward from other military families thanking her for her steadfastness during Pinochet's funeral. There was still nostalgia for the former dictator among some of the older officers, but this was ebbing. The revelations of Pinochet's illicit fortune had disappointed many one-time supporters of the former dictator. There was, she said, a sense of "horror and frustration" over the case. And many military officials and their wives had been impressed by Bachelet during her time as defense minister and told Blanlot they had voted for her.[46]

VI

"In time my father will be given his true place in history," Lucía Pinochet told Chile's national television station. She was speaking after a mass held at a military chapel in Santiago on the first anniversary of her father's death on December 10. There had been no systematic human rights abuses during the regime, she said, "If there had been I would have noticed, and I didn't." She criticized former regime loyalists for distancing themselves from her father and said she was "absolutely certain" that *Pinochetismo* was alive and well in Chile and that she was considering running for a seat in congress as an independent candidate. The dictator's daughter did not run for congress but did win a seat on a municipal council in eastern Santiago.[47]

Bachelet's government seemed to shrug off the commemoration, saying it wasn't even an issue. "Pinochet is not something that moves the country," the interior minister remarked.[48] The memorial service did not attract much of a crowd: approximately one hundred people, including two retired generals, a senator, and a congressional deputy turned up at the mass, which was followed that evening by a gathering of fifteen hundred *Pinochetistas* at a conference center in eastern Santiago. Those in attendance held a moment of silence at the arrival of Pinochet's eighty-five-year old widow, who looked radiant despite having been hospitalized two months earlier.

That hospital stay happened just as Judge Cerda ordered her arrest, along with her five grown children and seventeen of Pinochet's closest collaborators, on charges of misappropriating public funds. In a sixty-page ruling, Cerda said that the Pinochet family and their associates had taken at least $20 million from presidential discretionary funds, the office of the commander in chief, and the Casa Militar, a group of Pinochet's closest advisors.[49]

Lucía Hiriart de Pinochet was rushed to the military hospital upon learning of the impending arrests, suffering from what was said to be high blood pressure. Her sons and daughters spent two days in prison, along with their father's former associates, before being released on bail. Among those detained was Chile's former consul in Los Angeles, whose sister was Pinochet's former justice minister, Monica Madariaga. "My brother is the only innocent man out of all these imbeciles," she snapped at a radio reporter outside the jail who ventured to ask if she would visit the Pinochets. "How can you even think such a thing!" Her brother's only involvement, she said, was purchasing a car for Pinochet's eldest son, Osvaldo Augusto.[50]

A few weeks later Pinochet's eldest son and the son of former DINA security chief Manuel Contreras were interviewed together on Chilean television. Both men bore their fathers' names, and both complained of people insulting them in public places, though the younger Contreras was more vocal. "The great mistake your father made was to hand over power," he told Augusto Pinochet. All the Chilean judges who had ruled against their fathers had done so out of revenge, he said, and they were all leftists and Marxists.[51]

On the same day that Pinochet's supporters were commemorating the anniversary of his death, Judge Cerda submitted his resignation. A lawyer for Pinochet's younger son, Marco Antonio, accused Cerda of bias against the family. But the investigation remained open, and Chilean authorities eventually filed a lawsuit in a U.S. federal court against four banks, including a Pittsburgh-based institution, PNC Financial Services, that had taken over the infamous Riggs Bank after its executives were fined. Bachelet had signed a decree in 2008 instructing the lawsuit to seek "adequate compensation for acts and omissions of United States banks" resulting from their transactions with Pinochet.[52]

TWELVE Chile, Post-Pinochet

I

It was the first presidential campaign since the dictator's death, and it initially looked like a tired political rerun featuring political actors already well known to Chilean voters. By law Michelle Bachelet was prohibited from running for a consecutive presidential term, though her approval ratings had ascended to 78 percent, according to a survey by the Centro de Estudios Públicos (CEP). The same poll ranked Bachelet as the Chilean public's best-liked political figure, with 83 percent of respondents giving her a positive evaluation. The second best-liked leader was her finance minister, Andrés Velasco (58 percent), a reflection of how her administration had managed the Chilean economy through the global financial crisis.[1] Her informal style had drawn criticism at the beginning of her administration, but by the end of her term, Bachelet was being credited with bringing the presidency closer to the Chilean public. The election campaign to choose her successor showed a changed political culture.

There had been speculation that either former president Ricardo Lagos or Organization of American States secretary general Jose Miguel Insulza might become the Concertación's candidate, but both men opted out of the race. There had been no primary or open process of candidate selection, and the Center-Left coalition eventually selected former president Eduardo Frei. After two decades in power, the Concertación seemed not to have cultivated the next generation of leaders and at times appeared to be teetering on the verge of political exhaustion.

The Center-Right Alianza coalition once again picked Sebastián Piñera, the Chilean billionaire and former senator who had lost the January 2006 runoff vote to Michelle Bachelet. Since then Piñera had maintained his high public profile, occasionally encountering legal or political problems. In 2007 Chile's securities regulatory agency fined him $680,000 for insider trading, charging that while serving on the board of Chile's national airline, LAN, he had purchased three million shares a few days before the company issued its earnings report for the first half of 2006. Finance Minister Velasco said the fine was based on technical considerations, while Piñera maintained that the charge was politically motivated because he was "a person with political expectations, with an important political situation." He announced he would not appeal the fine, since it could take five years for the case to go through the courts—an oblique reference to his plans to make another run for the Chilean presidency.[2]

There would be other suggestions of financial wrongdoing, including an accusation from the Pinochet regime's former justice minister Monica Madariaga about his actions during Chile's 1982 banking crisis. According to Madariaga, she had helped Piñera avoid going to jail when authorities took administrative control of a bank he had managed and uncovered evidence that the institution had made millions in bad loans. When a judge issued an arrest warrant for Piñera, he went into hiding for twenty-four days while his lawyers tried to get the order overturned. Madariaga said Piñera's brother, a former regime cabinet minister, sought her intervention. She contacted the judge in the case, asking that Piñera not be arrested, and the judge in question confirmed that Madariaga had indeed called him. Chile's Supreme Court later acquitted Piñera of the charges, after an extensive legal battle.[3]

Piñera rejected this version of events, accusing the Frei campaign of attempting to smear him as opinion polls showed him enjoying a considerable lead over the former president. To his critics, the billionaire was a Chilean edition of Italy's flamboyant Silvio Berlusconi, coming to power atop a business and media empire—though unlike Berlusconi, Piñera was able to present himself as an exemplary family man and was frequently photographed with his wife and four grown children. A practicing Catholic, he described his political philosophy as Christian humanism and frequently referred to his opposition of Pinochet's reelection in 1988.

Piñera was also one of the few business leaders in the country to become involved in nature conservation. He established a philanthropic organization, Fundación Futuro, that offered arts and education programs and funded research into urban renewal projects such as a proposal to build public recreation areas along Santiago's Mapocho River. The foundation also funded a 290,000-acre park and nature reserve on Chiloé, the largest of the country's southern archipelago islands. Parque Tantauco's stated objectives include preserving the local ecosystems and species and promoting "ecologically sustainable productive activities."[4]

Perhaps not so coincidentally, the park lies just northwest of the nature reserve founded and funded by Douglas Tompkins, the California billionaire and environmental activist. Over the years many of Tompkins's critics had retreated as more and more Chileans had visited Parque Pumalin and enjoyed the well-marked trails through pristine rainforest and along waterfalls and had gone kayaking in pools with dolphins and sea lions. Chilean environmental activist Sara Larrain praised Piñera's Parque Tantauco, noting that it might not have happened without Tompkins's example.[5]

II

There were two more candidates in the race. Jorge Arrate was an economist and former doctoral candidate at Harvard University and a senior member of Chile's Socialist Party. He had held cabinet posts in the Aylwin and Frei government and then became the Lagos administration's ambassador to Argentina, but he had become disenchanted with the Concertación governments' economic policies. By 2007 he was urging that it was time for the Chilean Left to break away from the Concertación to form a new political movement. Arrate subsequently became the candidate of Juntos Podemos, a coalition comprised of the Chilean Communist Party and smaller leftist organizations. The CEP poll showed that of those Chileans who could identify Arrate, 32 percent had a favorable impression of him—which was not the same thing as supporting him politically.[6]

His stated policies included support for small- and medium-sized businesses, tax cuts, and a vague plan to restructure the economy and amend the constitution to benefit underserved segments of the Chilean population such as students, retirees, and workers. The Concertación was unwilling to make such changes, and the Chilean Right, even less so, Arrate wrote on his campaign Web site.[7]

Frei, Piñera, and Arrate may have seemed all too familiar to Chilean voters, but the fourth candidate injected a blast of fresh air into what had threatened to be a stale campaign. Marco Enríquez-Ominami, age thirty-six, was a first-term member of congress who had resigned from the Socialist Party to run for president as an independent. He had been born a few months before the 1973 military coup, the child of Movement of the Revolutionary Left (MIR) founder Miguel Enríquez. His mother fled with him to France while his father remained in Chile, attempting to organize resistance to the new military regime. The following year DINA agents discovered his hideout in Santiago and surrounded the house. Enríquez refused to surrender and died in the ensuing shootout, becoming something of a legend among the Chilean Left. His mother later married Carlos Ominami, the Aylwin government's future economy minister and senator, who legally adopted him.

Enríquez-Ominami spent his early years speaking more French than Spanish, eventually acquiring French citizenship. Toward the end of the Pinochet regime, he returned to Chile with his family, studying philosophy at the University of Chile. He later went back to France and took a filmmaking course in Paris. His French upbringing, his family's dramatic history, and his adoptive father's Japanese surname meant that MEO, he came to be known, was bound to attract attention. Before launching his political career, he told a Chilean magazine interviewer that he regretted his dual French-Chilean citizenship, that he would have preferred to be French-Italian, and that while Paris was one of the world's most beautiful cities, Santiago was surely one of the ugliest.[8] He amended his comments in a later interview by saying that he had had to fight for his Chilean identity.[9]

Enríquez-Ominami had a short but successful career as a filmmaker, and in 2002 produced a somewhat irreverent look at what had become of his late father's leftist colleagues. *Chile, los héroes están fatigados (Chile, the Heroes Are Exhausted)* was screened at several international film festivals and retraced the careers of a half-dozen former would-be revolutionaries who, by late middle age, had become business consultants or officials in post-Pinochet governments that were decidedly less radical than their younger selves would have desired.[10]

Enríquez-Ominami began his campaign with no party organization but with thousands of enthusiastic supporters, especially young Chilean voters disenchanted with the country's political establishment. He spoke of legalizing gay marriage, improving the public education system, and raising taxes on businesses—while insisting he supported free enterprise. "I don't believe in market societies but I do believe in societies with markets," he told Reuters news agency, adding that as a film producer he benefited from the market himself. "I believe in the market, but not for distributing wealth." As for his chances of winning the election, he pointed out that Bachelet had also seemed to be a long shot.[11]

Less than two months before the election, polls showed Enríquez-Ominami closing in on Frei, and although Piñera was ahead of both candidates, some polls suggested that Enríquez-Ominami would do better than Frei in a runoff with Piñera. (The same polls showed that 14 to 23 percent of Chileans planned to either abstain or to cast blank ballots.)[12]

Enríquez-Ominami's candidacy seemed like a heartening sign that the Chilean electoral system was capable of renewing itself, though he was embarrassed when a former advisor was found guilty of using state funds to finance campaign activities during the 2005 elections. According to prosecutors, the advisor funneled the equivalent of $42,000 in state money to a Socialist Party member working for Enríquez-Ominami and another candidate, though it was not clear how or if the money was spent in either politician's campaign. But the advisor, Edgardo Lepe, had played an important role in Enríquez-Ominami's congressional race and afterward had worked as chief of staff for Enríquez-Ominami's adoptive father, now a member of the Chilean senate. Enríquez-Ominami sought to distance himself from Lepe, saying that he had nothing to do with his former advisor and that prosecutors had been satisfied that neither he nor his adoptive father had any involvement in the fraud.[13]

As the election approached, the lines between Chile's governing bodies and political campaigns began to blur. Finance minister Andrés Velasco was photographed working on a document for the Frei campaign on his laptop during a Senate debate on the budget.[14] There were so many members of the chamber of deputies out campaigning that it became difficult to reach a quorum, so party leaders voted first to take Thursdays off and then to suspend congressional sessions altogether until after the election. Attendance had dwindled during the run-ups to previous elections, but this was the first time the Chilean congress had officially shut down—though the deputies insisted they were still working in their constituencies.[15]

There were a series of televised debates featuring the four candidates, and some of the most dramatic exchanges took place between Piñera and Enríquez-Ominami, as if each had recognized the other as the biggest challenger. Piñera accused the filmmaker of suffering from "Peter Pan syndrome," of imagining that he was a completely fresh leader unencumbered by any political past. "I want to remind you that you were a member of the Concertación these past twenty years, you were a deputy," he said. "I ask you to accept your own history, but not to get trapped by it." He noted that if the Concertación had held a primary, Enríquez-Ominami would have either been its candidate or have been backing Frei. The filmmaker shot back that Peter Pan had the advantage of not being a liar, and that he'd noticed that Piñera's campaign posters did not bear the logos of the conservative political parties—Renovación Nacional and the Union Democrática Independiente (UDI)—who were backing his candidacy.[16] At times Piñera seemed an unlikely choice for conservative Chilean voters—one of his television advertisements showed him with a gay couple, part of a diversity sequence that included a Mapuche representative, workers, the elderly, students, and disabled Chileans. The words "he will be our voice" appeared as one of the gay men, holding hands with his partner, puts an arm around Piñera, who tells viewers, "People accept them; now we need a country that respects them."[17] Several UDI leaders expressed their displeasure with this television spot, as did the head of Chile's Roman Catholic bishops conference, who said "there were limits" to what candidates should do to win votes. Piñera said he had met with the bishop and assured him that his government would work to strengthen the Chilean family. But he seemed blithely unconcerned by the conservative criticism, saying that his government was not going to discriminate against anyone "for their economic condition, ethnic origin, religious belief or sexual orientation."[18]

For conservative Chilean voters, Piñera was still the only possible choice, but their support would not be enough to win the election. His outreach to Chilean gays, women, and other groups was in marked contrast to the slightly sexist undertones during his 2005 race against Bachelet. It was also another sign of how much Chile was changing. A spokesman for the Frei campaign also reacted to the bishops' concerns, saying, "Homosexuals are everywhere, including the Catholic Church," and that their candidate also supported pluralism.[19]

Indeed, Piñera's campaign called itself the coalition for change, and it borrowed and reworded a slogan from the Concertación's 1988 campaign for a "no" vote against Pinochet ("Chile, happiness is on its way"): "Chile, happiness never retires." The Enríquez-Ominami campaign borrowed the slogan "Yes We Can" from the previous year's presidential election, keeping the words in English but using the Spanish phonetic spelling to print posters that read, "Yes Gui Can."

III

"Chile will be immensely rich in 21st century energy, which is basically new, renewable, clean energy." On his campaign Web site, Piñera noted that Chile had an abundance of sunshine for solar power, volcanoes for geothermic energy, and a long Pacific coastline that might be ideal for wind and wave power. His administration would work toward the goal of having 20 percent of the country's electrical energy come from such sources.[20] The other three presidential candidates also promised more investment and research in green energy; even Frei, once the nemesis of Chilean environmentalists, pledged support for solar panels and subsidies for small- and medium-sized businesses using renewable energy.[21]

The vulnerable underside of Chile's economic growth has been its lack of traditional energy sources. It has limited reserves of oil, and production has been gradually falling since 1987, when it produced less than half of what it consumed. That consumption has since increased by 150 percent. And despite extensive exploration by Chile's Empresa Nacional de Petroleo, there is little natural gas in the country. Chile's consumption of natural gas remained level with its domestic production until 1997, when it began importing gas from Argentina, and by 2004 consumption levels had quadrupled.[22] But that same year Argentina reduced its exports in the wake of its own rising domestic consumption. The supply of natural gas arriving through the seven pipelines linking the two countries began to dry up, at times falling as much as 50 percent below contracted volume and sometimes ceasing altogether. During one two-week period in August 2006, Argentina completely cut off natural gas exports to Chile, forcing at least one power plant to shut down. Bolivia also has a good supply of natural gas to be exported, conveniently near Chile's northern mining region, but old resentments from the 1879 War of the Pacific, when the country lost its sea outlet, make it an unlikely supplier.

What Chile does have is some hydroelectric power and the potential for more, but proposed new dams and plants have met with fierce opposition from environmental groups and a national and international campaign to stop such projects from going ahead. In the early 1990s environmental groups had tried to stop the Spanish electrical company ENDESA from constructing two dams on the Bio Bio, Chile's second-largest river, which lies roughly 250 miles south of Santiago and flows from the Andes to the Pacific. The area is the traditional home of many isolated indigenous communities and had become increasingly popular with whitewater rafters and adventure tourists. The campaign to stop construction did not succeed, and in 1996 ENDESA built the Pangue hydroelectric plant, harnessing the upper Bio Bio to produce 467 megawatts of electricity. A coalition of environmental and indigenous activists managed to delay ENDESA's second project in the region, the Ralco dam, but construction eventually went ahead; the plant began operating at the end of 2004, becoming Chile's second-largest power plant.[23]

Hydroelectric power accounts for well over half the energy consumed in Chile, and environmentalists decried the apparent lack of government strategy for the future or serious consideration of alternative energy sources. When Argentina reduced its natural gas shipments, ENDESA revealed plans to develop a $4 billion hydroelectric project in two rivers in the Aysen region of northern Patagonia. The project involved four power plants that together would produce 2,400 megawatts of electricity, covering the estimated increase in demand for at least five years. A transmission line over seven hundred miles long would have to pass through five national parks and two nature reserves to reach Santiago.

The Patagonia dam project, HidroAysen, was bigger than the Bio Bio dams, but so was the campaign against the project. The Aysen region is sparsely populated, with approximately one hundred thousand residents who have often complained that Santiago plays little attention to their needs. The project threatened to flood grazing lands and hurt tourism, which had become increasingly important to the local economy. A poll published in April 2008 by the Centro de Estudios de la Realidad Contemporanea showed that of those Chileans familiar with the HidroAysen project, 53 percent were opposed—an increase of 15 percent over those who had opposed the Bio Bio dams. An even larger majority, 70 percent, believed the hydroelectric projects would damage the environment.[24]

The bishop of the Aysen Catholic diocese, Monsignor Luis Infanti, composed a lengthy pastoral letter in which he decried the project's environmental, social, and economic costs. Entitled "Give Us This Day Our Daily Water," Infanti warned of the dangers to local businesses, tourism, and flora and fauna posed by the quest for "profit, exploitation and destruction." "In every corner of the immense Patagonia, one can see the mark of God the creator," he wrote. "Patagonia is contemplation and praise. It is exuberant life." The bishop said the ENDESA electric company had a virtual monopoly over local water rights and urged the government to replace the Pinochet regime's water law, which allowed water rights to be sold to the highest bidder, and renationalize the country's water resources.[25]

Of the four presidential candidates, Marco Enríquez-Ominami was the most outspoken critic of the HidroAysen project, and, faced with growing opposition to the plant, Frei and Piñera seemed to play down their earlier expressed support. Campaigners published a coffee-table book of compelling photographs of Aysen and other parts of Patagonia, showing areas devastated by illegal logging, overgrazing, and erosion. There were breathtaking photos of the region's lakes and other scenic attractions, interspersed with photomontages showing what the views would be with the proposed power lines running through the area.[26] Similar images appeared in posters at Santiago's airport and other public areas.

The antidam campaign brought Chilean environmental groups under increased official scrutiny, with the Interior Ministry's Agencia Nacional de Inteligencia (ANI), a division of the Interior Ministry, stepping up its monitoring in 2007. At least three ANI officials were gathering information on environmental NGOs' activities, members, and funding. One antidam campaigner said that several of his groups' computers had been stolen and that their office had received phone calls saying "we should be careful about what we do."[27]

The director of one NGO, the Latin American Observatory on Environmental Conflicts, said he had been contacted several times by ANI officials looking for information—which he had declined to provide. "They are keeping a close eye on our activities," he said. "But we refuse to cooperate with them. It is extremely worrying that, even though we are in a democracy, environmental movements are considered a threat to the State."[28]

IV

Piñera's fortune might have distanced him from the everyday lives of most Chileans, but his three opponents also came from relatively privileged backgrounds and had also been educated at private schools. Although poverty levels had declined under the Concertación governments, roughly one-sixth of the Chilean population still lived below the poverty line, according to government figures, and this had proved resistant to change.[29] A newspaper survey of the mayors of Chile's ten poorest municipalities—all located in rural areas outside the capital—suggested there had been little improvement in local living conditions in recent years: there were still high levels of unemployment and illiteracy and poor transportation and public services.[30]

"The poor are less poor, and fewer in number," a Catholic priest who had served a poor Santiago parish told me. "But they are also better informed and less submissive." The Bachelet administration had extended health-care coverage for low-income Chileans and built thousands of free or low-cost child care centers throughout the country. There had not been any significant reform of the public education system, but Bachelet had pushed the Chilean congress to approve the biggest budget ever for education--$8 billion—and Piñera had urged his political allies to support the bill, emphasizing its importance to Chile's future.[31]

Income disparities had also persisted, as much of the Chilean labor market seemed reluctant to adopt meritocratic criteria in its hiring practices. The richest 20 percent of the population earned 61 percent of the GDP, while the poorest 20 percent earned 3.3 percent. One study by the University of Chile found that although academic performance was rewarded in the labor market, socioeconomic background was a better predictor of future earnings. The researchers compiled data on graduates of an economics and business degree program and found that a low-performing student who had been raised in a high-income neighborhood, had attended a prestigious private secondary school, and whose surname suggested upper-class ancestry could expect significantly higher earnings than a student who had graduated at the head of his or her university class but had come from a poor or even an average socioeconomic background.[32] The author met a couple whose son, a recent college graduate, was looking for his first job. The family was experiencing financial difficulties but had opted not to move from their affluent Santiago neighborhood to a less expensive location, for fear that an address in a more modest part of the city would look bad on their son's curriculum vitae—and thus hurt his job prospects. Economic growth and democratic processes have yet to bring about anything approaching an egalitarian society in Chile.

V

On March 8, 2010, Bachelet appointed a new commander for the Chilean army, which over the years had shrunk from around seventy thousand troops under Pinochet to forty thousand but had become the best-equipped army in Latin America. It was also becoming a more professional fighting force, with conscripts replaced by volunteers and an emphasis on international peacekeeping and civil defense during natural disasters.

A few weeks earlier many of those former conscripts had confronted the Bachelet government with a proposition. If they could be protected from retaliation from both their former commanding officers and the Chilean courts, they would tell what they knew of crimes committed during the Pinochet regime. Many of them had horrifying experiences of being forced to torture and kill or risk being killed themselves. Some had approached Chile's civilian courts with offers to testify, only to be referred to military courts, and vice versa. The former teenage soldiers were also hoping for some psychiatric care for their long-untreated traumas. "We were executors and witnesses of many brutalities and now we're willing to talk about them for our own personal redemption," said Fernando Mellado, president of the Santiago chapter of the Former Soldiers of 1973 group.[33] Chilean Defense Ministry officials later met with the group's representatives, but it seemed unlikely there would be any clear resolution to the embittered soldiers' concerns.

General Juan Fuente-Alba was appointed to succeed General Oscar Izurieta as army commander, and an official photograph showed the two men, among the last of the generation that had served under Pinochet, standing alongside Bachelet and her defense minister. Fuente-Alba had been chosen in part for his apparently clean human rights record, but not everyone agreed with his appointment.

As a young officer stationed in northern Chile, Fuente-Alba had been present during General Sergio Arellano's visit to the town of Calama during the infamous Caravan of Death tour, in which one hundred twenty prisoners were summarily executed. A government spokeswoman said Fuente-Alba had voluntarily testified in a judicial investigation into the case and had been cleared of any wrongdoing. Fuente-Alba told the judge that while he had been in the town of Calama during the executions, he had been assigned to patrol the nearby Chuquicamata copper mine and had had no contact with prisoners. The only witness to have placed Fuente-Alba at the scene of the crimes was another military officer found guilty of human rights abuses and known to have lied during his testimony. The Families of the Detained and Disappeared were skeptical and issued a statement saying that Chile's new army commander should have a spotless reputation. Marco Enríquez-Ominami defended Bachelet's appointee, noting that as a former victim of the dictatorship, her judgment should be respected.[34]

Sebastián Piñera, speaking to a group of retired military officers, offered a rather different view, telling them that if elected he would take steps to see justice applied in "an appropriate manner, without proceedings that go on ad eternum, that never finish." While his statement was textually vague, it was enough for Piñera to receive hearty applause from the group, which included some former officers under judicial investigation for human rights abuses. It also earned the conservative presidential candidate a rebuke from Chile's Supreme Court president, who noted that such cases were now moving more swiftly through the country's courts. "If someone believes some of our citizens are not getting their due process rights, he should cite the cases or situations where this has not been respected," he said.[35]

Nearly two decades had elapsed since the military regime had ended, but there was still no consensus on how to confront Chile's past or even what that past comprised. And yet there was broad agreement on all sides that past abuses should not be repeated under any future government. On November 24, 2009, Bachelet presided over the opening of a new human rights institute, whose creation had been proposed four years earlier but had only recently approved by Chile's congress. The institute would be an autonomous government body, presided over by officials appointed by the president and congress but who could only be removed by the Supreme Court.

The new agency would have the power to investigate human rights cases, including those from the military regime. In addition, the institute would reopen the investigations of earlier government commissions into killings and torture, inviting more victims and witnesses to come forward to testify. The institute would present an annual report of its findings to the United Nations and other international human rights organizations. "We are keeping a promise made by the government, a moral and political promise the country made to itself," Bachelet said.[36]

On December 13, 2009, Chileans went to the polls and gave Sebastián Piñera 44.05 percent of the vote. Eduardo Frei received 29.6 percent, with independent candidate Marco Enríquez-Ominami getting 20 percent and Jorge Arrate, 6.2 percent. As Piñera had not received an outright majority, the election went to a runoff vote two months later, as had happened in Chile's two previous presidential elections. Frei continued to campaign, courting voters from both the Arrate and Enríquez-Ominami camps, and after he agreed to include some of their proposals in his program, Arrate and his leftist coalition agreed to support him. Just three days before the runoff, Enríquez-Ominami said he would vote for Frei but stopped short of calling on his supporters to do so.[37] On January 17, 2010, Piñera, who had invested over $16 million of his own money in the campaign, won the second round, receiving 51.61 percent to Frei's 48.39 percent.[38] The results suggested that a majority of Chilean voters felt the Center-Left coalition that presided over the country's return to democracy had served its purpose and that it was time to move on.

Tragedy struck less than two weeks before Piñera's inauguration. On February 27 a massive earthquake occurred off the coast of southern Chile, measuring eight on the twelve-point Mercalli scale, triggering a tsunami that devastated several coastal towns and sending tremors to neighboring Peru and Argentina. It was the worst seismological disaster to hit the country since the catastrophic 1960 earthquake near Valdivia. The country's second-largest city, Concepción, lay seventy miles southeast of the earthquake's epicenter, with its electricity cut off along with supplies of food and water. Looters began ransacking supermarkets and other businesses, and lawlessness soon spread to residential areas, where thieves began breaking into homes and setting fires.

Concepción had once been a leftist stronghold and had suffered more than its share of repression during the Pinochet regime. In Santiago Bachelet's critics accused her of letting her own painful memories delay the decision to send in the army to restore order, ignoring the fact that her air force general father had coordinated relief efforts following the 1960 earthquake. And when some six thousand troops arrived in Concepción two days after the earthquake, they were welcomed by most of the city's five hundred thousand distressed residents. The army imposed a curfew from six p.m. to noon, positioned tanks outside supermarkets, and organized lines of people waiting to shop for food, use banks, or buy gasoline. The young soldiers, born and raised under civilian government, interacted respectfully with the local residents, who thanked them and sometimes patted them on the back or attempted to hug them. An army corporal at a military checkpoint commented that what happened in 1973, the year of Chile's coup, "was another time."[39]

A Chilean Chronology

September 4, 1970 Salvador Allende, a Socialist, wins a plurality of votes in the Chilean presidential election and, after being confirmed by congress, becomes president on November 3, 1970.

August 23, 1973 General Augusto Pinochet becomes Chilean army commander, replacing General Carlos Prats, who was forced out of office following protests by military wives backing a coup against the Allende government.

September 11, 1973 The Chilean military, led by the navy, seize power from Allende, who commits suicide while air force planes strafe the La Moneda presidential palace. A junta composed of Pinochet, naval commander José Merino, air force commander Gustavo Leigh, and carabinero commander Cesar Mendoza assume control of the government.

June 14, 1974 Official creation of the Dirección de Inteligencia Nacional (DINA) by junta decree law. The new intelligence service is led by army colonel Manuel Contreras, who reports only to Pinochet.

June 27, 1974 Pinochet is declared "supreme leader of the nation," receiving a presidential sash, in a ceremony prepared without the other junta members' knowledge.

October 1, 1974 DINA agents kill former Chilean army commander Carlos Prats and his wife, Sofia, in a car bomb explosion in Buenos Aires.

October 6, 1975 DINA agents operating in Italy shoot and critically wound Bernardo Leighton (a former cabinet minister under the Christian Democratic government of Eduardo Frei [1964–70]) and his wife, Anita, who had taken political refuge in Rome.

June 16, 1976 The U.S. Senate passes a bill banning all arms sales to Chile.

July 16, 1976 The body of Spanish diplomat Carmelo Soria, who had helped numerous Chileans and other nationals flee the country in the wake of the coup, is found in Santiago, two days after his kidnapping by DINA agents.

September 21, 1976 DINA agents in Washington, D.C., plant a car bomb that kills Chilean exile leader and former Allende cabinet minister Orlando Letelier and his American coworker Ronni Moffitt.

August 13, 1977 The Pinochet regime announces the dissolution of DINA, to be replaced by a new security agency, the Central Nacional de Informaciones (CNI).

December 16, 1977 The United Nations General Assembly approves a resolution condemning Chile's military regime for human rights abuses.

January 4, 1978 Following a United Nations resolution condemning human rights violations in Chile, a referendum is held by the regime in which Chileans are asked to cast "yes" or "no" votes in support of Pinochet. The official results of the vote, held without an electoral registry, show 75 percent in favor of the resolution.

July 24, 1978 Pinochet forces the resignation of junta member and air force commander General Gustavo Leigh, who is replaced by General Fernando Matthei.

October 1979 Chile's Supreme Court rejects a U.S. extradition request for DINA chief Manuel Contreras and two other DINA agents for the 1976 car bomb assassination in Washington, D.C., of Orlando Letelier and Ronni Moffitt.

September 11, 1980 The regime holds a plebiscite in which Chileans are asked to vote "yes" or "no" on a new constitution and an extension of Pinochet's rule for eight more years. Official results show the "yes" ballots total 67 percent of the vote.

September 12, 1980 Pinochet tells reporters he will not seek reelection in 1988.

March 11, 1981 Pinochet leads a ceremony in which the commanders of Chile's navy, air force, and police force, along with another army general, are sworn in as members of the junta, which will act as a legislative body under Pinochet's presidency. The regime moves its headquarters into the La Moneda presidential palace, which had been closed since the 1973 coup.

January 22, 1982 President Eduardo Frei (1964–70) dies in the hospital following a minor surgery. His family suspects foul play. At Frei's state funeral, Pinochet is confronted with hundreds of protestors screaming "Murderer!"

February 25, 1982 The president of Chile's public employees union, Tucapel Jimenez, is found murdered in his car on the outskirts of Santiago. The previous week he had called for a coalition against Pinochet's economic policies.

May 11, 1983 The first mass protests against the regime are held, organized by a coalition of labor and political groups.

August 2, 1985 Junta member and carabinero commander General Cesar Mendoza resigns when a judicial investigation links members of his police force to the murders of three Chilean leftists earlier that year. He is replaced by General Rodolfo Stange.

September 7, 1986 The Manuel Rodriguez Patriotic Front ambush Pinochet's motorcade as it leaves his country retreat, using rocket launchers and automatic weapons. The attack kills five bodyguards, but Pinochet is uninjured and launches a crackdown.

October 5, 1988 Pinochet is defeated in the one-man presidential plebiscite.

October 1989 Pinochet dissolves the security agency, the CNI, incorporating it into the army's intelligence services.

December 14, 1989 Patricio Aylwin, former senate leader during the Allende government and president of the Christian Democrats and the Concertación de Partidos por la Democracia, wins the presidential election with 55.17 percent of the votes cast.

March 11, 1990 Pinochet turns the Chilean presidency over to Patricio Aylwin but remains army commander.

December 19, 1990 Pinochet orders troops throughout the country to be placed on a state of alert, following a congressional investigation into payments his son received from the Chilean army.

March 4, 1991 President Aylwin goes on national television to report the findings of the National Commission on Truth and Reconciliation, which uncovered at least thirty-two hundred killings and disappearances during the Pinochet regime and describes the circumstances of their torture and executions.

December 1991 An eleven-ton cargo of arms from Chile's army munitions company is intercepted on its way to Croatia, in violation of a UN ban on weapons sales to that country.

February 20, 1992 The body of Colonel Gerardo Huber, the army's director of logistics, is found on the outskirts of Santiago. He had disappeared shortly before he was due to testify in the Croatia arms case.

May 28, 1993 Responding to reports that an investigation into army payments to his son has been reopened, Pinochet places armed paratroopers in full combat gear on the streets near the armed forces building in Santiago.

December 11, 1993 Christian Democrat Eduardo Frei wins the presidential election, receiving 58 percent of the vote.

May 30, 1995 Former secret police chief Manuel Contreras and another DINA official are sentenced to prison for their role in the 1976 car bomb assassination of Chilean exile Orlando Letelier and Ronni Moffitt in Washington, D.C.

January 20, 1998 Judge Juan Guzmán Tapia files criminal charges against Pinochet for the 1976 disappearance of five Communist Party members.

March 10, 1998 Pinochet retires after twenty-five years as Chile's army commander. The following day he takes a seat in the Chilean senate as a lifetime member, amid protests by some members of congress and thousands of street demonstrators.

October 16, 1998 Pinochet is arrested at the London Clinic after Spanish judge Baltasar Garzón requests his extradition to Spain.

January 16, 2000 Ricardo Lagos, a Socialist whom Pinochet had imprisoned during his regime, wins a runoff election to become president.

March 2, 2000 Britain's home secretary Jack Straw informs parliament that he is dropping extradition proceedings against Pinochet, citing the former dictator's memory deficit.

March 3, 2000 Pinochet arrives in Santiago and immediately becomes the object of multiple human rights lawsuits.

May 23, 2000 The Appeals Court revokes Pinochet's immunity as a senator for life by a vote of thirteen to nine, opening the way for him to be tried for crimes committed during his regime.

January 31, 2001 Pinochet is placed under house arrest following orders from a court judge investigating his role in the Caravan of Death.

July 9, 2001 An Appeals Court panel of judges rules two to one that Pinochet suffers from dementia and is unfit to stand trial.

June 13, 2003 Chilean army commander General Juan Emilio Cheyre gives a speech in which he promises that the country's military will "never again" repeat the human rights violations of the past.

November 29, 2004 The National Commission on Political Imprisonment and Torture publishes a detailed report into torture and abuses suffered by those imprisoned under the Pinochet regime, drawing upon testimonies by 35,868 people.

March 16, 2005 A U.S. Senate committee investigating money laundering publishes a report on Pinochet's secret bank accounts in U.S. financial institutions.

November 23, 2005 Judge Carlos Cerda issues four indictments against Pinochet for tax evasion, falsifying official documents, the use of false passports, and failing to report his financial and real estate transactions on his tax returns.

January 16, 2006 Michelle Bachelet, a pediatrician, Socialist, and former political prisoner who had been Latin America's first female defense minister, wins a runoff vote in the presidential election.

August 19, 2006 Chile's Supreme Court votes to strip Pinochet of immunity from prosecution, allowing him to be tried on corruption charges for his unexplained fortune deposited in foreign bank accounts.

December 10, 2006 Pinochet dies in Santiago's military hospital.

Notes

INTRODUCTION

1. *El Mercurio,* February 22, 2006. Unless otherwise indicated, all translations are mine.

2. Jorge Burgos, interview with author, London, England, July 2, 2007.

3. Patricio Rojas, interview with author, Santiago, Chile, October 24, 2007.

4. Quoted in Raquel Correa and Elizabeth Subercaseaux, *Ego Sum Pinochet* (Santiago: Editorial Zig Zag, 1989), p. 141.

5. Indicador de la Sociedad de la Información (ISI), 2009, study by Everis consulting company and the University of Navarra, Spain, http://www.everis.cl/Images/91936%20ISI%20DICIEMBRE%2009_tcm40–65345.pdf, accessed September 7, 2010.

6. Remarks by OECD Secretary General Angel Gurría on the accession of Chile to the organization, January 11, 2010, http://www.oecd.org/document/50/0,3343,en_21571361_44315115_44369330_1_1_1_1,00.html, accessed September 6, 2010.

7. Balance de la Delincuencia 2009, Fundación Paz Ciudadana, http://www.pazciudadana.cl/docs/pub_20100527153035.pdf, accessed September 5, 2010.

8. Marta Lagos, interview with author, Santiago, Chile, November 16, 2007.

9. www. Carabineros.cl, accessed November 14, 2007.

10. Isabel del Campo, interview with author, Santiago, Chile, October 23, 2007.

11. Juan Maureira, interview with author, Paine, Chile, November 7, 2007.

12. Genaro Roman, interview with author, Paine, Chile, October 14, 2007.

13. Author's observation at meeting in Paine, Chile, November 7, 2007.

14. Author's conversations with members of the Paine association of relatives of the disappeared, November 7, 2007.

15. http://ospped.blogspot.com/, accessed November 19, 2007.

16. Funa al Asesino de Victor Jara "Edwin Dimiter Bianchi" Buena, May 25, 2006, http://www.youtube.com/watch?v=UA9IGZMg0Qc&feature=related, accessed October 17, 2007 and September 8, 2010.

17. http://www.globalpost.com/video/general/090310/defending-the-dictator-history-gets-rewrite-at-the-pinochet-museum, accessed March 11, 2009.

CHAPTER ONE

1. Author's observations in Santiago, October 5–6, 1988.

2. The Chilean press reported the explosives were discovered at the La Serena airport on February 27, 1988. A declassified Central Intelligence Agency cable and a Department of Defense cable two days later analyzed the incident, citing Chilean Communist sources, and concluded the affair was a hoax. See the partially redacted cable "Denying Leftist Responsibility for Reported Assassination Attempt against Pinochet," March 2, 1988, http://foia.state.gov/documents/Pcia3/000092A7.pdf, and "Possible Government Hoax," a partially redacted Defense Intelligence summary, March 4, 1988, http://foia.state.gov/documents/Pdod3/000098C4.pdf.

3. Fernando Matthei, interview with author, Santiago, Chile, October 29, 2009.

4. Macroeconomic indicators from the Chilean Ministry of Finance and the Central Bank, http://www.minhda.cl/english/informacion_inversionista/economic_information_macro.php.

5. Centro de Estudios Públicos, Encuesta Nacional de Opinión Pública Mayo–Junio 1988, Santiago, Chile, pp. 87, 88, and 93, http://www.cepchile.cl/dms/lang_1/cat_443_pag_5.html, accessed March 12, 2008.

6. Estimates of the number of Chileans living in exile during the regime vary greatly. Alan Angell of Oxford University notes that the Office of the United Nations High Commissioner for Refugees put the figure at thirty thousand

while the Chilean-based support group, the Comite Pro-Retorno, put the figure as high as two hundred thousand. See *Democracy after Pinochet: Politics, Parties and Elections in Chile* (London: Institute for the Study of the Americas, 2006), p. 8.

7. For a complete account of the Pinochet regime's efforts to assassinate its opponents abroad, see John Dinges, *The Condor Years: How Pinochet and His Allies Brought Terror to Three Continents* (New York: New Press, 2004).

8. Rafael Moreno, interview with the author, London, England, September 24, 2007.

9. Patricia Arancibia Clavel and Isabel de la Maza Cave, *Matthei: Mi testimonio* (Santiago: Random House Mondadori, 2003), pp. 402–403.

10. State Department cables, "Imminent Possibility of a Staged Coup," September 30, 1988, http://foia.state.gov/documents/StateChile3/00007B33.pdf, and "Pinochet Determined to Use Violence on Whatever Scale Is Necessary," October 2, 1988, http://foia.state.gov/documents/StateChile3/00007B46.pdf.

11. Ricardo Lagos, interview with author, Santiago, Chile, November 15, 2007. Stange also told the U.S. Embassy that several buses of the type used by carabineros had mysteriously disappeared prior to the plebiscite and that "some elements posing as carabineros" might cause disruptions. See the declassified State Department cable, "Conversation with Junta Member Stange," October 19, 1988, http://foia.state.gov/documents/StateChile3/00007C08.pdf.

12. According to "no" campaign leader Genaro Arriagada, his organization offered to share its own counting of the returns with the Chilean military. The air force and navy accepted this offer; the army did not. Genaro Arriagada, interview with the author, Santiago, Chile, November 20, 2007.

13. Declassified State Department cable, "The Chilean Plebiscite, SITREP Four," October 6, 1989, http://foia.state.gov/documents/StateChile3/00007B72.pdf.

14. As reported in a declassified State Department cable, "Pinochet Looks Ahead," February 23, 1989, http://foia.state.gov/documents/StateChile3/00007F6A.pdf.

15. Matthei, interview.

16. Author's observations in Santiago, October 6, 1988.

17. This speech on October 25, 1988, was widely reported in the Chilean news media.

18. Genaro Arriagada, interview with author, Santiago, Chile, November 13, 2007.

19. Matthei, interview.

20. The 1991 National Commission for Truth and Reconciliation listed 2,279 people killed for political reasons and another 641 suspicious deaths that the commission could not conclusively determine were politically motivated. In another 449 cases there was no information uncovered apart from the missing person's name. See page 1122 of the *Report of the National Commission on Truth and*

Reconciliation, appendix 2, available in English translation at http://www.usip.org/files/resources/collections/truths_commissions/Chile90-Report/Chile90-Report.pdf.

21. Declassified State Department cable, "Offer/Threat by Manuel Contreras," February 10, 1989, http://foia.state.gov/documents/StateChile3/000094F4.pdf. A handwritten note attached to the cable proposes informing the Chilean foreign ministry of Contreras's threat, warning, "We will hold the [government of Chile] responsible if any of this is carried out."

22. *El Mercurio,* February 15, 1989.

23. *El Mercurio,* March 12, 1989.

24. Declassified State Department cable, "Pinochet Loyalists Named to Constitutional Court," April 4, 1989, http://foia.state.gov/documents/StateChile3/00007A8B.pdf.

25. Arancibia Clavel and de la Maza Cave, *Matthei,* p. 413.

26. Caceres stuck to this mild version of events fifteen years later during a television interview with historian Patricia Arancibia Clavel on October 10, 2004, on Chile's ARTV. Quoted in Patricia Arancibia Clavel, *Cita con la historia* (Santiago: Editorial Biblioteca Americana, 2006), p. 521.

27. *El Mercurio,* May 5, 1989.

28. See the profile of Büchi in *La Época,* December 3, 1989.

29. Alan Angell, *Democracy after Pinochet: Politics, Parties and Elections in Chile* (London: Institute for the Study of the Americas, 2007), p. 42.

30. Declassified State Department cable, "Aylwin Addresses AmCham," April 28, 1989, http://foia.state.gov/documents/StateChile3/00007E5B.pdf.

31. *El Mercurio* of July 23, 1989, carried a front-page color photograph of Büchi at this event; the sight of the candidate in riding attire may have helped to offset his semi-bohemian image among conservative voters.

32. Centro de Estudios Públicos, Estudio Social y de Opinion Publica, Septiembre–Octubre 1989, Documento de Trabajo 127, November 1989, Santiago, Chile, p. 4.

33. *El Mercurio,* August 24, 1989.

34. Arancibia Clavel and de la Maza Cave, *Matthei,* pp. 325–26. Matthei also told me during our interview that the Aylwin government's human rights investigation had found no cases of abuse committed by the Chilean air force since 1978.

35. *Santiago Times,* May 16, 2005.

36. *El Mercurio,* September 12, 1989.

37. "Army's 'Politicos' Gain Upper Hand; Professionalist Zincke Is Replaced by 'Tame' Lucar," *Latin American Regional Reports: Southern Cone,* November 16, 1989, p. 6.

38. *El Mercurio, La Tercera,* and other Chilean news media carried Aylwin's remarks on October 14, 1989, as well as Pinochet's warning the previous day.

39. Declassified State Department cable, "Chile Democratic Transition: Worst Case Scenarios," November 7, 1989, http://foia.state.gov/documents/StateChile3/00007F2D.pdf.

40. These incidents were widely covered in the Chilean press, especially in the December 16, 1989, edition of *El Mercurio.*

41. Declassified State Department cable, "Ambassador Meeting with President-Elect Aylwin," December 15, 1989, http://foia.state.gov/documents/StateChile3/00007F97.pdf.

CHAPTER TWO

1. Ascanio Cavallo, *La historia oculta de la transición* (Santiago: Editorial Grijalbo, 1998), p. 12.

2. Patricio Alywin, interview with the author, Santiago, Chile, October 18, 2007.

3. Edmundo Pérez Zujovic, Frei's former interior minister, was shot and killed on June 8, 1971, by the Vanguardia Organizada del Pueblo, a left-wing fringe group. The assassination was purportedly a revenge attack for the killing of eleven peasant farmers by police during the Frei government.

4. In *Hostile Intent: U.S. Covert Operations in Chile, 1964–1974* (Washington, D.C.: Potomac Books, 2007), Kristian Gustafson interviewed former secretary of state and National Security Council chairman Henry Kissinger, who coordinated the Nixon administration's anti-Allende campaign. Kissinger says, "We did not know Pinochet . . . we thought he might be someone favorable to Allende" (p. 214). The author notes that this statement is consistent with information contained in CIA and other declassified U.S. documents.

5. This resolution is often touted as a direct call for a military takeover, but a careful reading of the text suggests otherwise: it is addressed to cabinet ministers as well as the police and armed forces, urging that they "put an immediate end to all situations herein referred to that breach the Constitution and the laws of the land with the goal of redirecting government activity toward the path of law and ensuring the constitutional order of our Nation and the essential underpinnings of democratic coexistence among Chileans." The full text of the resolution on August 23, 1973, "Grave quebrantamiento del orden constitucional y legal de la república," can be accessed at http://es.wikisource.org/wiki/Grave_Quebrantamiento_del_Orden_Constitucional_y_Legal_De_La_Rep%C3%BAblica_del_Gobierno_Socialista_representado_por_Salvador_Allende.

6. According to a partially declassified Central Intelligence Agency report, extreme rightist elements in the Chilean army had discussed assassinating Aylwin as part of a plan to disrupt the democratic transition and give Pinochet a pretext for continuing in office. The report notes, "Only the most hard-core, fanatical Pinochet supporters who feel themselves threatened by the possibility of human rights persecutions by a civilian government would contemplate derailing the democratic transition. In the past their plans have not been approved by Pinochet" (partially declassified Central Intelligence cable, "Plans by the Extreme Right to Disrupt the Democratic Transition by an Assassination Attempt against Aylwin," December 13, 1989, http://foia.state.gov/documents/Pcia3/000092BA.pdf).

7. Arancibia Clavel, *Cita con la historia*, p. 551.

8. Emilio Rojo Orrego, *La otra cara de La Moneda: Los cuatro años de Aylwin* (Santiago: Ediciones ChileAmerica CESOC, n.d.), p. 9.

9. Aylwin, interview.

10. Declassified State Department cable, "The Chilean Inauguration and Vice President Quayle Visit," March 16, 1990, p. 5, http://foia.state.gov/documents/StateChile3/00007FF0.pdf.

11. Veronica Ahumada, interview with the author, Santiago, Chile, November 16, 2007.

12. Rafael Otano, *Nueva crónica de la transición* (Santiago: LOM Ediciones, 2006), p. 123, and "Reporter's Notebook: The Quayle Trip: Jaguars and Palms," *New York Times,* March 16, 1990.

13. *El Mercurio,* March 12, 1990.

14. Aylwin's speech was broadcast on Chilean television, and portions can be seen at http://www.museodeprensa.cl/1990/discurso-de-patricio-aylwin-en-el-estadio-nacional.

15. Tucapel Jimenez was fired from his civil service job in 1980 after urging a "no" vote in that year's constitutional plebiscite, which also extended Pinochet's rule for eight more years. He supported himself by driving a taxi, and on February 25, 1982, his vehicle was commandeered by security agents who killed him and later murdered an illiterate workman, staging a hoax in which the victim purportedly hung himself after leaving a note confessing to the union leader's murder. See *Report of the National Commission on Truth and Reconciliation,* p. 866, http://www.usip.org/files/resources/collections/truth_commissions/Chile90-Report/Chile90-Report.pdf.

16. Arancibia Clavel, *Cita con la historia*, pp. 625–26.

17. Felipe G. Morande, "A Decade of Inflation Targeting in Chile: Main Developments and Lessons," Central Bank of Chile, Santiago, 2000, http://www.bcentral.cl/eng/policies/presentations/executives/pdf/2000/morandejulio132002.pdf.

18. Quoted in Arancibia Clavel, *Cita con la historia*, p. 626.

19. Alberto Espina, interview with the author, London, United Kingdom, July 29, 2007. Espina later became a senator.

20. Cavallo, *La historia oculta,* p. 60.

21. For an account of Mexican-Chilean relations during this period, see Ximena Ortuzar, *México y Pinochet: La ruptura* (Mexico City: Editorial Nueva Imagen, 1986).

22. Peter Kornbluh, *The Pinochet File: A Declassified Dossier on Atrocity and Accountability* (New York: New Press, 2004), p. 176, and John Dinges, *The Condor Years: How Pinochet and His Allies Brought Terrorism to Three Continents* (New York: New Press, 2004), p. 73.

23. From a transcript of the Bush-Aylwin conversation on October 2, 1990, contained in a declassified National Security Council memorandum dated October 3, 1990, p. 5, http://foia.state.gov/documents/StateChile3/0000980A.pdf.

24. David R. Mares and Francisco Rojas Aravena, *The United States and Chile: Coming in from the Cold* (New York: Routledge, 2001), p. 91.

25. The assassination attempt against Leigh was widely covered in the Chilean press.

26. The most spectacular attack occurred December 14, 1983, when the FPMR blew up five electricity towers.

27. Declassified State Department report, "Analysis of Terrorist Arms Discovered in Chile," September 9, 1986, http://foia.state.gov/documents/StateChile3/00006DBE.pdf.

28. A former member of the FPMR in Santiago told me that his organization's ill-fated management of the weapons "caused us a lot of problems with Cuba."

29. *New York Times,* February 2, 1990.

30. Quoted in Arancibia Clavel and de la Maza Cave, *Matthei,* p. 420.

31. Declassified State Department report, "Assassination Attempt against Air Force General Gustavo Leigh," March 26, 1990, p. 5, http://foia.state.gov/documents/StateChile3/0000801E.pdf.

32. The assassination of Jaime Guzmán was widely covered in the Chilean press, April 1 and 2, 1991.

33. Partially redacted CIA report, "Government Believes Chile Is Targeting Figures of Major Political Importance," April 11, 1991, p. 2, http://foia.state.gov/documents/Pcia3/00009237.pdf.

34. Jorge Burgos, interview with the author, London, United Kingdom, July 2, 2007.

35. Partially redacted CIA report, "Terrorism in Chile," August 10, 1991, p. 5, http://foia.state.gov/documents/Pcia3/000091FE.pdf.

36. Declassified State Department cables, "Chilean Government Protests Terrorism Report," May 3, 1991, http://foia.state.gov/documents/StateChile3/

000082D1.pdf, and "Patterns of Global Terrorism Report on Chile," May 3, 1991, http://foia.state.gov/documents/StateChile3/000082D2.pdf.

37. Today the FPMR operates in Chile as a small political organization.

38. *New York Times,* January 15, 1992.

39. Cavallo, *La historia oculta,* pp. 150–51.

CHAPTER THREE

1. In his book *Pinochet: El gran comisionista,* journalist Benedicto Castillo, citing accounts by former Chilean army officers, writes that Pinochet disappeared the day of the uprising and only appeared, dressed in combat fatigues and brandishing a submachine gun, later in the afternoon, when the rebellious officers had already surrendered (Santiago: Editorial Mare Nostrum, 2007), pp. 40–41.

2. Patricio Rojas, interview with the author, Santiago, Chile, October 24, 2007.

3. Aylwin, interview.

4. A partially redacted U.S. Department of Defense report, "State of Civil-Military Relations in Chile," dated March 18, 1991, observed that "paradoxically, the degree of sympathy for a modern U.S. or Western European model of intra-military and civil-military relations is probably greater among the older generation of Chilean officers than their younger colleagues. Younger generations of military officers have had limited contact with democratic rule and an institutional approach to civilian-military relationships, and there is a presumed allegiance to the military government, if not Pinochet himself. " See http://foia.state.gov/documents/Pdod3/00009889.pdf, pp. 0053–54.

5. Rojas, interview.

6. Cavallo, *La historia oculta,* pp. 24–25.

7. "Pinochet Gets Told Off by President; After a Week of Tension, Army Is Told to Eschew Politics," *Latin America Weekly Report,* London, June 7, 1990.

8. Cavallo, *La historia oculta,* p. 44

9. Statement by Chilean bishops, quoted in the Jesuit magazine *Mensaje,* June 21, 1990.

10. Partially redacted U.S. Department of Defense cable, "Army Officer Attitudes," July 10, 1990, http://foia.state.gov/documents/Pdod3/00009788.pdf.

11. *El Mercurio,* September 1, 1990, and *La Tercera,* September 1, 1990.

12. Augusto Pinochet Ugarte, *Camino recorrido: Memorias de un soldado,* vol. 1 (Santiago: Imprenta Geografia Military de Chile, 1990). At least one Chilean academic told me the book was almost certainly ghostwritten, and Pinochet's version of the night before the September 11, 1973, coup on p. 192 is almost identical to that of *The Crucial Day,* an account of the coup released in 1980 that consists of a question-and-answer session with Pinochet by an anonymous interviewer.

13. "Pinochet Told to Hold His Tongue: Armed Forces 'Must Stick' to Their Constitutional Duties," *Latin American Regional Report: Southern Cone,* London, October 18, 1990, p. 2.

14. In fact, the Chilean army uniform is modeled on the Prussian design, gray in color, and Chilean soldiers march using the *paso regular,* or goose step.

15. Aylwin recalled during our interview that the air force invitation had been deliberately timed to allow him to be out of Santiago during the coup anniversary. On September 11 of the following year, the Chilean navy followed suit with a presidential visit to Easter Island.

16. *Latin America Regional Reports: Southern Cone;* October 18, 1990, p. 2.

17. Cavallo, *La historia oculta,* pp. 52–53. The incident in which the officer salutes but does not ask Aylwin's permission to begin the parade was seen on Chilean national television.

18. "Aylwin Backs Down on Pinochet; Private September Deal to Call Off the Pressure," *Latin America Weekly Report,* London, October 18, 1990, p. 10.

19. "Ex-CNI Officers in Finance Scandal; Pinochet Claims Generals Had No Part in 'Cutufa' Activities," *Latin America Regional Report: Southern Cone,* London, November 22, 1990, p. 2.

20. Claudia Farfán and Fernando Vega, *La familia: Historia privada de los Pinochet* (Santiago: Random House Mondadori, 2009), pp. 72–73.

21. Ozren Agnic, *Pinochet, S.A.: La base de la fortuna* (Santiago: RIL Editors, 2006), pp. 38–39.

22. Castillo, *Pinochet,* pp. 116–17.

23. Cavallo, *La historia oculta,* pp. 67–68.

24. Espina, interview.

25. José Antonio Viera Gallo, interview with the author, Santiago, Chile, November 16, 2007.

26. Cavallo, *La historia oculta,* p. 73.

27. Aylwin, interview.

28. Rojas, interview.

29. The army statement was widely reported in the Chilean press on December 20, 1990.

30. Partially redacted Central Intelligence Agency report, "Internal Army Reactions to 19 December Alert," January 4, 1991, http://foia.state.gov/documents/Pcia3/00009221.pdf.

31. Viera Gallo, interview.

32. Declassified State Department cable, "Chile Minister of Defense Visit: The Rojas Agenda," March 8, 1991, http://foia.state.gov/documents/StateChile3/00008252.pdf.

33. Rojas, interview.

34. Declassified State Department cable, "Proposed Travel by General Pino-

chet to the US: Chilean Army Advisors Seek Information on Legal Status," August 8, 1991, pp. 2–3, http://foia.state.gov/documents/StateChile3/0000836C.pdf.

35. *El Mercurio,* May 12, 1991.

36. "So Who Really Did Invite Pinochet; Government Looks Away, Then Turns on General's Critics," *Latin America Weekly Report,* May 23, 1991, and May 30, 1991.

37. Declassified State Department cable, "Not So Innocents Abroad," May 28, 1991, pp. 3–5, http://foia.state.gov/documents/StateChile3/000082EC.pdf.

38. Maria Irene Soto, "Entrevista exclusiva a Pinochet en Portugal: El misterio no lo he hecho yo," *Hoy,* May 20–26, 1991.

39. Cavallo, *La historia oculta,* p. 131.

40. Rojas, interview.

41. Quoted in the *New York Times,* June 19, 2006.

42. U.S. Senate Permanent Subcommittee on Investigations, *Money Laundering and Foreign Corruption: Enforcement and Effectiveness of the Patriot Act,* supplemental staff report on U.S. accounts used by Augusto Pinochet, 109th Cong., 1st sess., March 16, 2005.

43. Castillo, *Pinochet,* p. 75.

CHAPTER FOUR

1. Luz Arce, *The Inferno: A Story of Terror and Survival in Chile,* trans. Stacey Alba Skar (Madison: University of Wisconsin Press, 2004), p. 328.

2. Ibid., p. 240. On July 18, 2007, the Chilean Senate voted to award a compensatory payment to Soria's family.

3. *Supreme Decree No. 355: Creation of the Commission on Truth and Reconciliation,* April 25, 1990, *Report of the Chilean National Commission on Truth and Reconciliation,* pp. 22–27, http://www.usip.org/files/resources/collections/truth_commissions/Chile90-Report/Chile90-Report.pdf.

4. Mark Ensalaco, *Chile under Pinochet: Recovering the Truth* (Philadelphia: University of Pennsylvania Press, 1999), p. 191.

5. *Report of the Chilean National Commission on Truth and Reconciliation,* part 1, chapter 1, sect. B: "Staff Organization," p. 31, http://www.usip.org/files/resources/collections/truth_commissions/Chile90-Report/Chile90-Report.pdf.

6. Ibid., pp. 33–34.

7. Ensalaco, *Chile under Pinochet,* p. 200.

8. *Report of the Chilean National Commission on Truth and Reconciliation,* part 2, chapter 1, p. 70, http://www.usip.org/files/resources/collections/truth_commissions/Chile90-Report/Chile90-Report.pdf.

9. Ibid., part 2, chapter 4, p. 141.

10. Ibid., part 3, chapter 2, pp. 620–21.

11. Ibid., part 3, chapter 3, p. 841.

12. Ibid., part 3, chapter 4, p. 1023.

13. President Aylwin's speech was widely reported in the Chilean press, and a part can be viewed online at http://www.museodeprensa.cl/node/336.

14. Matthei read a prepared statement to the press on March 8, 1991, that was widely publicized in the media. See *El Mercurio,* March 9, 1991. The commission report did not cite any cases involving the Chilean air force after 1978, when Matthei took command of the service. During the author's interview with Matthei, he recalled that he was recovering from an illness when the report was released a few days earlier and that Aylwin had visited him at his home to discuss it.

15. *El Mercurio,* March 28, 1991.

16. None of the three magazines—*Hoy, APSI,* and *Página Abierta*—are still being published, but the *APSI* story can be read online at http://www.memoriaviva.com/culpables/agentes/arce.htm.

17. A translation of Contreras's interview is contained in a declassified State Department cable, "Ex DINA Chief Contreras Comments on Human Rights Violations, Letelier and DINA," March 28, 1991, pp. 2–38, http://foia.state.gov/documents/StateChile3/00008FEC.pdf.

18. Various Chilean newspaper reports from March 26 and 27, 1991.

19. Olga Weisfeiler, e-mail message to the author, April 7, 2008.

20. Olga Weisfeiler to Truth and Reconciliation staffer Jorge Correa Sutil, November 1991, http://foia.state.gov/documents/StateChile3/000082B7.pdf.

21. Partially redacted State Department cable, "Welfare Whereabouts Case of Boris Weisfeiler," October 17, 1985, p. 6, http://foia.state.gov/documents/StateChile3/000068EC.pdf.

22. Claudio R. Salinas and Hans Stange, *Los amigos del "Dr." Schafer: La complicidad entre el estado chileno y Colonia Dignidad* (Santiago: Random House Mondadori, 2006), pp. 62–63.

23. Amnesty International document 3 O 123/77, October 1997, *Colonia Dignidad: Chronicle of a Process.*

24. One notorious Nazi lived openly in Chile from 1958 until his death in 1984: Walter Rauff, an SS officer credited with the invention of mobile gas chambers. Chile's Supreme Court rejected a West German extradition request in 1963, and even Salvador Allende made no move to expel Rauff from the country.

25. Partially redacted State Department cable, "Case of Boris Weisfeiler/Colonia Dignidad—New Information," August 23, 1987, http://foia.state.gov/documents/StateChile3/00007520.pdf, pp. 1–12.

26. Ministry of Justice Decree 143, published in the Chilean news media, January 1–2, 1992.

27. Marcia Alejandra Merino Vega, *Mi verdad: Más allá del horror, yo acuso* (Santiago: A.T.G., 1993).

28. "Unsettled Business: Human Rights in Chile at the Start of the Frei Presidency," Human Rights Watch 1994, New York, p. 4, http://www.hrw.org/en/reports/1994/05/01/unsettled-business.

29. A Chilean editor told me that following Pinochet's defeat in the 1988 plebiscite, the editor's magazine had been approached on at least two occasions by security agents offering to sell their stories in exchange for safe passage out of the country. As the magazine had no funds for any such informal witness protection, these offers were declined.

30. Rojas, interview.

31. Otano, *Nueva crónica de la transición,* p. 361.

32. Alberto Luengo, "Mi historia personal del boinazo," *La Nación,* December 17, 2006.

33. Rojas, interview.

34. Centro de Estudios Públicos, Social Study and Opinion Poll, August 1993, working document 200, http://www.cepchile.cl/dms/lang_1/doc_2925.html.

35. *El Mercurio,* September 8, 1993.

36. Ibid., September 9, 1993.

37. Quoted in *La Segunda,* September 9, 1993.

38. Pinochet Ugarte, *Camino recorrido,* 3:21.

39. "Unsettled Business: Human Rights in Chile at the Start of the Frei Presidency," Human Rights Watch 1994, New York, p. 27, http://www.hrw.org/en/reports/1994/05/01/unsettled-business.

CHAPTER FIVE

1. Centro de Estudios Públicos, Social Study and Opinion Poll, March 1993, p. 5, http://www.cepchile.cl/dms/lang_1/doc_2926.html.

2. Felipe Morandé, "Una década de metas de inflación en Chile: Desarrollos, lecciónes y desafiós," p. 40, http://www.bcentral.cl/estudios/revista-economia/2001/abril2001/rec_v4n1_pp35_62.pdf.

3. Monica Gonzalez, "Medico de la DINA y CNI opero a Eduardo Frei Montalva," March 5, 2009, Centro de Investigación e Información Periodistica, http://ciperchile.cl/2009/03/05/medico-de-la-dina-y-cni-opero-a-eduardo-frei-montalva/, accessed March 6, 2009.

4. Arturo Alessandri Besa was also the grandson of a former president by the same name. Arturo Alessandri Palma served two terms in office, from 1920 to 1925 and from 1932 to 1938.

5. Arancibia Clavel, *Cita con la historia,* pp. 635–42.

6. Angell, *Democracy after Pinochet,* p. 78.

7. Matthei later joined Chile's other main right-wing party, the Union Democrática Independiente (UDI), and continued her political career; she is today one of Chile's best-known senators.

8. Cavallo, *La historia oculta,* p. 176.

9. "Army Embarrassed, RN Badly Damaged; Eduardo Frei Emerges as Only Clear Winner in Bugging Row," *Latin America Weekly Report,* London, November 26, 1992, pp. 8–9.

10. Edmundo Pérez Yoma, interview with the author, Santiago, Chile, November 20, 2007.

11. Francisco Ledantec, interview with the author, Santiago, Chile, October 17, 2007.

12. Partially redacted Department of Defense document, "Committee for the Truth on Human Rights," January 1, 1990, pp. 2–3, http://foia.state.gov/documents/Pdod3/000086D4.pdf.

13. Ledantec, interview.

14. The May–August 1996 issue of ANEPE's quarterly magazine contains a photograph of Bachelet giving the valedictory address at a ceremony marking the completion of the course and another of her shaking hands with Defense Minister Edmundo Pérez Yoma. During my meeting with Francisco Ledantec, ANEPE staff tried to find a copy of Bachelet's speech somewhere in their archive and apologized, saying they had never been able to locate the speech when other journalists inquired.

15. According to the Chile section of the 1996 World Report by Human Rights Watch, "Police, particularly the uniformed carabineros, operated without effective judicial control, often arbitrarily arresting, mistreating or torturing detainees." See http://www.hrw.org/reports/1996/WR96/Americas-02.htm#P210_51347, accessed January 15, 2008.

16. Cavallo, *La historia oculta,* p. 249.

17. Matthei, interview. Matthei told me that resentment on the part of Pinochet and his supporters over Matthei's actions on the night of the 1988 plebiscite ("I was the man who stopped him") were starting to hurt relations between the Chilean army and the air force, and this influenced his decision to retire.

18. "Carabinero Chief Stange Bows Out; Of the Old Guard Only Pinochet Hangs On," *Latin America Weekly Report,* London, October 19, 1995.

19. *La Nación,* July 29, 2007.

20. *La Nación,* December 23, 2007.

21. Human Rights Watch, 1996 World Report, Chile, http://www.hrw.org/reports/1996/WR96/Americas-02.htm#P210_51347, accessed January 15, 2008.

22. Anthony De Palma, "Separate Trade Pact by Canada and Chile," *New York Times,* November 19, 1996.

23. See data as of March 1994, "Chile: Narcotics Trafficking," www.country-data.com/cgi-bin/query/r-2559.html, accessed March 5, 2008.

24. Cavallo, *La historia oculta,* pp. 231–35.

25. Calvin Sims, "Has Wealth Ruined Chile? Neighbors Think So," *New York Times,* November 17, 1996.

26. "Poverty and Social Stratification in Chile: Motivations, Perceptions and Realizations," social study and opinion poll, June to July 1996, work document 263 (Santiago: Centro de Estudios Públicos, 1996).

27. Julieta Palma and Raul Urua, "Anti-poverty Policies and Citizenry: The 'Chile Solidario' Experience" (Santiago: Department of Public Policy, Institute of Public Affairs, University of Chile, 2005), p. 15.

28. Bart Ostr, José Miguel Sanchez, Carlos Aranda, and Gunnar S. Eskeland, "Air Pollution and Mortality Results from Santiago, Chile," vol. 1 (working paper, World Bank, May 31, 1995).

29. Jeffrey Sachs and Gordon C. McCord, "Time for Chile's Next Step in Economic Development," *Business CHILE Magazine,* Santiago, November 2004.

30. From the U.S. Geological Survey, found at http://earthquake.usgs.gov/regional/world/events/1960_05_22.php, accessed August 15, 2008.

31. http://www.ancientforests.org/chile.htm, accessed August 17, 2008.

32. Andres Azocar, *Tompkins: El millonario verde* (Santiago: Editorial La Copa Rota, 2007), p. 104.

33. John Ryle, "Lord of All Her Surveys," *Outside,* June 1998.

34. Calvin Sims, "America's Parkland in Chile Draws Opposition," *New York Times,* May 15, 1995.

35. Agnic, *Pinochet,* pp. 215–16.

36. *La Nación,* August 7, 2005.

37. U.S. Senate, Permanent Subcommittee on Investigations, *Money Laundering and Foreign Corruption: Enforcement and Effectiveness of the Patriot Act,* supplemental staff report on U.S. accounts used by Augusto Pinochet," 109th Congress, 1st sess., March 16, 2005, p. 31.

38. Ibid., pp. 39–41.

39. Ibid., p. 38.

40. Carol Thompson, memorandum, November 3, 1994, in ibid., pp. 171, 172, and 175.

41. Timothy Coughlin to Augusto Pinochet, November 4, 1994, in ibid, p. 180.

42. Ibid., pp. 7 and 10–12.

43. See www.fundacionpinochet.cl, accessed September 11, 2009.

44. Cristóbal Peña, "Exclusivo: Viaje al fondo de la biblioteca de Pinochet," December 6, 2007, Centro de Investigación e Información Periodistica, http://ciperchile.cl/2007/12/06/exclusivo-viaje-al-fondo-de-la-biblioteca-de-pinochet/, accessed December 15, 2008.

45. Carol Thompson, memorandum, March 3, 1997, in U.S. Senate Permanent Subcommittee on Investigations, "Supplemental Staff Report on U.S. Accounts Used by Augusto Pinochet," p. 195.

46. U.S. Senate Permanent Subcommittee on Investigations, "Supplemental Staff Report on U.S. Accounts Used by Augusto Pinochet," pp. 21–22.

47. Maria Carol Thompson to Joe Allbritton, memorandum, "Chile Country Overview," October 14, 1997, in U.S. Senate Permanent Subcommittee on Investigations, "Supplemental Staff Report on U.S. Accounts Used by Augusto Pinochet," p. 217.

48. Maria Carol Thompson, memorandum, "Call Report," November 6, 1997, in U.S. Senate Permanent Subcommittee on Investigations, "Supplemental Staff Report on U.S. Accounts Used by Augusto Pinochet," p. 211.

49. Joseph Allbritton to Pinochet, November 14, 1997, and Barbara Allbritton to Pinochet, October 31, 1997, in U.S. Senate Permanent Subcommittee on Investigations, "Supplemental Staff Report on U.S. Accounts Used by Augusto Pinochet," pp. 217–18.

50. Timothy Coughlin to Pinochet, November 10, 1997, in U.S. Senate Permanent Subcommittee on Investigations, "Supplemental Staff Report on U.S. Accounts Used by Augusto Pinochet," p. 219.

CHAPTER SIX

1. In justifying the city's inscription as a World Heritage Site, UNESCO notes that Valparaíso is "an exceptional testimony to the early phase of globalization in the late nineteenth century, when it became the leading merchant port on the sea routes of the Pacific coast of South America" (http://whc.unesco.org/en/list/959/, accessed July 30, 2008).

2. According to election returns, on December 14, 1989, Lagos received 399,408 votes, while Guzman received 223,302 votes. See *El Mercurio* and *La Tercera,* December 16, 1989.

3. Angell, *Democracy after Pinochet,* p. 127.

4. David Aronofsky, telephone interview with the author, July 14, 2008.

5. Ibid.

6. John M. Carey, "Parties, Coalitions and the Chilean Congress in the 1990s" (draft paper, Washington University, Saint Louis, September 22, 1998).

7. Declassified State Department cable, "The New Chilean Congress and Its Leaders," p. 2, August 6, 1990, http://foia.state.gov/documents/Pnara3/0000 97E4.pdf.

8. Peter M. Siavelis, *The President and Congress in Post Authoritarian Chile: Institutional Restraints to Democratic Consolidation* (University Park: Pennsylvania State University Press, 2000), p. 50.

9. Marialyse Delano, "Library of Congress of Chile: A Hands-on Modernization Experience" (paper presented at the 64th International Federation of Library Associations Conference, Amsterdam, August 16–21, 1998).

10. Quoted in Pascale Bonnefoy, "Chile's Secret Laws," *Global Post,* March 22, 2009.

11. Article 48 of the 1980 constitution states that to be elected to the chamber of deputies, a candidate must be at least twenty-one years old, have graduated from secondary school, and have resided in the corresponding electoral district "for a period no less than two years, counted backwards from the election day." Article 50 states that elected senators must be at least thirty-five years old, have completed high school, and also have lived in the district they represent for at least two years prior to the election Constitutión Politica de la República de Chile, pp. 49–50, http://wwwleychile.cl/Consulta/Exportar?radioExportar=Normas&exportar_formato=pdf&nombrearchivo=DTO-100_22SEP-2005&exportar_con_notas_bcn=True&exportar_con_notas_originales=True&exportar_con_notas_al_pie=True&hddResultadoExportar=242302.2010–01–07.0.0%23, accessed July 16, 2008.

12. Patricio Navia, telephone interview with the author, August 4, 2008.

13. Otano, *Nueva crónica,* p. 142.

14. Francisco Javier Cuadra, telephone interview with the author, August 6, 2008.

15. Cavallo, *La historia oculta,* p. 287.

16. Cristián Bofill, "Algunos parlamentarios consumen drogas," *Qué Pasa,* January 14, 1995.

17. See Human Rights Watch, "Limits of Tolerance: Freedom of Expression and the Public Debate," New York, November 1998, http://www.hrw.org/legacy/reports98/chile/Chilerpt-02.htm#P434_87673.

18. Cavallo, *La historia oculta,* p. 294.

19. *La Nación,* April 25, 2004.

20. Cavallo, *La historia oculta,* p. 290.

21. Carlos Cerda was one of a small group of Chilean judges who was bravely investigating human rights abuses; he also oversaw a long and difficult inquiry into Pinochet's illegal bank accounts.

22. Human Rights Watch, "Limits of Tolerance."

23. Written correspondence from Francisco Javier Cuadra with the author, August 8, 2008.

24. Human Rights Watch, "Limits of Tolerance."

25. Cavallo, *La historia oculta,* p. 291.

26. Otano, *Nueva crónica,* pp. 128–29.

27. Human Rights Watch, "Limits of Tolerance."

28. Ken Leon-Dermota, . . . *And Well-Tied Down: Chile's Press under Democracy* (Westport, CT: Praeger Publishers, 2003), p. 24.

29. Calvin Sims, "Chileans Are Prosecuted for Criticizing Officials," *New York Times,* November 10, 1996.

30. Human Rights Watch, "Limits of Tolerance."

31. Marin died of a brain tumor in 2005. The government declared two days of mourning, and her funeral was attended by at least two hundred thousand people, including President Ricardo Lagos and even some right-wing political leaders, who praised her integrity and courage. See *El Mercurio,* March 9, 2005.

32. *El Mercurio,* August 24, 1997.

33. Ibid., October 12, 1997.

34. Cavallo, *La historia oculta,* p. 347.

35. *El Mercurio,* October 19, 1997.

36. Massad, "The Chilean Economy: Strengths and Perspectives," http://www.bcentral.cl/politicas/presentaciones/consejeros/pdf/1998/massadooctubre001998.pdf.

37. Carlos Huneeus, "Malestar y desencanto en Chile: Legados del autoritarianismo y costos de la transicion" (paper, Centro de Estudios de la Realidad Contemporanea, Santiago, n.d.).

38. *The Economist,* December 18, 1997.

39. Centro de Estudios de la Realidad Contemporánea poll, June 1997, p. 4, http://www.cerc.cl/Encuestas/97Mar.pdf.

40. Patricio Navia, "Participación electoral en Chile, 1998–2001," *Revista de ciencia politicia* 24, no. 1 (2004): 92–93, http://www.scielo.cl/pdf/revcipol/v24n1/art04.pdf.

CHAPTER SEVEN

1. The author lived for a time in the area badly served by Telefónica Manquehue, one of several private companies that had sprung up to work in areas not covered by the soon-to-be privatized Telefonos de Chile. The company enjoyed a monopoly in the area and did not have enough telephone lines for all the customers it enrolled. However, it was the only service available.

2. Pérez Yoma, interview.

3. Otano, *Nueva crónica,* p. 442.

4. Pérez Yoma, interview.

5. Various Chilean newspaper reports of June 1, 1995.

6. Calvin Sims, "Chilean Vows to Avoid Prison in Letelier Case," *New York Times,* June 1, 1995.

7. Cavallo, *La historia oculta,* pp. 277–80.

8. Pérez Yoma, interview.

9. Cavallo, *La historia oculta,* p. 286.

10. Eduardo Gallardo, "General in Solitary as Chile Debates Imprisoning Pinochet's Henchman," *Los Angeles Times,* September 17, 1995.

11. *Latin America Weekly Report,* July 29, 1995, and various Chilean newspaper reports of July 23, 1995.

12. Burgos, interview.

13. Pérez Yoma, interview.

14. Ibid.

15. Cavallo, *La historia oculta,* pp. 280–82.

16. Dinges, *The Condor Years,* pp. 241–42.

17. Cavallo, *La historia oculta,* p. 283.

18. Pérez Yoma, interview.

19. Human Rights Watch, "Chile: Human Rights Development," 1996, http://www.hrw.org/reports/1996/WR96/Americas-02.htm#P210_51347.

20. President Eduardo Frei's televised speech of August 21, 1995, was widely covered in the Chilean press. See *El Mercurio,* August 22, 1995.

21. Human Rights Watch, "Chile: Human Rights Development."

22. Otano, *Nueva cronica,* pp. 445–47.

23. In an open letter to the Chilean congress, Human Rights Watch criticized the government's failure "to establish clear norms ensuring that cases were kept open until the fate of the victims had been determined." See http://www. hrw .org/reports/1996/WR96/Americas-02.htm#P210_51347.

24. From a brief history of Villa Grimaldi on the park's Web site, www.villa grimaldi.cl, accessed July 30, 2008.

25. Father Jose Aldunate, interview with the author, Santiago, Chile, November 20, 2007. See also Jose Aldunate, "Villa Grimaldi, un memorial de nuestra historia," *Mensaje,* May 1997.

26. Rodrigo del Vilar, president of the Villa Grimaldi board of directors, interview with the author, Santiago, Chile, October 16, 2007. The case of Carlos Carrasco, the kind young guard, is detailed in *Report of the Chilean National Commission on Truth and Reconciliation,* chapter 2, "DINA Agents Who Disappeared at the Hand of Their Own Colleagues," pp. 794–96, http://www.usip.org/files/resources/collections/truth_commissions/Chile90-Report/Chile90-Report.pdf.

27. Cavallo, *La historia oculta,* p. 349.

28. From various news reports in the Chilean media of Pinochet's comments, December 27, 1997.

29. "Pinochet Has Seat in Senate; But His Enemies Remain Determined to Bring Him Down," *Latin America Regional Reports: Southern Cone,* p. 2, London, April 21, 1998.

30. Pinochet regime officials began a kind of whispering campaign against

Lavandero following the attack, with regime supporters spreading the rumor that the Christian Democrat had been set upon by the male relatives of a young woman he was seeing. The author was told this version of events on at least two occasions in 1984.

31. British Broadcasting Corporation report, March 6, 1998, http://news.bbc.co.uk/1/hi/world/americas/62724.stm.

32. Agence France Press, March 11, 1998.

33. Timothy Coughlin to Pinochet, April 23, 1998, in *Money Laundering and Foreign Corruption,* p. 226.

34. Otano, *Nueva crónica,* pp. 455–56.

35. *Report of the Chilean National Commission on Truth and Reconciliation,* pp. 741–45, http://www.usip.org/files/resources/collections/truth_commissions/Chile90-Report/Chile90-Report.pdf.

36. Ibid., p. 745.

37. Juan Guzmán Tapia, interview with the author, Santiago, Chile, November 14, 2007.

38. Quoted in Patricia Verdugo, *Chile, Pinochet and the Caravan of Death* (Miami: North-South Center Press, 2001), p. 112.

39. Ibid., p. 109

40. Guzmán, interview.

CHAPTER EIGHT

1. The photograph of Thatcher and Pinochet at the 1994 British embassy reception in Santiago can be found on various Internet sites.

2. Quoted in John B. Dunlop, "Alexandr Lebed and Russian Foreign Policy," *SAIS Review* 17, no. 1 (Winter–Spring 1997): 47–72.

3. Jon Lee Anderson, "The Dictator," *New Yorker,* October 19, 1998, http://www.newyorker.com/archive/1998/10/19/1998_10_19_044_TNY_LIBRY_000016635?currentPage=all.

4. Monica Perez and Felipe Gerdtzen, *Augusto Pinochet: 503 días atrapados en Londres* (Santiago: Editorial Los Andes, 2000), p. 83.

5. Raul Sohr, *La industria militar Chilena* (Santiago: Comision Sudamericana de Paz, 1993), p. 66.

6. Duncan Campbell, Nick Hopkins, Ian Black, and Ewan MacAskill, "Diplomatic Crisis over Pinochet," *Guardian,* October 20, 1998.

7. Anderson, "The Dictator."

8. Ernesto Ekaizer, "Viaje a la corte de Augusto," *El País Digital,* Madrid, February 14, 1999.

9. www.thelondonclinic.co.uk, accessed July 30, 2008.

10. Diana Woodhouse, "The Progress of Pinochet through the UK Extradition Process: An Analysis of the Legal Challenges and Judicial Decisions," in *The Pinochet Case: Origins, Progress and Implications,* ed. Madeleine Davies (London: Institute of Latin American Studies, 2003), p. 90.

11. "Pinochet's Suicide Threat," *Daily Mirror,* November 30, 1998.

12. Warren Hoge, "Pinochet Is Shown the Door by a Vexed London Hospital," *New York Times,* December 2, 1998.

13. Perez and Gerdtzen, *Augusto Pinochet,* p. 4.

14. Esteban Catalan M., "Pinochet: Las voces que se levantaron en Chile tras la detención," Radio Cooperativa, October 16, 2008, http://www.cooperativa.cl/prontus_nots/site/artic/20081015/pags/20081015194115.html.

15. Trade figures from the Banco Central de Chile, www.bcentral.cl.

16. Investment figures from the Comite de Inversiones de Chile, http://www.inversionextranjera.cl/.

17. Programa Economica de Trabajo, "The Chilean Economy: From Crisis to Stagnation," Global Policy Network, January 8, 2002, Santiago, http://www.gpn.org/data/chile/chile-analysis.pdf.

18. *Qué Pasa,* December 19, 1998.

19. José Tohá was Allende's defense minister and frequently socialized with Pinochet and his wife before the 1973 coup. Tohá's wife pleaded with Pinochet to release her husband from detention, to no avail.

20. *El Mercurio,* December 3, 1999.

21. *La Segunda,* October 26, 1998.

22. These unofficial estimates were published in the *Guardian,* March 26, 1999.

23. U.S. Senate Permanent Subcommittee on Investigations, Riggs memorandum, "Chairman's Trip to Latin America, March 1999, Gift Ideas," in *Money Laundering and Foreign Corruption,* p. 227.

24. U.S. Senate Permanent Subcommittee on Investigations, *Money Laundering and Foreign Corruption,* pp. 59–60.

25. British Broadcasting Corporation broadcast, December 11, 1998, http://news.bbc.co.uk/1/hi/world/233307.stm.

26. The complete text of Pinochet's "Letter to the Chilean People" can be found at http://es.wikisource.org/wiki/Carta_a_los_Chilenos,_de_Augusto_Pinochet.

27. *Telegraph,* January 20, 1999.

28. "Thatcher Visits Her Old Friend Pinochet," *Guardian,* March 26, 1999. Officially, Chile claimed neutrality during the 1982 Falklands War, but, unbeknownst to the regime's own Foreign Ministry, Pinochet authorized air force commander Fernando Matthei to allow a British air force official to set up a communications post in southern Chile. British officials first contacted Matthei, who had once been air force attaché at the Chilean embassy in London, and Pinochet

appears to have had a very limited involvement in the matter. See Arancibia Clavel and de la Maza Cave, *Matthei*, pp. 349–60.

29. The Academia Judicial Web site is www.academiajudicial.cl.

30. Alejandra Matus, *El libro negro de la justicia Chilena* (Santiago: Grupo Editorial Planeta, 1999), p. 13.

31. Human Rights Watch, "Chile Progress Stalled: Setbacks in Freedom of Expression Reform," March 2001, pp. 21–25, http://www.hrw.org/en/reports/2001/03/01/chile-progress-stalled.

32. Arriagada, interview.

33. Partially redacted State Department cable, "Chilean Request for Detention Advisor and Equipment," September 28, 1973, pp. 1–2, http://foia.state.gov/documents/Pinochet/8d5d.pdf. Interestingly, one of the two Chilean officers mentioned in this cable, air force general Nicanor Diaz, is not among those officials accused by former political prisoners or human rights groups of having taken part in torture or killings.

34. Declassified State Department briefing memorandum, "Chilean Executions," November 16, 1973, pp. 1–2, http://foia.state.gov/documents/Pnara/9da4.pdf.

35. Declassified National Security Council memorandum, "Disarray in Chile Policy," July 1, 1975, http://www.gwu.edu/~nsarchiv/NSAEBB/NSAEBB8/ch04–01.htm.

36. Declassified National Security Council memorandum,"Chilean President's Visit to U.S.," August 8, 1975, http://www.gwu.edu/~nsarchiv/NSAEBB/NSAEBB8/ch07–01.htm.

37. Partially redacted CIA biographic handbook, November 1974, http://www.gwu.edu/~nsarchiv/NSAEBB/NSAEBB212/197411%20CIA%20Pinochet%20Bio.pdf.

38. Declassified State Department report, "Report Concerning Pinochet," June 2, 1989, http://foia.state.gov/documents/StateChile3/00007D4E.pdf.

39. U.S. State Department daily press briefing, Tuesday, December 1, 1998, http://www.fas.org/sgp/news/dos120198.html.

40. Tim Weiner, "U.S. Weighs Extradition of Pinochet," *New York Times*, November 7, 1998.

41. The Rome Statute of the International Criminal Court was passed by a vote of one hundred twenty to seven, with twenty-one countries abstaining. In addition to the United States, China, Iraq, Israel, Libya, Qatar, and Yemen voted against the measure.

42. Madeline Davis, ed., *The Pinochet Case: Origins, Progress and Implications* (London: Institute of Latin American Studies, 2003), p. 179.

43. *Sunday Telegraph*, July 18, 1999.

44. *Guardian*, August 4, 1999.

45. *Observer,* August 15, 1999.

46. Juan Guzmán Tapia, *En el borde del mundo: Memorias del juez que procesó a Pinochet* (Barcelona: Editorial Anagrama, 2005), p. 166.

47. The full text of Thatcher's speech appeared in the *Guardian* and other British media, October 6, 1999.

48. *Observer,* March 13, 2000.

49. *Observer,* January 16, 2000.

50. Letter to the *Times* (London) from British Medical Association ethics committee chairman Michael Wilks, January 20, 2000.

51. Warren Hoge, "After 16 Months of House Arrest, Pinochet Quits England," *New York Times, March* 3, 2000.

52. "Chile: Pinochet's Legacy May End Up Aiding Victims," Human Rights Watch, December 10, 2006, http://www.hrw.org/en/news/2006/12/10/chile-pinochet-s-legacy-may-end-aiding-victims.

CHAPTER NINE

1. *La Tercera,* September 21, 1999.

2. Lagos, interview.

3. See Lagos's biography on http://www.cidob.org/es/documentacion/biografias_lideres_politicos/america_del_sur/chile/ricardo_lagos_escobar.

4. *El Mercurio,* September 12, 1980.

5. Lagos, interview.

6. Angell, *Democracy after Pinochet,* p. 94.

7. Lagos, interview. The author also sought but could not obtain an interview with Lavín.

8. Corporacion de Estudios Públicos, Cuestionario estudio social y de opinión pública, September–October 1999, Tema especial: Elecciones 1999, pp. 6 and 9, http://www.cepchile.cl/dms/lang_1/doc_2906.html.

9. Juan Guzmán, *En el borde del mundo: Memorias del juez que procesó a Pinochet* (Barcelona: Editorial Anagrama, 2005), p. 160.

10. Reuters, Santiago, March 3, 2000.

11. "Defending Human Rights," *Human Rights Watch World Report 2001: Chile,* http://www.hrw.org/wr2k1/americas/chile2.html.

12. See Sebastian Brett, "Impunity on Trial in Chile," North American Congress on Latin America, *Report on the Americas,* July–August 2000, New York. Brett quotes Chilean human rights lawyer Roberto Garretón, who said that his country's judges "saw the dynamic style and independence of their colleagues in Madrid and London as a challenge to their own professional pride."

13. Guzmán, *En el borde del mundo,* p. 189.

14. Guzmán, interview.

15. Ibid.

16. The complete Spanish text of the Chilean Supreme Court ruling can be found at http://216.72.168.65/p4_plinea/site/20010709/pags/19800102153952.html.

17. Inter-American Commission on Human Rights, *Third Report on the Situation of Human Rights in Chile,* chapter 2, "Right to Life," February 11, 1977, http://www.cidh.org/countryrep/Chile77eng/INDEX.htm.

18. "Confesiones de un agente de seguridad," pamphlet published by the Agrupación de Familiares de Detenidos-Desaparecidos, Santiago, December 1984.

19. The complete Spanish text of Lagos's speech can be found at http://216.72.168.65/p4_plinea/site/20010107/pags/19800101202346.html.

20. *La Nación,* November 23, 2003.

21. The railings are on display at Villa Grimaldi's museum.

22. "Estuve encerrada en un cajón, vendada y atada: Conmovedor relato de la madre de Michelle Bachelet, Angela Jeria," *Diario Clarín,* January 19, 2006, http://edant.clarin.com/diario/2006/01/19/elmundo/i-02201.htm. Also see the interview in the documentary film *Cruel Separation,* directed by Sarah Boston, Fuse Films Ltd. (www.fusefilms.co.uk), 2006.

23. Felipe Aguero to Dr. Alfredo Rehren, director of the Instituto de Ciencia Politica, Universidad Catolica de Chile, undated. Excerpts published in various Chilean media, including the digital newspaper *El Mostrador,* on March 27, 2001.

24. Michael Easterbrook, "Justice, Memory and a Professor's Accusation," *Chronicle of Higher Education,* August 17, 2001.

25. Lagos, interview.

26. *La Tercera,* January 5, 2003.

27. Ibid., June 14, 2003

28. Ibid., July 3, 2003.

29. Human Rights Watch, "Letter to President Lagos on Judicial Investigations in Chile," June 15, 2003, http://www.hrw.org/en/news/2003/07/15/letter-president-lagos-judicial-investigations-chile.

30. Lagos, interview.

31. *New York Times,* December 30, 2002.

32. Salinas and Stange, *Los amigos del "Dr." Schafer,* p. 103.

33. Bruce Falconer, "The Torture Colony," *American Scholar* (Autumn 2008), www.theamericanscholar.org/the-torture-colony/.

34. *Santiago Times,* April 20, 2006.

35. U.S. Senate Permanent Subcommittee on Investigations, *Money Laundering and Foreign Corruption,* p. 2.

36. *Washington Post,* November 20, 2004.

37. Ibid., February 26, 2005.

38. U.S. Senate Permanent Subcommittee on Investigations, *Money Laundering and Foreign Corruption,* p. 5.

39. *Clinic,* July 22, 2004.

40. Quoted in "Caso Riggs: El procesamiento del clan Pinochet," *El Mercurio,* http://www.emol.com/especiales/pinochet_riggs/procesados.htm.

41. These include accounts in Jacqueline Pinochet's name at the Banco de Chile's Miami branch and in Veronica's name at Citigroup's Miami branch, in addition to more extensive holdings managed by Pinochet's children Lucia and Marco Antonio Pinochet.

42. Castillo, *Pinochet,* p. 29.

43. From court records of Cerda's interview with Pinochet of November 8, 2005, quoted in ibid., pp. 229–33.

44. From court records of Cerda's interview with Pinochet of November 15, 2005, quoted in ibid., pp. 239–43.

45. From court records of Cerda's interview with Pinochet of November 17, 2005, quoted in ibid., pp. 246–54.

46. From court records of Cerda's interview of November 8, 10, 15, and 17, 2005, reproduced in ibid., pp. 231–54.

47. Dinges, *The Condor Years,* pp. 235–36. On June 21, 2008, Chile's National Journalists Union issued a public apology for the news media's role in Operation Colombo.

48. From court records of Judge Victor Montiglio's interrogation of Pinochet and Contreras, November 18, 2005. Reproduced in Castillo, *Pinochet,* pp. 255–60.

49. Peña, "Exclusivo."

50. Rodrigo García Pinochet, *Caso Riggs: La ultima persecución* (Santiago: Editorial Maya, 2007), p. 206.

51. Pascale Bonnefoy, "World Briefing/Americas: Chile: U.S. Officials Detain Pinochet's Daughter," *New York Times,* January 26, 2006.

52. Pinochet, *Caso Riggs,* p. 213.

53. "Lucia Pinochet pide asilo politico en EE.UU," *Teletrece Internet,* http://teletrece.canal13.cl/t13/html/Noticias/Chile/251819paginaq3.html.

54. Reuters, "Pinochet's Daughter Returns to Face Charges in Chile," *New York Times,* January 28, 2006.

CHAPTER TEN

1. Quoted in Larry Rohter, "Hints of Cruel Fate for American Lost in Chile," *New York Times,* May 19, 2002, p. 432.

2. U.S. State Department memorandum, "Ambassador Barnes/Minister Del

Valle Appointment on April 10, 1987," April 10, 1987, http://foia.state.gov/documents/StateChile3/000072B3.pdf.

3. Central Intelligence Agency memorandum, "Boris Weisfeiler Case," November 15, 1987, p. 2, http://foia.state.gov/documents/Pcia3/00009282.pdf.

4. Notes from the Weisfeilers' trip to Chile in December 2000, posted on the family's Web site: http://boris.weisfeiler.com/Weisfeilers_Chile_trip_report_2000.htm, accessed January 30, 2008.

5. Quoted in the *Santiago Times,* March 28, 2006.

6. *El Mercurio,* March 23, 2005.

7. *La Tercera,* November 28, 2008.

8. Ibid., April 8, 2007.

9. Kelly's interview with Radio Bio Bio was quoted in the *Santiago Times,* August 6, 2007.

10. *Santiago Times,* January 29, 2008.

11. Guillaume Boccara, "The Struggle of the Mapuche People: Deepening Democracy in Chile," *ReVista* (Spring 2004): 31–32.

12. *Diario Austral,* June 4, 2001.

13. Boccara, "The Struggle of the Mapuche People."

14. Quoted by Inca Garcilaso de la Vega in *Comentarios reales,* book 7, chapter 19, pp. 376–77, http://www.scribd.com/doc/14659195/Inca-Garcilaso-de-La-Vega-Comentarios-Reales-Obra-Completa, accessed March 3, 2008.

15. Alonso de Ercilla, *La Araucana,* canto 24, verses 20–24. Reprinted on www.bibliotecasvirtuales.com, accessed February 12, 2008.

16. Pablo Neruda, "Education of a Chieftain," from *Selected Poems by Pablo Neruda,* ed. Nathaniel Tarn, trans. Anthony Kerrigan (London: Jonathan Cape Ltd., 1970), p. 217.

17. Louis C. Faron, *The Mapuche Indians of Chile* (Prospect Heights, IL: Waveland Press, 1968), p. 17.

18. *La Nación,* March 11, 2007.

19. Reynaldo Mariqueo, telephone interview with the author, March 31, 2009.

20. Amnesty International, "Chile: Extreme Cruelty: The Plight of the Mapuche Indians during the Years of Military Rule," June 30, 1992, http://www.amnesty.org/en/library/info/AMR22/009/1992/en.

21. American Anthropological Association Committee for Human Rights, "The Pehuenche, the World Bank Group and ENDESA S.A.: Violations of Human Rights in the Pangue and Ralco Dam Projects on the Bio Bio River, Chile," http://www.aaanet.org/committees/cfhr/rptpehuenc.htm.

22. See the foundation's Web site, http://www.fundacionpinochet.cl/1024_768.html.

23. A 2002 population census showed that 4.7 percent of the Chilean popula-

tion described itself as indigenous. The real figure may be higher, and because of persistent social discrimination, many Mapuches prefer not to identify themselves as such. The National Corporation for Indigenous Development, CONADI, puts the figure at 10 percent.

24. Franz Lidz, "The Most Hated Man in Tennis," *Sports Illustrated,* March 28, 1998.

25. Marta Lagos, interview with the author, Santiago, Chile, November 16, 2007.

26. Jaime Andrade Guenchocoy, interview with the author, Santiago, Chile, October 5, 2007.

27. Patricia Bustos, Hugo Amigo, Sergio Munoz, and Reynaldo Martorell, "Growth in Indigenous and Nonindigenous Chilean Schoolchildren from 3 Poverty Strata," *American Journal of Public Health,* October 9, 2001, pp. 1646–49.

28. "Mapuche Indian records Bizet's *Carmen*—in Mapudungun," Reuters news agency, Santiago, March 12, 2009. The performance was also posted on the municipality's Web site, www.cerronavia.com.

29. Reynaldo Mariqueo, interview.

30. Sara Kerosky, "Chile's Senate Passes Native Forest Law," *Patagonia Times,* August 20, 2007.

31. *La Nación,* August 13, 2007.

32. The complete text of the law can be found at the Chilean congress's digital library at http://www.leychile.cl/Navegar?idNorma=274894.

33. "Chile y comunidad indigena se unen para crear un parque de Araucarias y promover el turismo en la Araucaria Andina," from the World Wildlife Fund Chile Web site (www.wwf.cl), accessed July 15, 2008.

34. *Santiago Times,* March 31, 2009.

35. Clifford Krauss. "Indians Make a Stand on a Historic River in Chile," *New York Times,* August 16, 1998.

36. American Anthropological Association Committee for Human Rights, "The Pehuenche, the World Bank Group and ENDESA S.A."

37. Ibid.

38. Human Rights Watch, "Undue Process: Terrorism Trials, Military Courts and the Mapuche in Southern Chile," report published October 26, 2004, http://www.hrw.org/en/reports/2004/10/26/undue-process.

39. José Aylwin, "The Ralco Dam and the Pehuenche People in Chile: Lessons from an Ethno-environmental Conflict" (paper presented at the Centre for the Study of Global Issues, University of British Columbia, Vancouver, Canada, September 25–27, 2002).

40. *The Economist,* September 2, 1999.

41. Human Rights Watch, "Undue Process."

42. From the Chilean Senate's Comisión de Constitución, Legislación, Justicia y Reglamento, p. 5. Quoted in Human Rights Watch, "Undue Process."

43. *La Tercera,* June 11, 2005.

44. Reuters news agency report, November 23, 2006.

45. Jaime Peña, "Who Are U, Aucan Huilcaman?" January 17, 2008, http://www.atinachile.cl/content/view/118869/Who-are-u-Aucan-Huilcaman.html.

46. Human Rights Watch, "Undue Process."

47. Ibid.

48. U.S. State Department, Country Reports on Terrorism 2007, published April 30, 2008, http://www.state.gov/s/ct/rls/crt/2007/103710.htm.

49. *Santiago Times,* March 30, 2009.

50. Reynaldo Mariqueo, interview.

51. *Santiago Times,* August 19, 2007.

52. *Patagonia Times,* August 25, 2008.

53. Cited by Human Rights Watch, "World Report Chapter: Chile: Events of 2008," http://www.hrw.org/en/world-report/2009/chile.

54. *El País,* May 8, 2006.

55. *La Segunda,* February 10, 2009.

56. *Patagonia Times,* June 16, 2008.

57. Amnesty International, "Amnesty International Assesses Human Rights in Chile," November 7, 2008, http://www.amnesty.org/en/news-and-updates/news/amnesty-international-assesses-human-rights-chile-20081107.

58. Rick Kearns, "School of Self Government Opens in Chile," *Indian Country Today,* February 27, 2009, http://www.indiancountrytoday.com/global/latin/40381522.html.

CHAPTER ELEVEN

1. Elizabeth Subercaseaux and Malu Sierra, *Michelle* (Santiago: Editorial Catalonia Ltd., 2005), pp. 82–86.

2. Lagos, interview.

3. Larry Rohter, "The Saturday Profile: Jailed by Pinochet, She Now Runs the Military," *New York Times,* January 4, 2003.

4. José De Gregorio, "Crecimiento Económico en Chile: Evidencia, Fuentes y Perspectiva," *Estudios Públicos* (Autumn 2005), http://www.cepchile.cl/dms/lang_1/doc_3536.html.

5. Only portions of the trail are open. See www.senderodechile.cl.

6. Encuesta Nacional CERC, August 2005, p. 6, http://www.cerc.cl/Encuestas/05AGOS.pdf.

7. Cited in *The Economist,* August 10, 2006.

8. Andrea Arango, "SERNAM and the Underrepresentation of Women in Chile" (Council on Hemispheric Affairs, Washington, D.C., May 8, 2008).

9. Quoted in U.S. State Department Bureau of Democracy, Human Rights and Labor, Country Reports on Human Rights Practices, Chile 2006, http://www.state.gov/g/drl/rls/hrrpt/2006/78884.htm.

10. For an overview of the Chilean pensions system, see Estelle James, "Private Pension Annuities in Chile," National Center for Policy Analysis, December 9, 2004, http://www.ncpa.org/pub/st271?pg=3.

11. CERC poll, November 2005, p. 6, http://www.cerc.cl/Encuestas/05NOV.pdf.

12. Tribunal Calificador de Elecciones-Chile, www.tribunalcalificador.cl.

13. Subercaseaux and Sierra, *Michelle,* p. 125. Bachelet told her biographers that during her first government job in the Health Ministry under Aylwin, she needed to supplement the very small paycheck with a private medical practice to pay for her children's needs and education.

14. Manuel Sierra, "Is Pinochet Dead?" *New Left Review,* September-October 2007.

15. Bess Keller, "Chile's Longtime Voucher Plan Provides No Pat Answers," *Education Week,* April 11, 2001.

16. *La Tercera,* April 26, 2006.

17. Tamara Gutierrez Portillo and Cristina Caviedes Reyes, "Revolución Pinguina: La primera gran movilización del siglo XXI en Chile" (Santiago: Editorial Ayun, 2006), p. 33.

18. *El Mercurio,* June 5, 2006.

19. Centro de Estudios Públicos, Estudio Nacional de Opinión Pública, Tema especial: Educación, June–July 2006, http://www.cepchile.cl/dms/lang_1/doc_3807.html.

20. Lori Azatani, "Chilean Leader Walks the Halls of Her Youth," *Washington Post,* June 9, 2006.

21. Jennifer Frey, "For Washington Women, Dinner with a Taste of Real Power," *Washington Post,* June 9, 2006.

22. *The View* episode was aired September 29, 2006.

23. "Colegio Médico llama a personas 'vulnerable' a no usar el Metro en hora punta," Radio Cooperativa, March 19, 2007, http://www.cooperativa.cl/p4_noticas/site/artic/20070319/pags/20073192013511.html.

24. German Correa, "Off to a Chilly Start: The Case of Transantiago Chile, or What Went Wrong?" (World Bank and World Resources Institute, 85th annual meeting, Washington, D.C., January 17, 2008).

25. *El Mercurio,* March 28, 2007.

26. Rodrigo Espinoza G., "Investigación: Usabilidad y pago de los usuarios al Transantiago 2008," Universidad Bernardo O'Higgins, Santiago, http://www.ubo.cl/pdf/ICI_Trans_EvasionV2.pdf.

27. Eugenio Tironi, "Evasores," *El Mercurio,* September 2, 2008.

28. Juan Forero, "Fujimori's Detention in Chile Was Just Part of His Plan," *New York Times,* November 10, 2005.

29. "Conditional Release for Fujimori," BBC broadcast, May 18, 2006, http://www.news.bbc.co.uk/2/hi/world/americas/4994908.stm.

30. The *Prensa Libre* interview with Michelle Bachelet was aired on July 28, 2006.

31. See Justin Vogler, "Bolivia Nears the Precipice," on http://www.opendemocracy.net/article/bolivia-nears-the-edge.

32. Adimark poll, February 2009, http://www.adimark.cl/medios/Evaluacion_Gobierno_Febrero09.pdf, accessed August 6, 2008.

33. Former defense minister Vivianne Blanlot, interview with the author, Santiago, Chile, November 21, 2007.

34. *La Nación,* December 5, 2006.

35. Ibid., December 4, 2006.

36. Blanlot, interview.

37. Ibid.

38. From multiple press reports; see for example http://news.bbc.co.uk/1/hi/world/americas/6167747.stm.

39. Chile's deputy interior minister publicly apologized to the Spanish television crew in wake of the incident. *El Mercurio,* December 13, 2006.

40. Radio Cooperative interview with Cuadrado Prats, December 13, 2006, http://www.cooperativa.cl/p4_noticias/site/artic/20061213/pags/20061213152506.html.

41. *El Mercurio,* December 21, 2006.

42. Blanlot, interview.

43. From multiple press reports and television broadcasts of Pinochet's funeral; see, for example, "Minuto a minuto del dia funeral de Pinochet," *El Mercurio,* December 12, 2006.

44. Ibid.

45. Blanlot, interview.

46. Ibid.

47. *El Mercurio,* December 11, 2007.

48. Ibid.

49. *La Nación,* October 4, 2007.

50. Radio Cooperativa, October 4, 2007, http://www.cooperativa.cl/monica-madariaga-califico-como-imbeciles-a-los-hermanos-pinochet/prontus_nots/2007-10-04/201733.html.

51. The interview can be seen online at http://wn.com/augusto_pinochet_y_manuel_contreras_jr.

52. "Florida: Lawsuit over Pinochet Money," *New York Times,* March 13, 2009.

CHAPTER TWELVE

1. The 78 percent approval figure was in response to a question about Bachelet's overall management of government; when asked about her government's economic management, the figure dropped to 69 percent. See Centro de Estudios Públicos (CEP), "Encuesta nacional de opinion publica," October 2009, www.cepchile.cl, accessed November 3, 2009.

2. Associated Press, "Ex-Chilean Presidential Candidate Fined," *USA Today*, July 6, 2007.

3. *Santiago Times*, July 26, 2009.

4. See www.fundacionfuturo.cl.

5. Sara Larrain, interview with the author, Santiago, Chile, November 16, 2007.

6. CEP, "Encuesta nacional de opinion publica."

7. See www.arratepresidente.cl.

8. *Revista Cosas*, June 11, 2003.

9. *El Mostrador*, September 15, 2009.

10. At the time of writing, *Los héroes están fatigados* could be viewed on various Internet sites, including www.video.google.com and www.youtube.com.

11. Louise Egan, "Chilean Leftist Says He Believes in Markets," Reuters report from Santiago, October 26, 2009.

12. CEP, "Encuesta nacional de opinion publica," accessed November 8, 2009.

13. *Santiago Times*, October 19, 2009.

14. *La Tercera*, November 4, 2009.

15. *Global Post*, October 30, 2009.

16. From multiple reports in the Chilean press on November 6, 2009.

17. The segment was entitled "Sebastian: The Voice of the Voiceless," http://www.youtube.com/watch?v = iUPd_sLPZ5g, accessed November 17, 2009.

18. *La Nación*, November 23, 2009.

19. *El Mercurio*, November 23, 2009.

20. http://pinera2010.cl/programa-de-gobierno/energia/2/, accessed November 17, 2009.

21. http://www.efrei.cl/laspropuestas/economia-verde-y-medioambiente, accessed November 20, 2009.

22. "Energy Profile of Chile," *Encyclopedia of the Earth*, September 4, 2008, http://www.eoearth.org/article/Energy_profile_of_Chile.

23. American Anthropological Association for Human Rights, "The Pehuence, the World Bank Group and ENDESA S.A.: Violations of Human Rights in the Pangue and Ralco Dam Projects on the Bio Bio River, Chile," http://www.aaanet.org/committees/cfhr/rptpehuenc.htm.

24. CERC poll, April 2008, pp. 9–10, http://www.cerc.cl/Encuestas/08ABR.pdf.

25. *Patagonia Times,* September 1, 2008.

26. Patricio Rodrigo and Juan Pablo Orrego, *Patagonia Chilena sin represas!* (Santiago: Ocho Libros Editorial, 2007).

27. *La Tercera,* December 7, 2007.

28. *Patagonia Times,* December 1, 2007.

29. According to the Chilean Planning Ministry, 15.1 percent of the country's inhabitants lived in poverty in 2009, and this figure is likely to increase to 19 percent in the wake of the 2010 earthquake. See "Gobierno prepara informe que revela alza de pobreza por terremoto," *La Tercera,* Spetember 26, 2010.

30. *El Mercurio,* November 16, 2009.

31. *La Nación,* November 24, 2009.

32. Roberto Gutierrez and Javier Nuñez, "Classism, Discrimination and Meritocracy in the Labor Market: The Case of Chile" (working paper, Department of Economics, Universidad de Chile, Santiago, 2004).

33. Associated Press report from Santiago, November 1, 2009.

34. *La Nación,* November 7, 2009.

35. *La Tercera,* November 11, 2009

36. *La Nación,* November 24, 2009.

37. "Marco Enríquez-Ominami declara su apoyo a Eduardo Frei pero déjà en libertad de accion a sus votantes," Radio Bio Bio, January 13, 2010.

38. Voting results from the Chilean Election Commission, http://elecciones.gob.cl/SitioHistorico/index2009_p2v.htm.

39. Alexei Barrionuevo, "Setting Chile's Past Aside, a City Welcomes Soldiers," *New York Times,* March 4, 2010.

Bibliography

ARTICLES

Aninat, Cristóbal, John Landregan, Patricio Navia, and Joaquin Vial. "Political Institutions, Policymaking Processes and Policy Outcomes in Chile." Research Working Paper R-521, Interamerican Development Bank, Washington, D.C., February 2006.

Delano, Marialyse. "Library of Congress of Chile: A Hands-on Modernization Experience." Paper presented at the 64th International Federation of Library Associations Conference, Amsterdam, August 16–21, 1998.

Fuentes, Claudio. "After Pinochet: Civilian Policies toward the Military in the 1990s Chilean Democracy." *Journal of Interamerican Studies and World Affairs* (Fall 2000): 111–42.

Gacitua-Mario, Estanislao. "Indigenous Peoples in Chile: Current Situation and Policy Issues." Background Paper 7, World Bank, Washington, D.C., August 2000.

Larrain, Felipe, Jeffrey Saches, and Andrew Warner. "A Structural Analysis of Chile's Long-Term Growth: History, Prospects and Policy Implications." Paper prepared for the government of Chile, Santiago, January 2000.

Navia, Patricio. "Incumbency in the Chilean Parliament: Candidates and Change." Paper presented at the Congress of the Latin American Studies Association, Miami, FL, March 16–18, 2000.

———. "Legislative Candidate Selection in Chile." Paper presented at Pathways to Power: Political Recruitment and Democracy in Latin America, Wake Forest University, Winston-Salem, NC, April 3–4, 2004.

Peña, Cristóbal. "Exclusivo: Viaje al fondo de la biblioteca de Pinochet." Centro de Investigación e Información Periodística CIPER, http://ciperchile.cl/2007/12/06/exclusivo-viaje-al-fondo-de-la-biblioteca-de-pinochet/, accessed November 15, 2007.

Silva, Eduardo. "Democracy, Market Economics and Environmental Policy in Chile." *Journal of Interamerican Studies and World Affairs* (Winter 1996–97): 1–33.

Weyland, Kurt. "Economic Policy in Chile's New Democracy." *Journal of Interamerican Studies and World Affairs* (Fall 1999): 67–96.

BOOKS

Agnic, Ozren. *Pinochet, S.A.: La base de la fortuna*. Santiago: RiL Editores, 2006.

Allamand, Andrés. *El desalojo: Porque la Concertación debe irse el 2010*. Santiago: Aguilar Chilena de Ediciones, 2007.

Angell, Alan. *Democracy after Pinochet: Politics, Parties and Elections in Chile*. London: Institute for the Study of the Americas, 2007.

Arancibia Clavel, Patricia. *Cita con la historia*. Santiago: Editorial Biblioteca Americana, 2006.

Arancibia Clavel, Patricia, and Isabel de la Maza Cave. *Matthei: Mi testimonio*. Santiago: CIDOC, Universidad Finis Terrae, 2003.

Arce, Luz. *The Inferno: A Story of Terror and Survival in Chile*. Translated by Stacey Alba Skar. Madison: University of Wisconsin Press, 2004.

Arriagada, Genaro. *Los empresarios y la política*. Santiago: LOM Ediciones, 2004.

———. *Por la razón o por la fuerza: Chile bajo Pinochet*. Santiago: Editorial Sudamericana, 1998.

Aylwin, Patricio. *El reencuentro de los democratas: Del golpe al triumfo del no*. Santiago: Ediciones B Chile, 1998.

Azocar, Andrés. *Tompkins: El millonario verde*. Santiago: Editorial La Copa Rota, 2007.

Castillo, Benedicto. *Pinochet: El gran comisionista*. Santiago: Editorial Mare Nostrom, 2007.

Cavallo, Ascanio. *La historia oculta de la transición.* Santiago: Editorial Grijalbo, 1999.

Davies, Madeleine, ed. *The Pinochet Case: Origins, Progress and Implications.* London: Institute of Latin American Studies, 2003.

Dinges, John. *The Condor Years: How Pinochet and His Allies Brought Terror to Three Continents.* New York: New Press, 2004.

Engel, Eduardo, and Patricio Navia. *Que gane "el más mejor": Mérito y competencia en el Chile de hoy.* Santiago: Random House Mondadori, 2006.

Ensalaco, Mark. *Chile under Pinochet: Recovering the Truth.* Philadelphia: University of Pennsylvania Press, 1999.

Farfán, Claudia, and Fernando Vega. *La familia: Historia privada de los Pinochet.* Santiago: Random House Mondadori, 2009.

Faron, Louis C. *The Mapuche Indians of Chile.* Prospect Heights, IL: Waveland Press, 1968.

García Pinochet, Rodrigo. *Caso Riggs: La última persecución.* Santiago: Editorial Maya, 2007.

Garreton, Manuel Antonio. *Del post-Pinochetismo a la sociedad democrática.* Santiago: Random House Mondadori, 2006.

Gustafson, Kristian. *Hostile Intent: U.S. Covert Operations in Chile, 1964–1974.* Washington, D.C.: Potomac Books, 2007.

Guzmán Tapia, Juan. *En el borde del mundo: Memorias del juez que procesó a Pinochet.* Barcelona: Editorial Anagrama, 2005.

Julio Reyes, Humberto L. *Hablan los militares: Operaciones de la Agrupación "Este" y de la Escuela de Artillería, 1973–1974.* Santiago: Editorial Biblioteca Americana, 2006.

Kornbluh, Peter. *The Pinochet File: A Declassified Dossier on Atrocity and Accountability.* New York: New Press, 2004.

Leon-Dermota, Ken. *. . . And Well-Tied Down: Chile's Press under Democracy.* Westport, CT: Praeger Publishers, 2003.

Mares, David R., and Francisco Rojas Aravena. *The United States and Chile: Coming in from the Cold.* New York: Routledge, 2001.

Matus, Alejandra. *El libro negro de la justicia Chilena.* Santiago: Grupo Editorial Planeta, 1999.

Merino Vega, Marcia Alejandra. *Mi verdad: Mas allá del horror, yo acuso.* Santiago: A.T.G., 1993.

Munoz, Oscar, and Carolina Stefoni. *El período del Presidente Frei Ruiz-Tagle.* Santiago: Editorial Universitaria, 2003.

Ortuzar, Ximena. *México y Pinochet: La ruptura.* Mexico City: Editorial Nueva Imagen, 1986.

Ostr, Bart, Jose Miguel Sanchez, Carlos Aranda, and Gunnar S. Eskeland. "Air

Pollution and Mortality Results from Santiago, Chile." Vol. 1. Working paper, World Bank, May 31, 1995.

Otano, Rafael. *Nueva crónica de la transición*. Santiago: LOM Ediciones, 2006.

Palma, Julieta, and Raul Urua. "Anti-poverty Policies and Citizenry: The 'Chile Solidario' Experience." Department of Public Policy, Institute of Public Affairs, University of Chile, Santiago, 2005.

Perez, Monica, and Felipe Gerdtzen. *Augusto Pinochet: 503 días atrapados en Londres*. Santiago: Editorial Los Andes, 2000.

Pinochet Ugarte, Augusto. *Camino recorrido: Memorias de un soldado*. Vol. 1. Santiago: Imprenta Geografia Military de Chile, 1990.

Rodrigo, Patricio, and Juan Pablo Orrego. *Patagonia Chilena sin represas!* Santiago: Ocho Libros Editores, 2007.

Rojo Orrego, Emilio. *La otra cara de La Moneda: Los cuatro años de Aylwin*. Santiago: Ediciones ChileAmerica CESOC, n.d.

Salinas, Claudio R., and Hans Stange. *Los amigos del "Dr." Shafer: La complicidad entre el estado chileno y Colonia Dignidad*. Santiago: Random House Mondadori, 2006.

Serrano, Margarita. *La historia de un "Bandido": Raul Rettig*. Santiago: Editorial Los Andes, 1999.

Siavelis, Peter M. *The President and Congress in Post Authoritarian Chile: Institutional Restraints to Democratic Consolidation*. University Park: Pennsylvania State University Press, 2000.

Subercaseaux, Elizabeth, and Malu Sierra. *Michelle*. Santiago: Editorial Catalonia Ltd., 2005.

Verdugo, Patricia. *Chile, Pinochet and the Caravan of Death*. Miami: North-South Center Press, 2001.

Villagran, Fernando. *Disparen a la bandada: Una crónica secreta de la FACH*. Santiago: Grupo Editorial Planeta, 2002.

REPORTS

Le Fort, Guillermo. "Los resultados macroeconómicos del gobierno de Eduardo Frei RT: Una evaluación comparativa." Banco Central de Chile, October 2000.

Human Rights Watch. "Limits of Tolerance: Freedom of Expression and the Public Debate in Chile," New York, November 1, 1998, http://www.hrw.org/en/reports/1998/11/01/limits-tolerance.

———. "Undue Process: Terrorism Trials, Military Courts and the Mapuche in Southern Chile." New York, October 27, 2004, http://www.hrw.org/en/reports/2004/10/27/undue-process.

———. "Unsettled Business: Human Rights in Chile at the Start of the Frei

Presidency." New York, May 1, 1994, http://www.hrw.org/en/reports/1994/05/01/unsettled-business.

U.S. Congress. Senate. Permanent Subcommittee on Investigations. *Money Laundering and Foreign Corruption: Enforcement and Effectiveness of the Patriot Act*. Supplemental staff report on U.S. accounts used by Augusto Pinochet. 109th Congress, 1st sess., March 16, 2005.

Index

Text: 10/14 Palatino
Display: Univers Condensed Light 47 and Bauer Bodoni
Compositor: BookMatters, Berkeley
Indexer: Kevin Millham
Printer and Binder: IBT Global

Made in the USA
Middletown, DE
02 October 2022